SERMONS PREACHED IN A UNIVERSITY CHURCH

SERMONS PREACHED IN A UNIVERSITY CHURCH

GEORGE ARTHUR BUTTRICK

ABINGDON PRESS
NEW YORK • NASHVILLE

159

SERMONS PREACHED IN A UNIVERSITY CHURCH

Copyright © MCMLIX by Abingdon Press

Library of Congress catalog entry on p. 223

PRINTED IN THE UNITED STATES OF AMERICA

For *my* grandchildren

ANNE, PETER, KAREN, STEPHEN, AND JEANNE

"Their angels always behold the face of
my Father who is in heaven."

FOREWORD

This is a book of sermons, all of which have been preached in the Memorial Church, Harvard University. Preaching is specific: its language is particular, and it is addressed to a particular congregation. The diction of the preacher is that of the historian and dramatist, not that of the philosopher, for preaching appeals *by* the history-drama of the Event of Christ *to* the willed drama of men's daily history. By the same token, preaching is never to people in general or to a crowd at large, but to an individual group or church. Only the pastor, or a man with pastoral imagination, can preach. Thus, though a true sermon may be in measure true anywhere, it is most centrally and sharply true in the congregation for whom it is prepared. These are *university sermons*. The title of this book is by deliberate intent.

It has seemed wise, therefore, to leave unchanged both the local references and the particular angle of approach. The references almost explain themselves, for many people are acquainted with the names of the Harvard buildings. In instances that might be baffling, a note has been added. As to the angle of approach, these sermons have been written primarily for university students, whose mingled idealism and realism, self-disparagement and self-assurance, naïveté and sophistication, turmoil of emotion and keenness of

7

mind, offer the hardest challenge for a preacher. These sermons tried to meet that challenge—and the attempt was joy, not least because of the probing questions which students afterward asked and because of their undeserved friendship. That these are college sermons may give them sharper point even for the average reader, if there is any average reader, for students state bluntly the doubts which other men may try to hide. Thus sermons addressed to students may interpret the average reader to himself; they may uncover and partly answer his otherwise inarticulate searchings.

There is particularity of *time* also in these sermons. They are University Sermons *in a Time of Crisis*. Counselors know that the dilemma of our generation has intensified the personal problem just as it has complicated the corporate responsibility. Our distractions and false norms of "success" have led, more than in other generations if we can judge aright, to a failure in home loyalties and parental love. Some student phrases occur with painful reiteration and reveal a malady of mind not easily healed: "I have not really known my father." "I guess I resented it because my mother never let me think for myself." "I went to church, but it didn't register." Meanwhile students are aware that man's misuse of atomic power may terminate the pageant, bedraggled and splendid, of man's life on earth; and they are tempted, their noble humanisms thus punctured, to ask, "What's the use?" Some of these sermons have been almost dictated by counseling experiences, as, for instance, "Home Ties and the Faith" and "God and Our Mixed Motives." Others are addressed to the personal problem today: "Our Times and the Resurrection," "Footnote on Freedom," and "Expiation." All are for a particular congregation in a particular crux in history. This particularity must mark any worthy preaching of the gospel.

I have long been reluctant to print sermons, even strongly resolved against it. Misgivings have not been removed as this manuscript goes to press. But the publishers, my wife, students and teachers in homiletics, and many friends in the university who have asked for copies of individual sermons have finally overborne my scruples—overborne them in kindness, not overcome them. There are hundreds of volumes of sermons on my shelves, but I cannot pretend that many of them "kindle" in the reading. Some of them follow the expected motions, with back-stage ropes and pulleys exposed. This is not said critically: the fault is in me and in the opaqueness of print. I know the authors of many of these books and so am sure that their sermons did "kindle" when they were preached. Why should I expect to succeed where better men have failed? So misgivings remain: they are temporarily yielded to the generous persuasions of my friends.

As for the opaqueness of print, sermons in book form run a hundred hazards. The preacher writes for the ear and must now rewrite for the eye. Writing for the ear is one task: the sentences are short and picture-esque and should be instantly clear because the ear has no chance to go back, saying, "I did not understand: say it again." Writing for the eye is another task: under the canons of good prose. These sermons have been partly rewritten for the eye, probably with no great success, for with me writing for the ear has become almost second nature. There are more serious hazards. A sermon is an "I-thou" transaction: the congregation "makes" the sermon almost as much as the preacher makes it; and often in this rewriting I have wished that I might bring the Memorial Church congregation, searching in mind yet gracious in spirit, to the printed page. Moreover, to instance a still deeper difficulty, a sermon is part of worship, is itself worship—the ascribing of worth to God, the celebration of all worthy life before the Unseen Eyes. Remove the prayer-worship, the brooding of the Spirit on the worshiping congregation, and how much of the sermon is left? A sermon is an "offering" on an altar. Perhaps it ought to be ephemeral. Perhaps it ought to perish in that sabbath's sacrifice. Perhaps no man has the right to draw it back, saying, "I want to print it." As to that, I do not know. I do know that misgivings about printed sermons are not easily erased.

It is a glad obligation to express gratitude to many helpers. I am debtor to the writers from whom I have quoted: the notes show the wide measure of that indebtedness but only half the thankfulness. I am debtor to my preacher-sons, George Robert Buttrick and David Gardner Buttrick, fine preachers in their own right, including the right to bring these sermons into judgment: they have read some of them and improved them. Had my other son, the economist-son, John Arthur, been near at hand, I would have trusted just as much his unparsonic comments! My thanks also to my secretary, Miss Elizabeth Stouffer, a most excellent secretary, who has typed the manuscript, offering betimes the illuminating comment. Most of all, I am grateful to my wife, Agnes Gardner Buttrick, who, as with each book that I have tried to write, has prepared the Notes. I would grow impatient, but she has a way with these items: meticulous quest, care, and loyalty in love. She has kept the house quiet and also her husband's alleged mind, and has steadfastly believed that there is some merit in this manuscript.

Perhaps these sermons have one dubious gift: they are not at second hand, however deep their indebtedness to better men and finer minds. There may be another merit: sympathy for the honest skeptic who will not side-step the apparent meaninglessness of our present world. Such skepticism wins me more than "little churchinesses." So perhaps these pages may offer, if not guidance, then understanding to readers who cannot easily dismiss their doubts and questions. Perhaps students in homiletics may find some help in this book, if only in its demonstration of how not to do it: for their sake Roman numerals have been used to accent the "sermon outline." The Revised Standard Version has been used in Bible quotations except in a few instances, which have been indicated, where the King James Version seemed immemorially "right." So in the hope that my misgivings are mistaken and that my friends are right in their trust that these chapters may serve the faith of Christ, I wish the reader Godspeed.

GEORGE A. BUTTRICK
Sequanota Club
Charlevoix, Michigan
August 22, 1958

CONTENTS

THE CHRISTIAN YEAR

1

LONELY VOYAGE

"Some went down to the sea in ships,
doing business on the great waters."
Ps. 107:23

"The eternal God is your dwelling place,
and underneath are the everlasting arms."
Deut. 33:27

Rupert Brooke, taking ship from Liverpool to New York, felt suddenly lonely, for he seemed the only passenger without friends on the dock to wave him good-by. So he ran back down the gangplank, picked out an urchin, and asked, "What's your name?" "Bill," said the boy. "Well, Bill, you are my friend, and here is sixpence. Wave to me when the ship goes." The boy waved a handkerchief in a very grubby hand.[1] Our human voyage is a still lonelier affair. The ship of this strange planet—should we say of the cosmos?—plunges on its way with no apparent port of departure, for nobody knows how or where or why our human life began; and no apparent port of arrival, for every passenger is buried in the deep. We are on a lonely voyage. When we confront that fact, biblical faith begins.

I

There is no dock and no "Bill" on the dock. So we try to build our securities (that is what the bank calls them) in the ship itself. It is a mammoth affair, and we can easily pretend that it is bastioned in rock. But it is not: it is a ship with no visible coast astern or ahead, an infinite sky above and an infinite sea beneath, the vessel's prow cutting the waters on an unstayed course—if there is a course. On shipboard we build our "securities"—on the personal level by means of hospital plans and the Red Cross, on the commercial level by cash and prestige, on the national level by law and order and defenses. These safeguards are right after their proper kind, for we should have due regard for life on board, but they cannot long hide the fact that we are not on shore. We are on a lonely voyage.

Some passengers paint out the porthole glass and refuse to walk on deck: they dare not confront the loneliness and the mystery. Yet they know there is a strange "beyond" and cannot help wondering what is out there below the sea and above the sky. Faith is not escape: it lives in confrontation of the abyss. Science can be valid or it can be escape: it is valid when it says: "We are here meanwhile, and may find the purpose of life by understanding the ship"; it is escape when it says: "No use asking about out there, for out there is a blank, and to make any guess about it is superstition." Culture also may be an escape, for it may be content to say: "Oh, well, we can live an enlightened and interesting life on shipboard." Perhaps the existentialists are right in this at least: that a non-authentic life runs away into abstractions or thinghood or the mass mind, conscience being a voice to make us aware of the cowardice, while an authentic life confronts apparent nothingness.

We may note a prime fact about passengers who say, "This world only: there is only life on shipboard": they do not add to the vessel's peace. For the more they try to build securities, the more they spread misgiving by contagion. When a man becomes too intent on his health, to postpone the day when his body shall be lowered into the deep, he becomes hypochondriac, so that other passengers begin to worry about their health. When first-class passengers try to perpetuate their economic privilege by means of tariffs and guns, they are beset by internal strains, and the steerage violently envies their comfort and pride. As for the other passengers, those who say, "We can learn something from the vessel but more from the Mystery and from our own loneliness," they first subtract from the vessel's peace and then greatly add to it, for their neighbors first resent being reminded of the voyage and of their own inner chaos, even to the point of making the would-be religious man walk the plank; but afterward they find stillness of spirit through the martyr, as they say of him, "Perhaps he knew, and knows." Wise men, it would seem, walk the deck, ask their questions about the vessel's port of departure and point of arrival, wonder who chartered it, and ponder the meaning of sea and sky. ✕

II

Suppose a man does not shrink from looking through the porthole or walking the deck. Suppose he confronts what Kierkegaard called "fear and trembling," [2] what Heidegger calls "basic care." [3] Then this or that may happen. He may commit suicide, which, if some modern thinkers are right, is the main issue: to go on living or to end life.[4] The man may fling himself into the endless waters. One such left a note saying, "I've seen everything." He meant everything in the ship. Beyond the ship he plunged into the Mystery, with whatever it may hide: certainly he did not plunge out of it. Or the man may give himself to slow suicide in one of its many forms—hatred for a vessel which he cannot understand, and self-hatred, and withdrawal from his fellow passengers. Perhaps the Mystery, from which we and the ship have come, understands slow or swift suicide but still requires ultimate confrontation.

Or the man may be afraid of the Mystery and thus retreat into the fascinating life on shipboard. As a philosopher he may say: "We know nothing except that which we can analyze and logically understand." As a businessman he may be an activist, always keeping busy or spending his leisure in the ship's tavern where he can "forget things." As an artist he may portray the ship's chaos, instead of setting up his easel on deck to catch the haunting lights and shadows of the sea. As a scientist he may scrutinize everything on board, saying meanwhile to his cabinmates: "Why not be realists? This is sole knowledge." Most people prefer the lighted lounge to the loneliness of the deck at night.

Or the man may live in an agnostic and stoic courage. The courage may be gay, as in the definition of an expert: "Ex—unknown quantity; spurt—a drip under pressure"—which seems to be a spoofing of our ignorance of the ship's purpose and destination. Or the courage may be sad:

> For men must work, and women must weep, ...
> And the sooner it's over, the sooner to sleep.[5]

Or it may be quiet and resigned: "Well, that's the way things are." Stoicism has a noble cast: it does not close the door against the Mystery. Agnosticism usually deals with its neighbors in a neighborly kindness. Meanwhile the ship plunges on its way through days and nights, with no coast line astern and no harbor light ahead and no easy answer from the infinite sky and the infinite deep.

III

No answer? Is there nothing else to be said? Much else, and to fail to say it is to fail in honesty. When the skeptic lecturer asked pretentiously, "What could be better than seeking truth?" the old lady on the front row made the obvious answer: "Why, finding it, of course." It is doubtful if we would have asked any question of the mystery of our life if we had not been already dimly aware of an answer.

This fact holds, and it is vital fact: men pray, and they pray harder when the vessel is tossed in tempest. To dismiss the universal fact of prayer as "projection" is not impressive: the tiny psychological cliché is not big enough to cover the agelong plea. Besides, the word "projection" begs the question. Is not all thought projection, including the psychological cliché? And does not the very word imply a solid screen on which the projection is flung? Prayer is native whenever men confront the Mystery. It is open to any man, when he has prayed or waited with open spirit in silence, to say, "I do not yet know"; and such a man usually moves to the side of the angels in any practical crux or choice. If he persists, he may yet know. But it is also right that a man should say in honest mind: "I received a secret answer, hard to construe, but clearly bidding me live for truth and love." Doubly right, when that answer requires a man thus to set himself against the capsuled shipboard mind. Why do men pray to the Timeless? Is it because of an eternal sense by which they know that time is time and that time is fleeting? Shall we say that when a man prays, God prays in him?

The prayer-fact leads on to that God-fact: men who pray have learned to say "God," and have declared themselves found of God. The Bible is a covenant book: it tells from end to end of a pledge which God has made with men. "The eternal God is your dwelling place, and underneath are the everlasting arms." Give the Bible an A grade for prodigious contours of thought. It claims that underneath the void of sky and the deeps of the sea, underneath the abyss of the past and the unknown future, are Hands and Arms, and above it all a Face. In *The Ball and the Cross* [6] G. K. Chesterton has said that he would contend for his friend, yet would remain were his friend to die; and that he would contend for his country, yet might persist were his country to be destroyed; but that if God were not, he, the man, would burst like a bubble. Of course, for a man's life is contingent and derived, and would disappear without its creative ground. So some men have told us by much prayer that the lonely voyage and the sea are held in God. They have spoken and lived in that certitude, which is better than propositional certainty, even as life is better than logic.

One Man in particular has thus spoken and lived: in the particular and in centrality and in a certain aloneness. There is debate about his exact words, and must be, for he spoke in Aramaic and was not careful to make any verbatim record. But his followers were undismayed by such uncertainties: they found in him, in the whole event of his life and death and abidingness, the eternal Word. As to the business of how to live on shipboard, as to the chaos that festers whenever men become obsessed with the ship, as to the strife that ensues whenever the first-class passengers defend their cabins against the steerage, when the steerage thus tries to seize that in which the first-class passengers have found no peace, as to all that, the Man spoke decisively: "Out there in the Mystery of sky and sea, and in you in equal Mystery, is the One. He loves us all, and so we should love Him, and our neighbors in Him, and ourselves in Him." He lived so, instant in crisis-prayer, constant in prayer's vigil; instant in love's crisis-deed, constant in love's attitude. The other passengers could not endure the ecstasy, the *ekstasis*, the Life that made them stand outside their own life to reappraise it. We are the other passengers. They said: "Our private cabin is enough; or if it isn't, we can forget our yearning by fighting for somebody else's cabin. Do not ask us to confront the Void." He answered, "Have faith in God." They made him walk the plank, but the sign of the plank has been set everywhere in the vessel since that day.

IV

Anything else to say? Yes, this: we shall not be sure of his way except at risk, as his love draws us. It is a venture of prayer, or of long silent waiting if a man cannot honestly pray. It is a venture in a new direction of life on shipboard. As instances of a new goal, even though we may yet be ignorant of any specific briefing, the wealthy of the world must address themselves to the problem of the world's poverty; and if they would thus spend themselves, they would not need to defend themselves by unconvincing panegyrics about "free enterprise." The labor unions, born in martyrdom but now aping the earthy comfort from which they wrested their freedom, must now be concerned with such issues as the nature of the work, the meaning of vocation, creative leisure, and the place of worship. Art must leave its little mirrors held up to nature and its entanglement with its inner distractions, and, like Dauber in the Masefield poem,[7] portray the fierce yet gleaming mystery of sea and sky. The Church must forswear its undue absorption in budgets and bricks and numbers, for this is a retreat into the seeemingly "safe" life of shipboard, and must once more confront men with God's sheer demand of love in Christ. And ourselves? It is asked that we let God's love in Christ have some free way in us. We cannot live only for the ship plus breath in our lungs. Every man goes at last into the Deep; every man is buried at sea. The real issue, for life or death, is the nature of the Deep.

People who live so, risking insecurity, have found themselves secure and can hardly tell why. "Father, into thy hands I commit my spirit!" [8] So he spoke, and was at home even on a cross. As for our text, there is a strange story of a man who dreamed almost nightly that he was falling into a bottomless void. His school hymn had required him to sing:

> Teach me to live, that I may dread
> The grave as little as my bed, [9]

when there was nothing he dreaded more than his bed with that recurrent dream! One day in a cemetery he saw an inscription on a grave: "The eternal God is Thy home, and underneath are the everlasting arms." Faith pierced him, then and there, savingly, so that the nightly dream was banished. Do not paint out the porthole: you will still see its outline and know there is a Beyond and a Within. Meanwhile the ship plunges on, for no man can escape the lonely voyage. Those who confront the Mystery have taken the first long step toward life—toward the knowledge that underneath sea and sky, underneath our shipboard selfishness and the fathomless deeps of our own yearning, underneath all that is underneath— God, and the power of God's love. Beyond distraction and stoicism —that kind of faith.

FAITH AND DOUBT

2

FAITH AND DOUBT

> "Straightway the father of the child cried out,
> and said with tears, Lord, I believe; help thou
> mine unbelief."   *Mark 9:24* (K.J.V.)

Raphael's "The Transfiguration," perhaps his greatest work,
shows in the upper half of the canvas the glorification of Christ
before the awe-struck eyes of three of his disciples; and, in the
lower half, a distraught father bringing his epileptic son to Christ
in the dim hope that Christ might heal him. Our life is lived on
those two levels: on Sunday the rapturous height of worship, if
only before a Raphael canvas; on Monday the anguish of a shadowed
valley. That father said to Christ: "If you can do anything, have
pity on us." Christ answered: "If you can! All things are possible
to him who believes." Could he mean that sometimes Divine power
waits on human faith? Thus we confront the whole issue of our
faith and doubt.

I

Everybody doubts, skeptic and believer, pulpit and pew. That
is a prime fact. In some eras doubt seems to have been the exception
and faith the rule; in other eras faith is the exception and doubt
the rule. From David Hume and the mid-eighteenth century, doubt

seems to have spread among men; and our own time, despite an alleged "revival of religion," seems to be a skeptic generation. We speak now of genuine doubt. Not the phlegm that follows shabby conduct: that is not doubt, but rather the scum that gathers on a locked-in lake, and it clears with honest confession. Not impatience with coercive or stultifying forms of religion: that is proper rebellion on the way to finer faith. Not the airing of brilliant denials: that is conceit, and conceit is its own desolation.

Genuine doubt is the reverse side of genuine faith. For just as genuine faith is not mere intellectual assent, but trust in ultimate Reality, so genuine doubt, as in the case of this father, is the fear that demonism and despair may have the last word (and the first word and all the essential words) in our life on earth. Epilepsy was in those days reckoned demonic, and the boy in the story was epileptic. "*If* you can do anything": there was the genuine doubt: perhaps the whole scheme of things is epileptic. In that sense everybody doubts at times, pulpit and pew, skeptic and believer. That a ski-lodge fire should kill four Harvard students (and they among our finest), that rationalism should make a vacuum in middle Europe and a megalomaniac paperhanger should fill the vacuum with obscene banners, that millions should follow him even to the depravity of Buchenwald, that the same perversion should be in every man's veins, is the darkness that breeds doubt. Meanwhile our fragile and fleeting life is suspended in apparent nothingness. How can we believe in anything? Sharper question: How can we believe in the God who cares? /

On the promontory of Malea stood a chapel to Michael, so that sailors rounding the cape when the storm struck declared that Michael was beating his archangel wings. Archangel? In our time the wings seem those of a huge black bat sending winds of anger and madness through our world. But notice: this genuine doubt is always a passionate *concern*. It says in effect: "In any rightful world things should not be callous or cruel." Even atheism must define itself by theism: it is a-theism, that is to say, not theism. Is doubt not always the doubt of our faith? If doubt is real, not the scum of shabby conduct, not rebellion against false piety, not intellectual conceit, then its only wickedness is the wickedness of the church that condemns it. To every preacher or peddler reading this page: Have you not doubted, times in a day?

24

II

But we may turn the table: everybody believes. Even David Hume, harbinger of an age of doubt, once declared, as he saw the piety of La Roche,[1] that he sometimes wished he had never doubted; and there is the saucy story of an atheist who, when asked if he were Christian, replied angrily: "No, I'm an atheist, thank God!" The farmer believes—in the fidelities of nature, or that he must so trust. The scientist believes—in the *uni-verse,* in an *esprit de corps* between his mind and the universe, and in a requirement resting on him to honor truth even though truth may shatter the presuppositions of a lifetime. The artist believes—in beauty and in devotion to beauty. The man who says "All is despair" still believes—in that which enables him to recognize despair, that is to say, in some ground of hope. Everybody believes.

The belief sometimes takes us unawares. Katherine Mansfield, unable to trust God, yet grateful for the sheer joy of life and of human love, exclaimed, "Thanks to someone. But who?"[2] We are not grateful to clouds or to the stuff of the ground. Perhaps all gratitude is belief—a person to Person call. Or the newspaper reports the aviator over Long Island who knew he was about to crash and who deliberately made for a sandpit where he could be sure that only his life would be lost: we read, and there is the break-through of a shining world beyond our world. Or for darker instance, *Peer Gynt*[3] shows us the scared lad who cut off his finger to avoid military service but who afterward always carried the shamed hand in his pocket. There is a "needs-must" within us and beyond us.

But this belief is always vulnerable, for we are finite, our sight dim and our faith faltering. One moment we trust God; the next moment we wonder if gratitude and sacrifice and conscience are any better than an affair of the glands. But we all believe, however fitfully and however dark our world. Even George Santayana, who in *The Last Puritan*[4] almost argued that wickedness is but the necessary sepia in the picture, could yet write:

> Columbus found a world, and had no chart
> Save one that faith deciphered in the skies;
> To trust the soul's invincible surmise
> Was all his science and his only art.[5]

25

So everybody doubts, skeptic and believer, pulpit and pew; and everybody believes. We should rightly speak not of a world divided between skeptics and believers, but of the "faith-doubt" tension in every man. Half of us is on the Mount of Transfiguration and half in the shadowed valley. Pascal spoke of the heart having reasons which the mind knew not,[6] and perhaps we should say that both heart and mind are in tension. The heart is grateful for love but indignant at the world's insensate cruelty; and for the mind tragedy is sometimes apocalypse and sometimes blank misgiving.

III

The faith and the doubt come to a crux in Jesus Christ. Most people would say of him that he is "the best." It is a strange acknowledgment, for unwittingly it reveals a scale of values, good-better-best, with Jesus as highest term to give meaning to the whole gamut. Thus the phrase becomes a vast faith. But it is hard for our age, weaned on scientific method, to find any special revelation in Jesus. Particularism is a road block for the modern man. Why, we ask, should God reveal himself through one Man in an ancient time in an inconsequential land? The question begs the question, for the word "revelation" is there taken to mean something arbitrary, such as a meteor falling uncouthly on our trim fields; and "ancient time" forgets that some items are timeless, such as the proportions of the Parthenon; and "inconsequential" harbors strange ideas of what is of consequence. Is not disclosure, even in science, always particular? That deed of the aviator, is it not axiomatic? In any event, we look at Christ, and all the faith-doubt comes to a turbulent crux, at least to any man who dares ponder Christ.

The crux has a still deeper dimension: From the side of doubt the Cross of Christ ought to be the terrible reinforcement of doubt, for there we see earth's "best" at the mercy of earth's "worst." But the Cross has not had that impact. It is set against the sky line of our raucous, anonymous cities. In our cemeteries it is a talisman against death. It quickens the world's finest art and music. Through it men have known that the bleakest tragedy may be the most piercing and healing light. It seems to give our doubts their best argument, and then to answer the argument not by a syllogism, but by an Event in love. Is there not a story of a statue on the banks of the Nile from which music came for the nerving of the nation, and that the enemy therefore destroyed it, only to find that still **more** kindling music came from the ruins? Albert Schweitzer, bravely confronting the doubts which modern biblical scholarship has raised, has this to say:

> He comes to us as One unknown, without a name, as of old, by the lake-side, He came to those men who knew Him not. . . . And to those who obey Him, . . . He will reveal Himself in the toils, the conflicts, the sufferings which they shall pass through in His fellowship, and as an ineffable mystery, they shall learn in their own experience Who He is.[7]

The word is autobiography, in the crux of the faith-doubt tension. The doubt is honestly admitted; the faith is courageously held.

IV

Can the tension be resolved? Not fully in this life but yet with great measure of certitude. We are finite creatures, deeps of mystery within us, deeps of mystery beyond us; and perhaps finite creatures must always doubt. Perhaps the only way to evade doubt is to stop thinking and feeling, and that attempt never fully succeeds. But we need not live on a seesaw, even though many never seem to go beyond that up and down of faith and doubt. There are no "scientific" proofs for faith, at least not in the strict sense of the word "scientific," because man is subject as well as object and must himself be tester as well as tested. The better reason is that God is Eternal Subject and never mere object. The scientific proof of faith is found in the scientist not in his science—in his devotion to truth, and in his awareness that science becomes chaos when scientists play fast and loose with truth.

In any event, the overt proofs do not prove. Sinclair Lewis some years ago on a public platform dared God to strike him dead. Then, when nothing happened, he said in effect: "There! You see: there is no such God."[8] But, of course, the argument could have gone in the other direction, as indeed Sinclair Lewis was there intent to prove: "Only a God of infinite patience and love would endure that nonsense and let him go on living." As for proofs, there is one kind of proof for potatoes, another for poems, another for persons, and another for God. Beyond all proofs and in lack of them we must go on living. What we need is a strategy rather than a proof, a strategy and a certain valor of the spirit. So let us look again at the father in our story, for his approach has its wisdom.

V

The man confessed his doubts and faced them: "Help my unbelief!" The creeds of the Church are magnificent, the harvest of minds harrowed and seeded by the pondering of Christ and by persecutions that came for his sake. But they are not coercive. No man has right to try to impose them on his neighbor—or on himself. Faith will always be doubted. Doubts are the odds that faith must meet. Otherwise faith would be a *dead* certainty, not faith. Someone has quipped that doubts are like the measles: health is served if they "come out." Well, they are a more serious issue than measles, much worse than a child's disease; but they are safer when they are acknowledged, and they are dangerous when they are hidden in the pretense which says, "I am not troubled by doubts." The father outrightly confessed his unbelief.

But we see him cleaving, nevertheless, to his faith: "Lord, I believe.'" The faith-doubt tension confronts us with an existential choice. This man chose his faith against his doubt. Faith as against doubt is venturous: a man has only to let go in order to doubt. Faith is creative: doubt could never have built Rheims Cathedral. Faith brings healing whereas doubt leaves a man at odds with himself and his world. Faith is community: perhaps doubt is doubt of love and so knows no deep bonds of friendship. This man chose his faith, as did Browning in a splendid word:

> With me, faith means perpetual unbelief
> Kept quiet like the snake 'neath Michael's foot
> Who stands calm just because he feels it writhe.[9]

> We're back on Christian ground. You call for faith:
> I show you doubt, to prove that faith exists.
> The more of doubt, the stronger faith, I say,
> If faith o'ercomes doubt. How I know it does?
> By life and man's free will, God gave for that! [10]

In the faith-doubt tension a man can still make his choice: "Lord, I believe."

The man flung his doubts on God. He prayed them: "Help my unbelief!" It is nobler to pray the doubt, flinging it on God in some kind of trust, than to splatter it on our neighbors. Horace Bushnell tells us that he was once so plunged in skepticism that he believed nothing beyond the abstract assertion that right is right. So he prayed to the abstract principle of right: "An awfully dark prayer in the look of it." [11] But it was an honest prayer with some vague notion of God hearing it, and it led on into light. So the father in the story vaguely understood that if faith should vanish from the earth, his son would go unhealed and demonisms would ride mankind. Only God Himself can ever cure the doubt of God. The man who thus prays opens life to God's self-disclosure and finds that in God there is mercy, not for his sins alone but also for his doubts.

VI

"Lord, I believe; help thou mine unbelief!" It is in certain ways the final prayer. To say "All is despair" is to acknowledge by inversion that we know hope—the hope without which we could not recognize despair. To say then, "I cleave to the hope as I cling to the Cross," is courage of a kind—of the only kind, perhaps: the root of all true courage. Faith is thus known to be the movement of God's life in us, that same life which is disclosed in Christ. Augustine spoke a final word: A man doubts, therefore God is.[12]

3

IT SHALL COME BACK

"Thus says the Lord of hosts, the God of Israel: Houses and fields and vineyards shall again be bought in this land." *Jer. 32:15*

A certain church has poured gifts and prayers for fifty years into a mission station in China. The project was not narrowly conceived. There was, for instance, a farm that by research added millions of dollars to crop values in that area, and schools and a hospital that gave friendly expression to the faith of the sanctuary, and the church itself was built in Chinese architecture, lest it should appear to represent "colonialism." The whole enterprise was largely under Chinese leadership.[1] Now the venture has been overrun by Communism. We are not interested at this moment either in any wholesale castigation of Communism or in any wholesale endorsement of the Church. But in that station brainwashing has taken the place of mutual trust; and a system obtains in which a man is regarded not as a child of God, but rather as the spawn of the economic process. What does now interest us is the apparent futility of good will in human history. Granted good will is always imperfect, why should it be eclipsed if God Himself is good? As another instance, remember that a recent flood wiped out an orphanage. What are we to say?

I

A story in the Bible is so pertinent that it might have been written for our purpose.[2] It has its touch of absurd, brave humor. The Chaldean invader was sweeping down on Israel, and one Hanamel saw that his farm would soon be engulfed. Cannily he said: "Perhaps I could sell it." So he appealed to his cousin Jeremiah to exercise the right of the next of kin and buy the land. Now Jeremiah was unmarried and did not need the farm. Moreover, he was in prison for views which conventional minds deemed traitorous, the enemy was almost at the gate, and all parties to the proposed real-estate deal would doubtless soon be carried captive to Babylon. But Jeremiah bought the farm, not because Hanamel was the world's supersalesman, but as an acted sermon on faith. "No panic price," said Jeremiah, "a fair market price!" He kept all the legalities: an open deed for public record and a sealed deed (in a Dead Sea cave kind of jar) for confirmation. Jeremiah thus thumbed his nose at events. He told us that there is no lost good and told us why: "For thus says the Lord . . . : Houses and fields and vineyards shall again be bought in this land."

II

The only comparable instance that comes quickly to mind is the sale of the farm on which the enemy Hannibal's tent was pitched, three miles from Rome, during his successful invasion.[3] That sale, in noble faith, was transacted in the Roman Forum. But Jeremiah's business has much deeper tones. He believed that God was using the Chaldean invasion as a scourge on Israel for her breach of God's covenant. He believed it and said it. That was why he was in prison. That perhaps was why he had never married. "How to Win Friends and Influence People!"[4] Let us hope that our grandchildren may not learn that we made *that* book a best seller! Besides, land meant far more to Israel than to us or to ancient Rome: the land and God's covenant with Israel were almost one: the land was the sign and seal of the covenant. Probably Jeremiah had little hope that he himself would ever live on his purchased farm. That was not the point. He was preaching a sermon in action (if only all preachers could so preach!) on the theme: "Lift up your hearts: the Lord God omnipotent reigneth";[5] or, rather, on his text: "Thus says the Lord . . . : Houses and fields and vineyards shall again be bought in this land." Did not the newspapers once tell of a lake being drained in Ireland to disclose a village 4,500 years old? Jeremiah said: "This flood shall pass, and the covenant land shall reappear washed clean of disobedience." Can you hear the story without a braver heart? All right: that braver beating of the heart is existential evidence, of perhaps the only kind that brave men will seek.

III

Let us look more closely at this matter of proof. Christian faith, or any worthy faith, can never be demonstrated by logic. God is not the end term of a syllogism. If He were, He could not be God. He would be in the power of *our* mind. He would be an existent among other existents; one term, however superior, among other terms. Logic does not establish truth: truth by its axioms enables logic to live. God is the whole axiom, the reason and ground by Whom we go on living, the kind of axiom which moves a man to say:

> For right is right, since God is God,
>   And right the day must win;
> To doubt would be disloyalty,
>   To falter would be sin.[6]

When Japan invaded China, Heywood Broun, a New York columnist, something of a sophisticate, and not then a religious man, wrote an indignant column entitled "They Will Come Back!" [7] How did he know? He knew, or else the whole scheme of things is mockery. From that latter alternative we shrink with a shudder of soul. If life were mockery, and we knew it, something other than mockery would thereby be in us, and we would still have to reckon with— with the very ground of our nature.

Of course, the mystery of time is here involved. God does not balance His books every month or year, except in strange hidden ways. He does bring insecurities on the proud, including the proud of mind, even in the instant of their victory; and He does draw the lowly into His light, even in the instant of their calamity. But *outwardly* His books are not balanced even with every generation. They seem never to be balanced in this planet, a fact that brings dismay on the man who lives only for this world. Of course the books are being balanced. Can you enter a Gothic cathedral, such as that in Durham, remembering how it was built by community labor at great cost—the wood carver working on a few inches of screen and hoping that some man in another age would complete the work: can you see such a shrine, the marching pillars leading on to the symbol of the Cross set in deep shadow, without being quickened at heart? It was built for nothing more substantial than a prayer, which is not man's act alone but the movement of God in man's life. Most men diced and drank, and laughed at "this religious bunk." But when you visit Europe, you do not seek out the place where men diced and drank. Maybe the "proof" of Christian faith can never be anything more solid than, let us say, the Bach *B Minor Mass.*

Yet there is always enough evidence that God will restore the waste places, enough evidence for our courage but never so much that we are spared the venture. Goodness is not a sure thing. If it were, there might be no goodness but only a shrewd bet, prudentially, on a sure thing. Again and again we are flung back on faith, which kindles reason, with ever and again some bright beckoning to cheer us on our way. This beckoning as an instance: the exiles *did* return from Babylon. They *did* reclaim their farms. Jeremiah's real-estate deed was not lost, at least not lost in this sense: the Scriptures record it, and you and I discuss it with a whimsical smile, saying to each other: "He bet his soul against history." If only the deed were in a museum and we could go to see it! We might more quickly take a new grip on courage. The whole episode is a foregleam of the Cross of Christ.

That mention reminds us that the land comes back, not as it once was but in new and changed form. Israel returned from Babylon and again broke the covenant. Then the covenant was renewed in Jesus: "This . . . is the new covenant in my blood" [8] Then the Church emerged, the new people of the covenant—under the same mission fulfilled in Christ, under the same judgment in their disobedience, under the same renewing mercy. As for Jesus, how much would you have bet on Him on the first Good Friday? The religious community traduced Him. Empire trod on Him as callously as on a moth. The crowd gaped at Him as they might at a dogfight. How much would you have bet? Of course, if Jeremiah had been there, he would have bought the land on which the cross stood. Other people would then have said: "The place of a crucifixion is accursed." The owner of the land, if anyone owned it, would then have said: "A fool and his money are soon parted." But Jeremiah would have said: "No panic price! A good round sum for it. Let it never be said that the place where he died was cheaply bought. And we will do it legally, for the world hereafter may wish to see this deed of transfer." "Thus says the Lord . . . : Houses and fields and vineyards shall again be bought in this land."

IV

There are subthemes and variations in this music. Would Jeremiah, living today, say that Communism is the scourge of God? And would we clap him in jail for subversion? That overrunning of the mission project in China is a troubling portent. It leaves us with uneasy conscience. We fail to ask how and why Communism came. We would have to say: from the lonely, fierce, and fiercely compassionate mind of Karl Marx—"out of" Engels, and he "out of" an arbitrary transfer of the Hegelian dialectic from philosophy to economics. But that would be the academic answer. Communism came from man's insensate pride, but also from the indignant sufferings of the mass of mankind in Russia. It sprang up in the desolation that followed one world war, and grew in the desolation that followed another world war. Meanwhile there was a church in Russia that may have been richer in ritual than in the courage of love. When was Communism most rife in America? In the "Depression." Where? In the poverty of Harlem. Meanwhile Western nations spent their substance in comfort and armaments. This account is a sweeping oversimplification of present history, but not, therefore, bereft of truth. Perhaps it was not surprising that compassionate but fuzzy-minded students, who had no safeguard in vital faith, should have turned to Communism. The whole portent leaves us uneasy. Perhaps the church in Russia and in America helped to provoke Communism, a fact that still does not condone the Russian heresy. Would Jeremiah say of modern Russia what he said of Babylon?—the scourge of the Lord on a wayward and selfish culture. No, for history does not repeat. But he might say things not palatable in the average church.

V

But these thoughts, though not unrelated to our theme, are not the central word. We are saying, as central word, in Jeremiah faith,

"There shall never be one lost good." That is the Browning phrase. It comes from the Browning illustration. An organist improvising, and suddenly music far better than he knew, such music as he could hardly have composed: it was given. He stopped, almost exhausted by very ecstasy. But now he could not recall what he had played. Try as he would, he could not recapture that wonder of sound: "Out of three sounds . . . not a fourth sound, but a star." [9] Was it therefore lost, like a friendly project in China, like an orphanage swept away in a flood? Browning's organist declares his faith:

> There shall never be one lost good!
> What was, shall live as before.

Then follows a line not fully convincing:

> The evil is null, is naught, is silence implying sound.

Then the poem resumes with strong power to convince:

> What was good, shall be good, with, for evil, so much good more;
> On the earth the broken arcs; in the heaven, a perfect round. [10]

To that faith we summon you. There is enough evidence of the right kind to warrant the venture; there is not enough to spare us the venture. The venture builds its own evidence.

This honest warning must be given. You may not see the farm recovered in your lifetime. How soon triumph comes is an item in God's books. He does not balance His books every year. Therefore, we live toward Him not toward the calendar. Man is not slave of the calendar. In a Cairo museum can be found a small clay tablet, thousands of years old, showing a queen with her arm protectingly round her legless husband. Perhaps some people said that such devotion was foolish, that with her youth and grace she might have married a warrior king. Centuries later the tablet speaks its truth: "Love never fails. . . !" [11] Much less God's love given in Jesus Christ. The seed sown in China or in a Pennsylvania orphanage springs to new life: "Houses and fields and vineyards shall again be bought in this land."

VI

Anybody care to buy a Jeremiah real-estate bond? I've one to offer: the Christian faith. What happened in Galilee and on a cross and in the Resurrection shall become a Kingdom. Anyone care to thumb his nose against the contemporary scene for the sake of Christ? Anyone care to take a "flier" on His Cross, against all cruelty, in a planet filled with griefs and graves? Years later they found Jeremiah's legal deed. Someone hereafter may even find this sermon. If it is found, someone may say: "He must have sounded a fool that morning, even more than usual. But as things have come to pass, he was right. Let's hope they listened to him!" It shall come back, in finer form—every lost good. "For thus says the Lord of hosts," sovereign ruler of history, "Houses and fields and vineyards shall again be bought in this land."

4

ANXIETY AND FAITH

"There is no fear in love, but perfect love casts out fear. For fear has to do with punishment, and he who fears is not perfected in love."

I John 4:18

"Therefore do not be anxious about tomorrow, for tomorrow will be anxious for itself."

Matt. 6:34

The sign "Shelter" is at our street corners, though no shelter would be much use against a sizable H-bomb. Another sign is set on our main highways advising that the road is reserved for military traffic in the event of enemy attack, but the sign has meaning only for an old-fashioned war: a bomb would hardly extend military courtesy to leave certain roads clear for military battle plans. We shall not speak much today about this crisis of our times. It is not the job of the Church to excite frenzy. We need not envy our forefathers their more placid world. We live at a crux in history, in what the New Testament calls *kairos,* a fulfillment of one order and the beginning of another way of life. If we are near destruction, we are near a proffered light. Our topic concerns the anxiety in which modern man is obliged to live: Anxiety and Faith. What are we to do in our anxiety?

I

What we should not do is fairly clear. We should *not* assume that "man's intelligence" will call a halt to the arms race. Intelligence is a wide, deep word; but since it is not as deep as the dynamics of depth psychology, it is no salvation. The mind is also vulnerable: it can rationalize. Besides, man is a creature of emotions: his angers and fears can overwhelm his intelligence. Modern man may set up a chain reaction in nuclear power by monkeying with destructive power, monkeying being the appropriate word. We should *not* get drunk on either whisky or art in the resolve to forget the whole business, for the whole business will be there when we "come to." We should *not* whine, "What can anyone do about it?" for we are not marionettes. We should *not* sell out to the demagogue who tells us that ferreting out a few Communists will solve the problem, for man's anxiety is as deep as human nature and as wide as all history—much wider and deeper than the childish-cruel simplification of Communism. Ferreting out men who would lay aside persuasion for violence is the necessary business of the police but not an answer to man's anxiety. We should *not* yield to newspapers which almost incite terror and gather in the cash: today's journalism, revolving round the two poles of conflict and sensation, has scant guidance for our deliverance. We should *not* cry, "Don't get frantic!" for that might be the best way to start a stampede. A loud horselaugh at the present result of "man's intelligence" would be better than these dead-end streets.

Psychiatry tells us what to do with anxiety, even though not on the profoundest level. It says "Face the anxiety." Actually it would be easier to face a fear, for fear is specific—as with a fire in the house when we can at least scream—whereas anxiety is inchoate like a clinging fog. But the counsel still holds: we can face anxiety to the measure of saying, "I am anxious. Why?" Certain fears might then shape themselves from the fog: fear of sickness or rejection or death; and the confrontation would, to some measure, grant us power. Psychiatry says also: "Take some action." There are perhaps times when any action in anxiety-fear is better than no action. No action in this issue is like a bird mesmerized under the fang of a serpent. In anxiety regarding health we can act, namely, go to a doctor and thus confront the worst or best. In vague misgiving it would be better to do anything worthy than to do nothing but moan, saying, "I am lost." Face the anxiety and act, says the psychiatrist. This summary does no justice to his fine realm of healing, and less to our topic, but it has some truth and value.

In our present anxiety this double counsel seems both useless and beyond our powers. Suppose the fog, as we face it, proves to be a blacker fog. It might then be wiser to get drunk, not on whisky but, let us say, on El Greco or astronomy. As for action, what action? If man is dust, idiotic dust, and doomed to dust, why stir up the dust and the idiocy? Now we are asking real questions. They go deeper than psychiatry or any other branch of medicine. The only answer to anxiety is faith. Science lives by faith—for instance, the faith that mind and cosmos live in a common medium and that the sensory world is susceptible to measurement. Social service lives by the faith that human beings are worth the trouble. When psychiatry says: "Face it, and then act on some life-strategy," it has a covert faith that the whole process of creation brings healing to a would-be open and honest mind. So in what faith shall we meet anxiety? But first, let us do the facing, even though in only a covert faith.

II

Our modern anxiety is modern only in its form, for anxiety is as old as human nature. The atomic bomb has not *caused* our fear-anxiety: it has only *awakened* it to give it new occasion. Men have always been anxious, even though some ages seem to have been more anxious than others. Dread seems to have been extreme in the Greek time just prior to Plato and in Luther's day, just as it seems to be extreme in our century. But in every age there is anxiety. The "right" event—such as the Orson Welles broadcast of the arrival of men from Mars, which sent thousands running to the streets because they took the broadcast for very fact [1]—will drive a shaft to that hidden reservoir of anxiety-fear, and it comes boiling to the top. Then what is anxiety?

There is no anatomy to this fog, but perhaps there are certain looming shapes. There is, for example, *ignorance*. We do not know our own deeps of mind, much less our neighbor's mind or "what goes" in Russia, for the very term "iron curtain" betrays our misgiving; or what the future holds, for such events as national socialism or economic depression always take us in some measure of surprise; and manifestly we do not know what may await us beyond death. Each of these items is signpost to a vast country, but all of them show man's constitutional ignorance—constitutional because our nature is finite and mortal. Another looming component of anxiety is *guilt*. By guilt I mean not essentially the breach of a moral code (Jesus broke codes from above them, as in the case of the Sabbath law)[2] but the denial of man's creaturehood. We walk a precarious line between the natural order in which we are set, but which never satisfies our deepest spirit, and a higher order which we know as our true home but to which we cannot lift ourselves by our own powers. We are neither animals nor angels. To pose as either is sin: to try to live as animals, however refined, is Baal-sin; to try to be our own God is pride-sin. This guilt takes us out of our proper nature, so that life becomes meaningless, and we feel lost—and anxious. The other looming component is *death*. Not somebody else's death, not death scientifically explained, not death philosophically considered, not death "sometime," but my death and your death—soon. For death speaks of judgment, if only because any event is judgment on preceding life ("Fear has to do with punishment"); and our life in regard to death seems to our mortal eyes to be a "Long Day's Journey into Night." [3] Once again these sentences tempt us to vast explorations, but we resist the tempting: our immediate job is the facing of anxiety.

Now let us probe more deeply into anxiety. The fog may hold hidden treasure. *Why* do we dread ignorance? Because of something in us that hungers to *know*. *Why* do we dread guilt? Because we hold some dim surmise of life beyond the "stigma of finitude." *Why* do we dread death? Because something in us "ought not" to die. Anxiety is not the ultimate word but only the penultimate word. We would not know ignorance for what it is but for some light of wisdom; or guilt, but for some norm of purity; or death, but for some dawn of life; or despair, if some hope were not in us. Anthropologists who say that religion began in fear need not dismay us. They do not know, for they were not there; but if we assume their guess is right, fear is still a correlative word: it betokens a prior peace and trust. The savage at the mouth of his cave, crying to the gods, "Save me!" took for granted that there was something in him that had claim to be saved. Has not Augustine said that fear is the needle that pierces us that it may carry a thread to bind us to heaven? [4] All right: this facing of anxiety begins to show some clearing in the fog, and it confronts us with a choice: we may choose the despair or its correlated hope, suicide or "The Courage to Be." [5]

III

But this Light by which we know our darkness must presumably shine on us, at least from time to time, or the light of life will utterly go out. Faith in God must know God's visitation, nay, must come from God's visitation, or faith will languish. Faith in any area of man's life is first a beckoning and then the valor of response. We may presently need the overwhelming by anxiety, if only to rebuke the impertinence-pride of the creature; but then the creature can live again only by the Creator's grace. Has not every man among us said to himself not once but many times, "If God would only give us some clear sign"? Granted *that*, we could walk through darkness or even stand in fog until the fog clears, or live in memory of the light until the light returns. If only we knew that our ignorance is held in Wisdom, our guilt in Mercy, and our death in Life and Love!

What kind of sign would we need? A *gentle* sign, for our manhood would vanish if it were coerced; we would become slaves under coercion, and then robots—if we still lived. The sign would have to be a *beckoning* sign to which we could give willing response, not a bludgeoning sign. The sign, we guess, would be *a lowly sign*, for, if our guilt is pride, the sin could hardly be cured by a vaster pride. A *loving sign*, yet set in power, we guess: a *gift* of some sort, for the native language of love is gift. The illustration might be a man offering a woman an engagement ring: we have no other parables than our life can provide. The man would be gentle in that instance: he would not seize the woman by the throat, saying, "You're going to wear this ring, and no other man shall ever get you!" He would be lowly: he would not strut with the ring in his hand as though he were about to bestow an eternal favor. He would give the ring at cost of sacrifice: he would not borrow it from a neighbor or charge it to the woman of his choice, or offer a "dime-store" ring. Thus he would say: "I love you." And she? She should not demand proof, as we demand "proof" of God, that life with him would always be secure. She would be coercive and a fool to demand "proof," and he would be wise in such a demand to run for our instanced "Shelter." No, she must trust the surge of her deepest nature and say: "I love *you!*" and then and there she must begin to wear the ring.

God has given men *this* sign: "God so loved the world, that he gave his only begotten Son." [6] So *gentle* is that gift that Jesus stole into our world at poor and conquered Bethlehem; so *lowly*, that he took upon himself the form of a slave [7] in lowliest service; so *costly* that it cost him all the passion-pains of Calvary. Does this account oversimplify the gospel? The proper tests remain: Does Christ judge and correct, and yet fulfill, God's previous gifts of light? Is he sovereign still over the disclosures of our time? Is God's revelation in Christ seminal, so that it always brings new harvests of light? Does he take us unawares as by the Ultimate, so that we are now required to stand outside ourselves to ask the ultimate question about the living of life? Does he speak to our deepest need of wisdom, mercy, and life beyond death? But our simple parable is yet at the core of the issue. And what of our response? It is the courage of faith, "I love You," not the shabby demand for "proof." Jesus asked his followers not, "Do you accept this rationale?" but "Do you love me?" "There is no fear in love, but perfect love" (God's love in Christ) "casts out fear."

IV

Now we can return to our strategy of "Face it, and act" but on much deeper ground. Let us *face* the anxiety which atomic power has aroused. Do you fear death by the bomb? You must die in any event. The bomb as portent of man's sin is as dark a portent as any man could wish—or never wish—but the bomb as the sign of death has made no change. To die wholesale is not different from dying retail, for each of us must die each for himself, and none of us is asked to die more than once. All who have lived before us seem to have managed the business of dying with at least this measure of success: they are dead. Then is it burning by the bomb that you and I fear? If so: man can bear only so much pain: then there is an "automatic cutout," and unconsciousness comes. Besides, the Christian martyrs, we have good reason to believe, turned death into joy as when the English martyr going to the stake, said: "Thanked be God. I am even at home." [8] Then is our fear a fear for the end of history? That is a nobler fear. But God, who brought our planet from primal fire and vapor and has led the human pilgrimage through the strange years, is not dismayed by our atomic firecrackers or by our sputnik toys. The Power-Love that fashioned us presumably can keep us—in more wonderful dimensions of life than this childish planet can give. So we face the fear.

And the action? On the world stage much more can be done than our poor, negative, defensive politics has yet dreamed. China sent a "cultural mission" to India and thus made a bond between the two lands. If we say that China's motives were mixed, we have yet to pursue that strategy to its far fine limits from better motives. The attempt may fail? Of course it may, but the man making it would not be anxious, for he would know God by response to God's beckonings of love. Meanwhile in our daily life we can let the "perfect love" have some path through us in home and friendship. This also may fail? Yes, though we do not know: God laid chaos and hate under a very large fee from one home in Nazareth. Fail or not, that kind of life would not breed anxiety: it would cast out fear. To these ends we can pray in the "flight of the alone to the Alone." [9] Perhaps prayer should be called "the flight of the Alone to the alone," for perhaps it is the movement of God's life in us. Age on age it has been triumph over anxiety, for by prayer our contingent and anxious freedom is at home in the Eternal Freedom. Someone still says that all action may fail? Perhaps the truer word is *must* fail. Why should we expect eternal permanence in a transient world? But God is never more Godlike than in "failure," as witness the utter "failure" of the Cross. So we can act, leaving the issue in God's hands.

V

When Jesus walked through Galilee, people talked about many things. They said, "Suppose harvest should fail," just as we discuss crop prospects. They bemoaned high taxes, as we in our time. They asked, "Have you seen Simon the Magician?" as we ask about Hollywood celebrities. They asked again, "Have you tried the Temple of Diana?" just as we run from one shallow cult to another. Meanwhile Jesus was on their roads, offering them deliverance from anxiety by sheer act of unbribed love. He said: "I love you." He asked in ultimate accent: "Do you love me?" Most people in those days never answered him, nay, never even pondered the meaning of him. And we? Over the fireplace of an old inn in Bray, England, there is a motto: "Fear knocked at the door. Faith answered. There was no one there."

5

PERSONAL WORTH

"Are not five sparrows sold for two pennies?
And not one of them is forgotten before God.
Why, even the hairs of your head are all num-
bered."   *Luke 12:6-7*

Two sparrows were sold for one penny. If a man wished to be reckless and spend *two* pennies, the storekeeper threw in an extra sparrow, so worthless were sparrows. "Not one of them is forgotten . . . ." The Matthew version says, "Not one of them will fall to the ground without your Father's will." [1] But they do fall, from high-tension wires and because cats plunder the nest. As for the hairs of our head, they too fall despite the promises made by hair-tonic manufacturers. That is part of the problem. The realities of our life do not seem to square with these assurances by Christ. Then we should not side-step: we should meet that issue.

I

God appears utterly careless over millions of sparrows that fall. Much worse: He seems careless of people caught in a tidal wave or an earthquake. In George Eliot's *Mr. Gilfil's Love Story*, she says of Tina:

While this poor little heart was being bruised with a weight too heavy for it, Nature was holding on her calm inexorable way, in unmoved and terrible beauty. The . . . great ships were laboring over the waves; the toiling eagerness of commerce, the fierce spirit of revolution, were only ebbing in brief rest; and sleepless statesmen were dreading the possible crisis of the morrow. What were our little Tina and her trouble in this mighty torrent, rushing from one awful unknown to another? [2]

The words might have been written yesterday, so true are they to our times.

The other part of the problem is hinted in that quotation: we ourselves aid and abet the seeming callousness of nature. We treat one another as if human life were worthless, as "hands" instead of persons in a factory, as "numbers" instead of men in a war. So nature and men conspire in unconcern for human life, let alone the life of sparrows. Our present world provides the convicting evidence. Armaments take on an almost fatalistic movement toward destruction. Technology with its vast wheels seems to eclipse individual life. As for the cosmos, blind and deaf,

> The heavens at last will end, as all things must—
> to let new heavens ripple out of dust.[3]

Then what becomes of the sparrow or the hair on a man's head? What becomes of the man? Jesus was offering comfort. "God not care for you?" he was exclaiming: "Why, He cares for the sparrow! Even the hairs of your head are all numbered!" But to be honest, as we should be, especially in church, we cannot see it. Nature and man conspire in callousness.

II

But there are other facts, and they also should be confronted. This fact, for instance: the creation is painstakingly and wonderfully individual. There are no duplicates. There is no mass production. The dust on a moth's wing when seen under a microscope is a copse of waving plumes, and each plume is different; each strand of each plume is after its own fashion. Every hair of our head is distinguishable in form and color from every other hair. Scholastic theology used to debate how many angels could dance on the point of a pin. The question was not utterly foolish, for modern thought now asks how many units of force are in incessant motion on a pin point and wonders if the whole race could count them in a thousand years. They tell me, I being no physicist, that one of the questions confronting modern physics is that of identity: Is each unit of force different from every other unit? Each sparrow is different. There is astonishing particularity in our world.

Furthermore, that fact appears still more strikingly in the realm of personality. Identical twins are never identical, for each lives in his own secret world, and that world is nonrecurrent: no other man will ever so live his life. In this realm assuredly there is no mass production; for that is one of man's conveniences which with all man's work partly falsifies the work of the Creator. Abraham Lincoln once commented that God must love the common people because He made so many of them.[4] The comment has its compassionate truth, but in strict fact God made none of them. He made each man with his own fingerprint, his own play of features, his own slant of mind, his own mysterious personhood. The universe may seem careless of your life or mine, but it has been careful enough to fashion each of us in individual craftsmanship.

Another fact: you and I, when we act halfway worthily, treat our neighbor as though he were precious, as though he were a new creation of God. Some time ago a child fell into a disused well shaft. Men quit their work to try to rescue one child. A nation waited to hear the news. When rescue was made, a whole nation rejoiced. It was a feature story in the newspapers. Why? Because we all know by some deep instinct that each human life is precious. Yes, we engage in mass slaughter in war, but we must then try endlessly to justify it—and we never succeed. We are uneasy about capital punishment. Some say "yes," and some say "no," and obviously the issue is ambiguous as is all our life; but if we say "yes," we must then wonder if we have not thrust the criminal out of life to hide from ourselves our own share in the guilt. Here is the criminal, a person, being led now to the electric chair, a man able to judge his own life, one who sees time from beyond the fret of time. What right have we . . . ? Axiomatically we know that each life is precious. Whence did we learn that knowledge? Is it the image of God in us?

Thus a further fact: we are above life even while we live it. Sometimes we say: "We and all things, gnats and men and stars alike, are held in natural law." But how do we know? We view the world thus, so there is a dimension in us above natural law. The sun is 330,000 times larger in mass than our planet, and flames leap from the sun 500,000 miles into space; but Sir Norman Lockyer discovered helium in the sun, and Sir William Ramsey used that clue to discover helium in our earth; [5] and we now use the gas in our dirigibles. Who is this "man" who thus contemplates and uses the cosmos? When Plato described man as a two-legged animal, Diogenes plucked the feathers from a rooster, so that it strutted in a comic nakedness; and then said: "Here is Plato's man." [6] That may not be a full answer to naturalism, but it will serve as a beginning. Perhaps there is no need of answer. Man is the being who views the cosmos. Man is the being who judges his own life. Man is the responsible creature: he listens to a voice of silence and then says: "I know I should treat my life and my neighbor's life as a center of freedom, above natural law, above time even while in it, held forever in the secrecies of the eternal."

III

Then why have we lost the sense of personal worth? This is the other part of the problem: Why do we aid and abet the seeming callousness of nature? "Inferiority" is a mark of our time. Our assertiveness only proves that fact. The followers of Hitler (and he himself) were plagued by a sense of littleness and sought compensation in marches and banners and a megalomaniac leader to whom they attributed almost messianic powers. On a smaller scale, the juvenile delinquent feels lost in the shuffle of our modern world and, therefore, tries to "register" by a zootsuit, sideburns, and gangsterism. We wonder if our forefathers were tormented by this complex of inferiority. We do not know, but we guess that they had a stancher sense of personhood than we can claim. Inferiority seems to be a sickness of our time. Why and whence?

Sometimes we attribute it to the traumatic shock of the new knowledge. We now know the lonely vastness of the universe, and we ask, "What is man in this play of worlds on worlds?" We now know the magnitudes of time and history, the long, slow, tortuous course of evolution, and again we ask of this myriad human midge-breed, "What is man?" Beyond much doubt this new knowledge is a factor in our doubt of human worth. But it may not be the main factor. Sight of stars in their music and majesty can ennoble rather than dwarf us, and we ourselves are the astronomers. As for the march of the generations, that is a proud pageant;

or if it is not, we still guess that we should not surrender to the vulgarity of numbers. The new knowledge is perhaps the *excuse* for our felt inferiority, not the real *reason*.

Then the real reason? It could be pride which leads us to treat our neighbor with contempt and which then makes our own life seem contemptible. Our cult of proud cities condemns the individual to become a digit in a multitude, one more sound in a cacophony of steps on echoing sidewalks. Our cult of business prestige loses each man in *The Organization Man*.[7] Our cult of money-arrogance stigmatizes the poor man as a failure; for in view of the fact of scarcity and the accompanying fact that few men can be rich, if money is the test of success, most men must fail. Our cult of national power puts men in uniform so that they become uniform, and meanwhile threatens the race of men with incineration. We have blamed on the new knowledge the loss of a sense of personal worth, but we ourselves are to blame. The loss is due to our sin, that is, to the egocentric pride of the creature, a pride which then becomes its own chaos since no man can for long pose as the center of the world.

IV

Then the antidote? The antidote is found only in a cure for human sin. Our text is the word of Christ, and what we say today we say in sight of him. Here we are in the "massisms" of our time, our nuclear powers, our impersonal technologies; here where we become bitter because we do not seem to matter and where in bitterness we turn upon our neighbors and thus add bitterness to bitterness. We are asking now how to fashion a way of life in which every person shall be regarded as a person, a center of freedom, a subject and not merely an object. The answer is not at first in some new economic structure or in any self-tinkering, but in renewal at the very springs of personhood. We are persons only when we know that we are confronted by God, when we know that He, the Eternal, has dealings with us. Does He not speak in Jesus Christ? If not there, then not anywhere. Some steps in recovery thus become clear.

We look on Jesus and repent. We have not treated our neighbor as he treated men such as I. We confront that fact and turn from our present life. "I've been wrong. I've treated my neighbor as a thing, or at best, as a name. I forget the face of the waiter in the restaurant, and it does not occur to me that I might be the waiter and he the customer. I have sunk into the pride of the times and failed in brave individual witness. So I have lost both my neighbor and myself." This repentance is not morbid: it confesses failure but also turns to the light. When I say, "I've been wrong," to Whom do I speak? The confession restores me to that Eternity from which a man views his own life and knows that he is better than a creature of time.

Then a man looks on Christ again, and his small human pride is melted in Christ's love. He said "not a sparrow," and he said, "the very hairs of your head," and he said "God misses nothing"; and so dealt with every man. Thus to the shabby collaborator Zacchaeus: "I must stay at your house today." [8] because it was as lonely and despised as any house in town. Or to some woman taken in adultery: "Neither do I condemn you." [9] Or to his disciples, men who often misunderstood him but whom he turned into saints: "Fear not, little flock, for it is your Father's good pleasure to give you the kingdom." [10] At the Cross all the self-hate of men whose pride made human life inferior was spewed on him, and he exposed his heart to it—soldiers secretly loathing their job, the dispossessed mob bitter because they were dispossessed, Temple leaders despising themselves because they knew the Temple asked of them a better loyalty. All this he accepted and, there in the alchemy of his own spirit, changed it into revelation and love. That self-same love, known by faith to be God's love for us, is our redemption. Was not the Giotto portrait of Dante discovered behind the whitewash and grime of a barn wall? [11] Jesus never averted his eyes from the grime or from the whitewash by which we try to cover our sins, but always he saw the picture. By him and in him we know ourselves held in eternal love and become sure again of personal worth.

Can the sense of personal worth ever be recovered except in faith in God's love? Robert Oppenheimer said in a moving lecture, as he confronted the anonymous brutalities of our time, that we can still find some solace in human love.[12] Yes, some measure of solace, for human love is sometimes the medium through which Divine love finds us. But human love is fitful and broken at best, and it is marked for death in this planet. We do not easily love our own life, for we know ourselves too well, and meanwhile there is that in us which can stand above all human love to appraise it at its best and worst. Unless human love is held in an ultimate Sanction, it is but a fading light. "Not one of them is forgotten *before God*": in that sanction we can at least begin by our deeds to love human nature in ourselves and in other men. Thus John Woolman quit business because he was making more money than he needed for a true life and because he feared that his money-making might brand other men as failures; and he crossed the Atlantic as a steerage passenger lest otherwise the steerage passengers might feel that he was looking down on them.[13] It is not Chamber of Commerce doctrine, but it is "the mind of Christ."

V

"But sparrows do fall," someone reminds us. Yes, but they are not forgotten of God, not one of them. They fall right into the care of God. "The hairs of our head fall," someone insists. Yes, but each is different; each is a separate and particular creation, and each falls into God's hands. "Men fall," our sad commentator continues, and he is right: they fall by swift death in fire and plague and battle. But even in this world each views the world from an eternity above the world. Each is even now in God. No man is ever outside God. At death each falls into the love of God, that same love, holy and merciful, revealed in Christ; that same triumph of love which turned Good Friday into Easter Day. Not one of us is forgotten before God. Trust that faith, try to live in it, and you will day by day become more sure of it.

6

GOD AND LAUGHTER

"He that sitteth in the heavens shall laugh: the Lord shall have them in derision."

Ps. 2:4 (K.J.V.)

"When the Lord turned again the captivity of Zion, we were like them that dream. Then was our mouth filled with laughter, and our tongue with singing." *Ps. 126:1-2 (K.J.V.)*

"Even so, I tell you, there is joy before the angels of God over one sinner who repents."

Luke 15:10

Laughter is a strange portent. In a world held in mystery, in seeming nothingness, a world in which we can neither prove God nor escape Him, our faces pucker in smiles. In a generation which competes in destructive weapons until final destruction looms, a cartoon appears in *The Boston Globe* [1] showing Uncle Sam as a hitchhiker while two Russian sputniks flash past him, one of them with a little grinning dog on board. We laugh at our own predicament. We joke even about death. A friend of mine, a bishop, is still chuckling over a pompous, humorless mortician who congratulated him on "your *graveside* manner." We can quip even in the act or moment of death, as when the not-so-saintly Charles II apologized for being "so unconscionable a time in dying." [2] In a world dark with griefs and hollow with graves we laugh. Even in war and sorrow we pity the man who cannot laugh. Why? Here are some comments which you can use to better purpose than I.

I

There seems to be laughter in creation itself, and if so, that is the basic laughter. On the first day of history, so the Bible tells us, "the morning stars sang together." [3] Every new springtime breaks into the gaiety of flowering meadows and purling streams. "The trees . . . clap their hands";[4] the little hills skip like lambs.[5] These phrases come, of course, from our minds but not without beckonings from nature. This laughter of creation may seem to us to be mockery when sorrow strikes, but it accords with our joyous moods. There is even a comic side to nature. A row of penguins looks for all the world like the speakers' table at the annual banquet of the National Association of Manufacturers. The small boy rightly exclaimed on first sight of a camel, "I don't believe it." Children's books, which are quite as important as our philosophies, feature this comic side of animal life. No somber God could ever have made a bullfrog or a giraffe.

This creation-laughter we see in little children. Nietzsche said gloomily: "Man . . . alone suffers so excruciatingly that he was compelled to invent laughter." [6] But man did not invent laughter, or anything else except from materials given to his hand. Who taught a child to laugh? Who needs to do any such teaching? You say that they imitate the chuckling of their parents? That only presses the question further back, even supposing it to be a valid question. Children laugh as birds sing: because they are made that way. We listen to a child's laughter, listen guiltily, and wish that our laughter were as unspoiled.

Theologians and preachers sometimes discuss the "duty of cheerfulness." It is a contradiction in terms and a horrible phrase in any event. Say, rather, that laughter is native and that our world has times and occasions that provoke it and that if we do not then laugh, we stultify ourselves. The Harvard man who placed an advertisement in *The Crimson*[7] for the sale of a bike, offering as inducement for the bike that it "knows its own way to Wellesley," is a benefactor in our community. The Anglican hymnbook has a

hymn which should be in every hymnbook, "Glad that I live am
I." [8] The Bible says again with deep wisdom: "There is . . . a time
to weep and a time to laugh." [9] We should not choke the laughter
because tears sometimes stain our days. The laughter has its own
rightful time and place. If people laugh even on the way home
from a funeral (as they do, as any wise pastor can tell you), perhaps they should: that release is given in our pent-up sorrow. We
believe despite our morbid moods that creation-laughter *is* basic.
There remains for us what Browning called "the wild joys of living." [10]

II

There is also the laughter of man's dilemma. We quip by nature
at our own predicament. Because the dilemma is a dilemma, because the predicament is always mixed with human guilt, this
laughter has elements of derision, and it is never far from tears.
Nature has cancer as well as flowering fields, death as well as birth;
and human nature has monumental self-idolatries as well as neighborly kindness. Who can doubt this ambiguity in nature? It confronts us wherever we walk and wherever we stay. Who can doubt
this ambiguity in human nature? Think of Hitler dancing a jig
when France surrendered, and think of the long failure of statesmanship which was left with no better expedient than to fight his
fire with fire. In "this ambiguous earth" [11] we can still laugh, but
the laughter is now inevitably "mixed." It has undertones of self-
condemnation and overtones of irony. In bad men it becomes a
bitter trampling sarcasm; in good men, a rueful smile.

We should examine with more care this typical laughter of our
adult life, for laughter also has gifts of wisdom. When are we ourselves comic? Whenever we try to live beyond the bounds of our
ordained nature. And these bounds? We are in the material order
and cannot escape it, even though we are never content with it; at
the same time we see ourselves in the natural order, from a stance
above our earthborn life which we still cannot escape. The bounds
of our nature are those of a precarious line between time—which
does not content us—and eternity—into which we cannot lift ourselves. Whenever we leave that line, we become comic. Henri Bergson argues that man becomes comic when he acts like a thing, that
is, when he sinks below the ordained line of creaturehood;[12] Alexander Bain likewise proposes that humor is always the humor of

man's "degradation." [13] Both are right, but both perhaps fail to see that man is comic when he tries to live above the line, when he poses as an angel or as his own god, as well as when he seeks a lower order of life.

Consider instances of a man becoming laughable because he is posing as a wiser or holier man than human nature grants—the comedy of his trying vainly to live above the line of precarious creaturehood. Ashes from a man's pipe on an upper balcony are carried by a whimsical wind into the dinner of a man eating on a lower balcony. Says the one: "Why do you knock your ashes on to my terrace?" Says the other: "Why do you place your terrace underneath my pipe?" [14] Neither man has power to control even the minor forces and vicissitudes of life, and both are angry in consequence because they are not gods or angels. Thus our "calculated risks" in statesmanship or in the building of apartment-house balconies are always miscalculated. Our terrifying defenses do not defend, for our adversary tries to outdo us in terror. Thus comedy, and irony, and guilt and tears. To take another instance: a hobo falling on a winter slide which boys are using would not be funny, for we would be sorry for him as victim of new misfortune piled on old misfortune; but if a bishop thus fell while wearing full regalia, or a professor dressed for a graduation ceremony, he would definitely be comic; for nobody can be as good as a bishop is supposed to be, or as wise as a professor sometimes thinks he is. We try to live above the line, and become comic.

Now take an instance of comedy and laughter that comes of life below the line of creaturehood. Two men imitating a horse, the one providing the forequarters and the other the hindquarters, with a horseskin thrown over them to complete the disguise, always bring merriment, especially in an ice show; for the men are acting as less than men by sinking into horse nature (what Bain calls "degradation"), and the pseudo-horse is trying to be more than a horse since horses do not skate. Similarly with the cartoon showing a man in the subway, with a pigeon on each shoulder. "Where are you taking them?" he was asked; and he answered, "Don't ask me: they got on at Fifty-ninth Street." The man was less than a man, for he had become a perch for pigeons; the pigeons were more than pigeons, for they were imitating foolish humans who bedevil themselves with subways. Naturalism merits no rebuttal, for men have always laughed it out of court. A man sinking into the natural

54

order is tragically comic (for example, the red nose of a drunkard: wood is painted red, not noses[15]) ; and that laughter against naturalism is a stronger retort than any argument.

But mark the tragedy of our thus leaving the line of our ordained nature. We know in these instances that we are neither animals nor angels. So we become self-estranged, and estranged from the true ground of our nature in God. In that self-estrangement we imagine that God is laughing at us: "He that sitteth in the heavens shall laugh: the Lord shall have them in derision." Perhaps God *is* laughing, perhaps He does hold us in derision, if there is that in God which in the deeps of His mystery answers to these human terms. There is "wrath" in God—the indignation of His "love." There is "derision" in God—the protest of His "pity." Always men have dimly sensed that derision. It is in *The Iliad*: "And unextinguishable laughter rose among the gods." [16] Heaven laughs, with tears, at our foolish attempts to be more than men or less than men. That our boasted defenses should now darken over us as a final threat, that our refusal to confront the real problem (our constitutional anxiety and pride) should lead us into a frenetic competition in sputniks, that our science should become instrument of our suicide, that our wealth should by our pursuit of it become taxed poverty, that our victories should reappear as defeat— this is the irony of history: "He that sitteth in the heavens shall laugh." Creation's laughter is sheer joy, but adult laughter in man's dilemma is close to tears and shame. A certain story tells of a doctor's impatience when he could find nothing wrong with his patient: "Why don't you forget yourself? Go see the clown Grumaldi, and laugh." Said the patient: "I am Grumaldi." [17]

III

But there is another kind of laughter, the healing laughter of redemption. It is not a child's laughter, and it is not man's dilemma-laughter. It is the joy of a new birth. Francis knew child's laughter in his earliest years in Assisi; and he knew adult laughter when as an unruly youth in that city he was the "life of the party," not without knowing and giving some real happiness; but the third laughter he did not know until with vows of poverty he gave himself to God before a high altar. Then and there joy was born in him by which he preached to the sparrows and danced in the village square. This laughter is the laughter of childlikeness beyond childishness. Perhaps our life is a pilgrimage from childish laughter, through the laughter of our guilty dilemma, to the childlike laughter that comes of God's forgiving and renewing grace. Many a man lives and dies only in the ruefulness of that middle term.

Can we find any parable of this best laughter? The small boy decided to run away from home: "I do not like this nasty house." Always we rebel against the walls of creaturehood. His mother told him that she was sorry for his desire but that she would help him pack. The lad was plucky: he left, scarcely able to lift the luggage. Where to go? When he reached the sidewalk, he sat there on the step between the garden path and the sidewalk. Where *shall* we go, where *can* we go, when we try to leave our humanness? His parents watched from behind window curtains. Soon he returned saving face cheerfully: "I've been away a long time." They agreed: "Was it a nice journey?" But, oh, the joy of the home-coming for them and for him! "Even so, I tell you, there is joy before the angels of God over one sinner who repents." This is the word of Christ. This is the joy which he revealed to our world. The bells of heaven ring whenever a man turns from his perverted skills and his insensate pride, from his poor attempts to live an animal life, to trust in the Power and the Love—the God who can lift him when he cannot lift himself.

Another parable, since here story is better far than argument? In the sequel to *The Pilgrim's Progress,* Christiana (Pilgrim's wife), her children, and a friend called Mercy follow him to the Celestial City. Christiana asks Mercy: "What was the matter that you did laugh in your sleep to-night? I suppose you was in a dream." Yes, Mercy had dreamed. She saw herself bemoaning the hardness of her heart, with people about her who were impatient of her complaint: "At this, some laughed at me, some called me fool, and some began to thrust me about"—the earthy answer to those ill-content with merely an earthy life. Then an angel came: "Mercy, what aileth thee?" As if she knew! Only angels know! "Peace be to thee!" Then she saw herself clothed in silver and gold, led by the angel through the skies to a Throne which was not "derision," for He who sat there said gently: "Welcome, daughter." Said Mercy: "So I woke . . . but did I laugh?" [18] She laughed and cried, with tears no longer bitter but rather childlike and at peace. "When the Lord turned again the captivity of Zion, we were like them that dream. Then was our mouth filled with laughter, and our tongue with singing."

IV

Even the laughter of our dilemma is still laughter, as if we knew unawares that the dilemma is always held in light. To the portent of laughter Christian faith gives the Christ-event, the historical drama of uncoercive love. So we may now choose how to laugh. We can laugh because life despite its darkness is good: "Glad that I live am I." That is basic laughter, and sadness may wait its turn. We can laugh too loud: that is dilemma-laughter, its loudness confessing its insecurity. We can laugh ruefully, with realism for man's failures, yet with kindly judgment since we also are "in the same condemnation," [19] well knowing that adult laughter is never far from tears. Are there not two faces over the proscenium arch of the theater which portray our mortal life—a laughing face and a weeping face?

But if we will, we may laugh in the midst of the storm in "unmixed" laughter. We can "become as little children",[20] in a new childlikeness, beyond childishness and beyond the adulthood that has known too many roads and too many doors. We can laugh even in an atomic age, even in the storm which we have raised by our own unruliness:

> Well roars the storm to those that hear
> A deeper voice across the storm.[21]

"Be of good cheer, I have overcome the world." [22] "Be of good cheer": laugh! Beyond the clinging doubt and beyond the unruly deed—God. Has He not "found" us in Jesus Christ? So *that* door is always open—into laughter.

7

FOOTNOTE ON FREEDOM

> "If you continue in my word, you are truly my
> disciples, and you will know the truth, and the
> truth will make you free. . . . If the Son makes
> you free, you will be free indeed."
>
> *John 8:31, 36*

The grandmother from Czechoslovakia tried to cross Third Avenue in New York City against the traffic light. We pulled her almost from the wheels of the oncoming bus, dusted her clothes, picked up her groceries, and said gently: "Mother, not against the lights." She said: "Free country!" She meant by implication that she had been reared in a land where *Verboten* met her at every turn and that now she was living just west of the Statue of Liberty. So her remark was not utterly foolish. If it were, she had lots of company, for the average American conceives freedom to mean doing just what he likes, with plenty of cash, and crossing the street against the traffic lights.

I

There is no absolute freedom. Always freedom is within pre-destined structure. Thus a man is free to go north from New York City to Albany or south to Philadelphia. But he is not free to go north to Philadelphia, or south to Albany, except by a long round-the-world journey; and he is not free to go either place by using the breast stroke through the air; and he is not free to go to both cities at one and the same time, despite the fact that in other realms of choice this is what we try (unsuccessfully) to do. If any decision is carefully examined, it will be found to be freedom within predestination. So no man can think wisely about his freedom until he has asked, "What is my destiny?" Suppose Christ is the word of destiny.

Take notice of the limits or structure of our human freedom. There are *physical* limits: we cannot walk through a brick wall or back pedal into the Middle Ages or grow cabbages from lead pellets. There are *social* limits: other people confine our freedom. If you doubt the fact, try crossing Harvard Square in the rush hour or passing a course without bothering about any books or any attendance at lectures. Jean Paul Sartre's "Hell is—other people," [1] is not true, but he had grounds for making it. We are limited by our own *past life*, so much so that we seem locked in a determinism. If in the past I have not studied maths, my prospects in a trigonometry exam are not exactly bright. Thus an era given to cash and gadgets will be uneasy with the word "God." Is not every act and thought the inevitable effect of long psychological cause? The *Second Mrs. Tanqueray* in the Pinero drama said despairingly, "The future is only the past again entered through another gate." [2] There are other limits, many of them, but we have instanced enough to show that freedom is always within destiny.

But by a strange paradox these limits are also doors. As for walls, through which we cannot walk, they not only give us privacy but are the very stuff of architecture. As for people, they are not necessarily "hell," for they make possible all that is implied in the word "community"—the theater and symphony, the treasure of friendship, the joys of human love, the solace of our homes. The country lad when he fell in love and when incredibly she loved him in return, proclaimed his new found freedom as he ran amuck with grammar: "Now I ain't got nothin' 'gin nobody." As for the bondage of the past, we are still free to survey it, being above the path as well as on it; and if we do no more than wish to walk another path, we are no longer slaves.

All of which means that we are always both free and destined. The two terms, freedom and destiny, are correlatives. They are two sides of one shield of life: the one cannot be without the other. Freedom is the chosen fulfillment of our destined nature. What *is* our destined nature? We begin to understand why the Augustine prayer wins our poignant "yes" in every generation: "Thou hast made us for Thyself, and our heart is restless until it rest in Thee";[3] or why the word in the Fourth Gospel so savingly disturbs us, "If the Son makes you free, you will be free indeed." Here is a gentle hint that may or may not shorten our interminable bull-sessions on the freedom of the will. That very phrase, freedom of the will, abstracts freedom from the person to make it an object; and an object almost by definition is not free. But freedom cannot thus be abstracted from the person, who is always subject as well as object and who himself still does the abstracting. We say, "Man is not free," but always assume that the bleak verdict is free! Thus we find "no end, in wand'ring mazes lost." [4] Christopher Morley once wrote, with his tongue in his cheek, "A human being: an ingenious assembly of portable plumbing." [5] But he and we would be startled if the kitchen sink took voice and said, "I am only a kitchen sink."

II

Let us look more closely at the fact of our being both destined and free. We instinctively assume the fact. We treat one another as such creatures. When we talk to a man in Harvard Yard, we know that he will not take wings over Widener Library; yet we know that he is not a robot. He is destined (a better word than limited, for these limits are still doors), but he is free. Thus—here we strike a mystery in our nature—even when we are bound, we know we are bound. We are finite and cannot escape finitude (if you think we can, try drinking neat whisky and eating Welsh rabbit as a steady diet: you will end in the hospital if the mortician does not intervene)—we are finite, but we know we are finite. We go to the movies, yet see ourselves going to the movies. We say, "Time is swift," because there is in us a stance above time—in eternity.

Our freedom lives in this self-transcendence. If we never pause to ponder our life, we become objects in a world of objects, and freedom ebbs. If we do nothing but ponder our lives, we do nothing, and once again freedom ebbs. If we pose as "only creatures," we sink into the natural order; if we pose as always above creaturehood, as God, we dissolve into sheer pretense. In a certain college a notice-board item announced a meeting of the Freethinkers Society. When I asked, "What is that?" I was told: "Just that: we had to throw out Sally So-and-so the other day because she had become an agnostic." That group was denying destiny, trying to play tennis without net, court, ball, racquet, or rules. They might have done even worse by denying freedom, by selling out to every passing impulse and every contemporary fashion. If we judge life by the past, thus falsely making the past a mere object, we are, of course, determined; but if we judge the past as a wave of consciousness, we are living at the front edge of the wave and then once more are free. Always free, always destined; and always aware of both from a stance above both freedom and destiny. Thus we live in a polarity of freedom and destiny, and we know it because . . . ? Because we are made in the likeness and image of God. Where do we see that image clear? In Christ? "If the Son makes you free . . . ."

III

This seeing ourselves, which is the vantage point of freedom: what happens there? There is *pondering,* as is obvious even in small issues. "Shall I take the subway to Boston, or the bus, or go by car?" In larger issues also we are in some small measure monarch of all we survey: "Shall I propose to this girl? Shall I choose teaching as a vocation? Shall I be agnostic in life-faith?" Thus the self ponders itself in a free-destined world. Moment by moment as we go through life, we engage in that strange conversation with ourself, which is perhaps more important than any we hold with our neighbors. The man above our strange paradox of freedom-destiny talks to the man within the paradox: "Why art thou cast down, O my soul? and why art thou disquieted in me?" [0] Thus the pondering.

Then the *purchase or choice.* The existentialists say that we must choose, that we are choosing creatures, who cannot live in a vague "tolerance"; and that if we do not choose, we shall sink into thinghood and the mass mind. The choice may be mistaken. A man may misread his gifts. He may misread the historical juncture, as many a statesman has found to his own loss and his country's misfortune. He may make a poor decision regarding vocation. But that is a risk which finite creatures take. The man may try even to deny destiny, whereas he ought first to ask, "What is my destined life?" But again that is the risk of freedom, which *is* free, as witness our phrase: "I cannot buy that," meaning that we cannot subscribe to that point of view. The choice always limits us more: a baseball catcher cannot be a dentist or a musician; but the choice always liberates: the catcher has the fun of the game and may even play in the world series. So purchase or choice.

Then *accountability*. Perhaps the word should be responsibility, the ability to respond—to that realm from which we see ourselves moving through this strange world of freedom-destiny. Do I enlist you in that comment? We speak about "the voice of conscience." The phrase is not the best in the world, for we all know instances of crimes committed in the name of conscience. Heidegger has defined conscience not as a police-court verdict but as the summons of the future, bidding us live the authentic life of choice beyond thinghood and the mass mind.[7] But even if a man should deny conscience, he would do so in the name of a higher truth: he would still be accountable. A doctor, if he should discover a cure for leukemia, could not rightly hide the cure, for he is responsible. It is doubtful if he would then have any right to patent the cure or grow rich on it. Always there is the seeing and choosing self, in a stance above life, and always that self is responsible—to a mysterious Aboveness. How shall that Aboveness be construed? Christian faith says that Jesus is the Eternal Word made flesh: "If the Son makes you free, you will be free indeed."

IV

No footnote on freedom can evade the fact of the abuse of freedom, of failure in responsibility. Nowadays we try to avoid the word "sin." We have some warrant, for the word has become the stock-in-trade of Mrs. Grundy; and, besides, we now know that so-called sin may be only psychotic guilt. But when we discard the word, we must find some synonym such as "the nonauthentic life." It is doubtful if the new terms are better than the old, for the old can be given its real meaning: failure in responsibility, the flouting of a *noblesse oblige* whereby we are required to live in love toward God and man. Suppose we fail in responsibility. There is no "suppose": we all fail. Then there is danger that we become slaves of the failure. Jesus, in the very context of our text, said that such failure is the worst slavery, worse than Israel's bondage at that time to the Roman power—worse because sin cuts the main contact, and we can no longer see and choose; worse because we thus threaten that stance above our life which is the seat of freedom.

Then? Then no help unless that Higher Realm moves to help us. "Whence cometh my help [?] My help cometh from the Lord which made heaven and earth" [8] and man's life on earth. Thus the immemorial cry, "Whence cometh my help?" and the immemorial sole answer to the cry, "From the Lord." Now we see the daringness of Christian faith: that God who has set responsibility in us and has beckoned us in all lovely things, who has laid on us the strange constraint to forgive one another, has gathered His whole intention in the fullness of the times into one Man. That intention now becomes plea, not coercion. Christ does not dissolve or dispel the mystery of God, for God's ways always go far beyond our ken; but though the mystery is not dispelled in Christ, it —or He—is disclosed, as light is light. When the bishop had saved Jean Valjean from arrest—you recall that Jean had stolen the bishop's silver knives and forks and that when the police had brought Jean with all evidence of the crime, the bishop gave Jean the candlesticks also and said that they were "silver like the rest" and he should take them as gifts along with the plate—he then spoke words which Christ with far better warrant has spoken to our race:

Jean Valjean, my brother: you belong no longer to evil, but to good. It is your soul that I am buying for you. I withdraw it from dark thoughts and from the spirit of perdition, and I give it to God! [9]

The daringness of Christian faith is that God has thus made common cause with us in Christ to bridge the gulf of alienation which our failure in responsibility always sets between man and man and between man and God.

But does not the crippleness of false choices remain? Are we not thus destined by our own past? Have we not said that our past limits us? Yes, but we have said also that limits can be a door. A sonnet is constricted as compared with a didactic poem. Indeed a Shakespearean sonnet must pour its essential word as quintessence into a final couplet. Masefield does just that when he pleads as in prayer for wisdom and passion:

> Give me but these, and though the darkness close
> Even the night will blossom as the rose.[10]

Our past may restrict, but it does not bind; and the very restriction may become a distillation of joy. Paul had on his hands the blood of the Church. But although he was burdened by the past, his burden became wings: he knew better than others both our human frailty and the sheer mercy of God.

V

We have not left our text in any word of this footnote on freedom. Said Jesus: "If you continue in my word, . . . you will know the truth." There the word "truth" does not mean university information, despite a thousand baccalaureate sermons. The nearest word in our language might be Reality, the Reality in which we and our world are always held. "The truth will make you free." Then the bold equation: "If the Son makes you free, you will be free indeed." The Son as the disclosure of our destiny, as the revelation of that realm from which we view our life, as the mercy to overcome every failure in responsibility. Great Book, its depths never sounded!

Any service of worship may be the moment of real freedom, for worship is exposure to ultimate Destiny, ultimate Light, ultimate Mercy. Somewhere I have read a strange story of a man who had been in prison for years and who had accepted his fate as hopeless, but who one day walked out into liberty because he tried the door and found that it was not locked. To say, "This I believe," or to say, "For this I pray," may be the trying of the door. Try it: the door is not locked. There is One "whose service is perfect freedom." [11]

8

HAS CHRIST LEFT US?

> "Nevertheless I tell you the truth: it is to your
> advantage that I go away, for if I do not go away,
> the Counselor will not come to you."
>
> *John 16:7*

How can it be to our advantage that Christ has left our earth? If he lived on our street, we could seek his door, whatever our sense of unworthiness. We could ply him with the questions that vex our age: "What are we to do in the dilemma of atomic arms? What about conscience and military service?" We could seek his counsel in matters far more personal: "Some compulsions are too strong for me, and some memories are not pleasant." If only we could ring his doorbell! "Nevertheless"—that word anticipates our bafflement—"it is to your advantage that I go away." His disciples probably answered him: "You mean go away to the hills for a while or to a quiet place beyond the Jordan?" But he: "No, I mean go away from this earth." There is our topic.

I

We ought perhaps to ask if we would know him were he still on our earth in the flesh. Most people saw no great light in him when he walked the roads of Galilee. They judged him by his unhistoric town: "Can there any good thing come out of Nazareth?" [1] Suppose he should come again as a bus driver between Boston and Revere Beach. He came once as carpenter. No historian of his time thought him worthy of more than passing mention. For that matter, most present-day historians ignore him. That is an astounding affair. Perhaps it reflects the scientific cast of our life, or perhaps it is because historians have tried to write "objective history." They cannot, for they must select only a few facts from millions, and selection implies a faith, if only a faith in what is important; and they then must marshal the facts, and that also implies an accepted principle of order. Every historian chooses his stance. The Bible as history takes its stance from Calvary and Easter.

There is a sharper question: If we knew Jesus in the flesh, would we follow him? Or kill him? Imagine him in a race riot in Little Rock, or at a Teamsters' convention, or at a directors' meeting of advertising moguls—or in Harvard Yard. People say sometimes that they wish they could have met Jesus in the flesh. I have never felt I was ready, even 5 per cent ready. To a lady who professed her wish to have met Christ, Carlyle gruffly replied that if Christ came preaching doctrines acceptable to the higher orders, he, Carlyle, might have received from her ladyship a card inscribed, "To meet our Savior." But if he came preaching what he once preached, her ladyship would join the cry, "Take Him to Newgate and hang Him." [2] Would we follow were he here today? We might be guilty of another Calvary, and that may be one reason why it is to our "advantage" that he has gone from sight. But there are more positive reasons.

II

He has gone from sight that we may see him more clearly. If you have lived, as I once, within sight of the three peaks of the Green Mountains, Killington, Pico, and Shrewsbury, you know how and where they can best be seen. Not from a trout stream with its overarching trees; not from any nearby point. No, from the wide valley, with the trees stripped of leaves, when snow has fallen. Contemporary events are like the cluttering woods: distance of years brings clarity. Lincoln's Gettysburg Address when first spoken was stigmatized in several American newspapers as a cheap political harangue that desecrated soldiers' graves; [3] but years have brought wisdom: the Address is now cut in enduring

stone in the Washington Memorial. This truth holds—does it not?
—of our own loved ones whom we have lost by death. We do not
pretend that they were free from fault. But their little idio-
syncrasies now are dear to us, and what seemed at the time their
great decisions may now seem small, and their blunders now seem
not to belong to their new nature.

This power of memory to clarify and interpret life, especially
memory after sorrow, Jesus knew. He would say: "What I am doing you do not know now, but afterward you will understand." [4]
Such ponderings bring us to the deeps of life where questions
throng: If history gives clearer understanding, is not history in
some sense alive? Do we not need a far more profound doctrine of
history? There are more poignant questions: If the death of our
friends brings both clarity and gentleness of judgment, is it right
to think of death as being dead? The "dim tracts of time" that
divide us from Christ do not divide. They set him in perspective
and at the same time draw him closer in new understanding. Other
things being equal, why should we unduly exercise ourselves to
discover the minutiae of his life on earth? That issue has importance, but we see Christ more clearly from the wide valley. Is that
why the epistles of Paul have no great concern to quote his very
words or retail his very deeds? He went from sight that we might
see him more clearly.

III

This reason follows: Jesus went away that all men might know
him. The emphasis is now on *all men,* in every land, in every
generation. Space and time are two prisons, though not without
their creative purpose. As for space, Jesus was held in his days of
flesh within what we call Palestine. Two or three times he went
beyond the bounds of his land but apparently felt that his work
could best be done mainly within and through Israel. As for time,
he was held within the thought-forms and culture of his age.
Otherwise he would not have been understood by his neighbors. Indeed, he could not have shared our mortal life on any other terms.
You and I take refuge in space and time, and yet yearn to trans-
cend them. But how dare a man venture the illimitable?

Darest thou now O Soul,
Walk out with me toward the unknown region,

Where neither ground is for the feet nor any path to follow? [5]

But Whitman in that poem knew that for mortal man the bounds of space and time must remain: "All but the ties eternal, Time and Space." [6] Our sputniks cannot break the time-space barrier, however they may break the sound barrier. Were a man to ride a sputnik, we would have to surround him in his little cabin with earth conditions. We cannot live in two places at once or in two eras. John Wesley said nobly: "I look upon all the world as my parish," but had to add, "I mean, that, in whatever part of it I am . . . ." [7] So Jesus was constrained by time and space: "The Word was made flesh." [8]

Imagine Jesus in our generation. Where shall we set him? In the land which once he walked? It is a troubled land in the midst of troubled lands, and few people could reach him. In Peru, then? He would have to speak one language, presumably that of the land which we might instance, and few people therefore would know what he said. Indeed, few people would be able to go to Peru. Most of us must work, and most of us lack the money to go to Peru. The rich could go; the poor would be denied. That is an old story, in which Jesus found no joy. Suppose all men could go to the place where Jesus lived in our time, how many could speak to him? If we knew him, and if we cared, both ifs being large ifs, the crowds would throng. Some years ago the grave of a young cleric in Malden, Massachusetts, was credited with healing power, and 200,000 people sought the grave and its alleged healing on one Sunday afternoon.[9] Even if we could see Jesus, our children and children's children would be thwarted: He would live in only one generation. Space and time are barriers.

But if Christ goes away, yet abides in Spirit, the space-time barrier is broken. Alice Meynell, at the Eucharist, meditated on the saving fact that Christ may be in every life, even in the life of every stranger, in the stranger in the same pew:

> O Christ, in this man's life—
> This stranger who is Thine—in all his strife,
> . . . .
> Christ in his numbered breath,
> Christ in his beating heart and in his death,
> Christ in his mystery! From that secret place
> And from that separate dwelling, give me grace! [10]

Christ was in that stranger and in Alice Meynell, even as he was mediated in Spirit through the Bread and Wine. The shaping of life, because Christ has gone from sight, is not now by outwardness of word and deed, which have perhaps always some tincture of compulsion, but by inwardness of welcomed Spirit—this for all men, rich and poor, of whatever race, in whatever generation. He went from sight because of his love for all men: "God so loved *the world* that he gave his only Son . . . ." [11]

IV

Thus the clinching reason: Christ went from sight that we might grow in free strength. If Christ lived on our street and we asked him always what to do, and always did as he commanded, we might end as echoes rather than as persons. He asked no blind obedience: "Why do you not judge for yourselves what is right?" [12] Sometimes we pretend that the Bible is a Book of specific and infallible advice. It is not. "Be obedient to the temporal powers," [13] does not solve the problem of military service, for it would require us, if we lived in Germany during Hitler's regime, to become Nazis. But supposing the Bible were a Book of specific and infallible counsels, as it is not, it might then be "our chain" and not "our guide." [14] The Book is a lamp to our feet, [15] not a strait jacket for our wills. To change the figure: we are not cash registers, with little enough cash, operated by a printed hand. Those who ask such infallibility know not what they ask: a God who turns both Bible writers and Bible readers into robots. Robots do not grow or ever understand, for they are robots; and such a God would not be Godlike.

Someone may rejoin that if we have freedom to find and follow "the mind of Christ," we may blunder. There is no "may": we do blunder. We shall blunder. What growing child does not blunder? Or what groping, hard-pressed parent? If the child never blundered, Little Lord Fauntleroy, velvet pants and all, might be better company. We grow by blundering. In a finite world, where memory trips us and the will becomes self-centered and the future is unforeseen, we shall always blunder. Even what we call "good deeds" are partial blunder. If we stand alone, we break community; if we always keep community, we become supinely "the organization man." When my wife feeds the birds in winter, she shows a characteristic kindness, and that is right; but she makes havoc of the weekly budget, for the birds consume granaries of food; and she deprives our neighbors of the sight of birds, for apparently all the birds in Cambridge have heard of her generosities and flock to our yard. Luther had the courage to say, "Sin boldly." [16] He meant, of course, that my wife should keep on feeding the birds even though goodness is never unmixed goodness. We try to obey in love the guidance of Christ's present Spirit and thus grow blunderingly; and Christ's Spirit is stronger than we, and he thus comes to his victory.

Nay, more: this Spirit of Christ, Advocate within and above, reproves "the world of sin, and of righteousness, and of judgment." [17] He is now universal, moving at the deeps of life. He convicts the wicked, so that they become chaotic and their power is broken; he sustains his own, giving them the word in season and a strength better than men can ever know in merely human power. "Of sin": that is to say, "right-minded people" thought that both God and the public peace would be served if he were crucified, but we see by the Spirit of Christ that they were wrong-minded. "Of righteousness": we see that he was right—in love. "Of judgment": his place and Pilate's are now reversed, for we see now that he was judging Pilate. How do we thus see and know? Not by our own virtue but because the Spirit is at work in every man's life. When the secret police came to take the names of Christians gathered in worship, one of those present said quietly: "There is one Name you have not got" [18] The truth struck home. Even the Russian police were "reproved."

This present Advocate is our hope. Ocean winds may be contrary, even to gale force, but the ground swell and the ground and the stars are set against the gale. Racial prejudice and greedy advertising and cheap politicians may seem to flourish, but other men have an "Advocate" who pleads for them in the court of heaven that their sins may be forgiven and their blunderings atoned. For the unruly ones the Advocate is judge until they turn. Their indifference to Christ is like that of the visitor to the famous art gallery who said that the pictures were "not much": the custodian made the only needed reply: "Sir, these pictures are not on trial; you are."

So we journey in free spirit guided by his Spirit. We blunder but are not unled. We are baffled but not bereft of his Presence. We travel toward the mountain ridge of death, beyond which mortal eyes cannot see, but that fact adds the grandeur of mystery to the journey, and he is there in light supernal. How may a blundering man confront that light? We may well ask:

> O! how shall I, whose native sphere
> Is dark, whose mind is dim,
> Before the Ineffable appear,
> And on my naked spirit bear
> That uncreated beam? [19]

But there is answer, and in the very language of the Epistle of John when it describes Christ as "advocate": [20]

> There is a way for man to rise
> To that sublime abode:—
> An offering and a sacrifice,
> A Holy Spirit's energies,
> An Advocate with God.[21]

The eternities now throb with a once-human heart. He now lives in heaven's spanlessness, ruler over our life in time and space. He has gone that we may grow into his likeness and image.

V

In a certain summer colony the favorite adult hymn at Vespers is a children's hymn, "I think when I read that sweet story of old," [22] with its longing, "I should like to have been with them then." Why is the hymn chosen—that the adults may obey Christ to "become as little children," [23] or in a childishness that should have "put away childish things"? [24] Who knows? All motives are mixed. The favorite children's hymn at that worship is an adult hymn, "Onward, Christian Soldiers." [25] Again we may guess that the motives are mixed: the children wish to grow up and meet the challenge—and fight. As an adult I sing the adult choice and the children's choice, but with misgivings. As to the soldier hymn, it reminds us of atomic war. As to the children's hymn, does it not go counter to Christ? He said: "I tell you the truth: it is to your advantage that I go away." Has Christ left us? Many are shrieking, "Look what the world is coming to!" The Church has glad answer: The world is coming to the triumph of Christ, who has left us that he may never leave us.

9

GOD'S WAYS AND MAN'S WAYS

> "For my thoughts are not your thoughts, neither are your ways my ways, saith the Lord. For as the heavens are higher than the earth, so are my ways higher than your ways, and my thoughts than your thoughts." *Isa. 55:8-9* (K.J.V.)

It is commonly charged against Christian faith that it makes God in man's image. Rupert Brooke has a poem in which fishes conceive God as a larger Fish:

> And under that Almighty Fin,
> The littlest fish may enter in.[1]

Robert G. Ingersoll had a much cleverer line: it reverses the well-known "An honest man's the noblest work of God," so that it reads, "An honest God is the noblest work of man." [2] The valid answers to the charge are not far to seek. Man, being a creature, must conceive God in part from materials given to his hand; and if he makes God, that material also is given. Nevertheless, if man's mind is self-transcendent, if he has power, as he has, to view time from beyond time, his notion of God can never be completely earth-bound. People do not know the Bible, or they would quickly realize that no book so sets its face against man-centered ideas of God. "For as the heavens are higher than the earth"—How high is that?—"so are my ways higher than your ways." To the Bible, God is both near in "the Word made flesh" and also "the Eternal Other."

I

We must not lose sight of the fact that God is like us as well as eternally beyond us.

> Speak to Him thou for He hears, and Spirit
> with Spirit can meet—
> Closer is He than breathing, and nearer than
> hands and feet.[3]

Otherwise the name of God with its thousand meanings could have found no place in our language. The repeated "your thoughts" and "my thoughts," despite the great gulf set between them, have a common term: thoughts. So man can in some measure "think God's thoughts after Him." [4] We live in response to Reality, and beckoning and response imply some commonalty. The words "finite" and "infinite" share two syllables. "When ye pray, say Our Father . . . ." There is likeness between our fatherhood and God's Fatherhood.

But the Lord's Prayer instantly safeguards that counsel, lest we should try to make God in our image: "Our Father which art in heaven. . . ." Our text tells this *unlikeness* of God, and its context relates an event which could be ascribed not to man but only to God's overruling. Israel had been carried captive into Babylon. Historians said: "It was by the clash of empires." Israel's prophets said: "It was because Israel broke covenant with God." One of the greatest prophets, author of our text, said: "In noble captives it was expiation for the sins of empires." Which view is true? Perhaps all of them. But the deepest is most deeply true. Suddenly in another clash of empires Babylon was defeated, and Israel was set free, even though the new conqueror had no concern at all for Israel's covenant or Israel's God. What a strange turn of events! Was it a mere quirk in history? Or God's act within history—from beyond history? Our author asked the question and believed that he heard God answer: "For my ways are not your ways."

II

Ponder God's ways in nature and history, nature being the stage of history. Our tiny planet swims in the void, dwarfed by its sun, as our whole solar system is dwarfed by constellations so immense that they beggar our imagining. We brag about Sputnik while God silently launches new orders of stars so distant that their light, traveling at incredible speed, will not reach us for millions of years. Meanwhile our tiny empires rise and fall. To angels they must appear smaller than street gangs, and, in many an instance, of the same kind. Man could not have made the cosmos, but few men on our planet are willingly governed by thoughts of God. Meanwhile those who do name His Name are sometimes made a captive sacrifice in Babylon. God's ways are vast and strange! A Welsh proverb tells us that there are three things which only God knows: the beginning, the cause, and the end. Only three? All things are known only to God. Are there higher orders, angelic ranks? Powers mightier than nuclear power? Silences which no violence can touch? Vistas on vistas beyond death? We do not know except by faith. Only God knows—anything.

We rail against God. But why? How much do we know or understand? We demand that He meet our time schedule, which is almost always present time: tyranny should be destroyed—now. We require that He suit our space measurements: His will be done, as I wish it, on my plot of land. We will not believe in Him until He plays lackey to our tiny questionings to answer them—in our answers. In childish conceit we dismiss Him, announcing ourselves atheists. We insist that only a secular assumption is framework for the Truth. How much do we know? Where were we when He laid the foundations of the world? Emerson imagined the stars saying to a group of politicians emerging from a frantic political convention: "Why so hot, little man?" [5] Yes, politicians such as we may still set our mark on history; and we should, for we are responsible, response-able, able to respond. But we do not initiate history, and history is not in our hands. He deals with Israel and Babylon as He wills. "The fear of the Lord is the beginning of wisdom": [6] not cringing fear, but awe-struck fear, which says wonderingly: "His ways are not our ways."

III

Now ponder God's ways in the strange gift of human freedom. The freedom is always crossed by unforeseen and unforeseeable contingencies, as when soldiers in a parachute descent could not know and could not guess that a sudden ground wind would blow them along the ground to danger and death. The freedom is always within an invincible structure of life: a man is free to be a liar but not free to win either his neighbor's trust or his own integrity by being a liar. Thus freedom is crossed by contingency and held in destiny. But it is a real freedom, even the freedom to mock God or to close our eyes on the cosmos or to end our days on earth. Why should Israel be free to break the covenant? Or pagan Babylon be free to make captive the covenant people? Why is Nikita Khrushchev free to brag about a tricky toy called Sputnik, and our State Department free to speak in nursemaid tones? Or both of them free to discuss life as if it were held in rigid ideologies, when clearly the ideologies are fluid rather than rigid? Why is our freedom to do good always entangled in an unwished and unintended bad, so that a man cannot even join a church without appearing to shut out other men? Why is our freedom to do evil always brightly mocked by some unintended good, as when roads built for military conquest sped the feet of the messengers of a Cross? God acts from above and below the paradox and ambiguity of human freedom.

All of which is not to say that our freedom is fantasy: it is real, and it is responsible. What we call "natural evil" may flout our freedom, and we ourselves may abuse freedom, but we still live in response. Oscar Wilde once remarked that there is enough misery in any London street to disprove God.[7] But that comment did not acquit Wilde: he knew it was his job to try to comfort the misery. Incidentally, neither the remark nor the misery disproved God, for Wilde, having made the remark, had then to account for the poignant indignation in him which protested the misery. What *are* God's ways in the strange gift of our freedom? Sometimes we brashly believe that we could have made a better world—with one hand tied behind our back:

Ah Love, could thou and I with Fate conspire
To grasp this Sorry Scheme of Things entire,

Would not we shatter it to bits—and then
Re-mould it nearer to the Heart's Desire! [8]

But what kind of world would we make? Just what do we have
in mind? A man must be free in order to be a man. So there must
be choice with risk and danger. How shall we make a risk that is
not risky or a danger that is not dangerous? Nietzsche wrote in
The Antichrist:

If we ever encountered a god who always cured us of a cold in the head
at just the right time, or got us into our carriage at the very instant
heavy rain began to fall, he would seem so absurd a god that he'd have to
be abolished even if he existed.[9]

Then what kind of world would we make? We can remake
it in part and should, but we can do that much only by gifts which
He has given.

His ways in our freedom are not entirely hidden. The hinterland
of the vast continent is both unseen and unexplored, but a jutting
promontory is clear to sight and action. For we and Oscar Wilde do
protest cruelty in any street, and we know thereby and by Jesus
Christ that we should try to live in love. We should press toward
our justice on earth (which ceases to be justice unless it is sublima-
ted in love), even though God's justice always crosses and transcends
our justice. Where these words are written, the little summer colony
has been shocked by a fire in one of the cottages, which killed a
mother and two daughters. Can we understand God's ways in our
strange freedom to risk fire? No. But that we must try to "stand
by" the sorrowing, none of us can doubt. Meanwhile we *dimly*
trace God's ways. If suffering makes us gentle and turns us to
heaven's help, is it *mis*fortune? If prosperity quickens in us an arrant pride and a false self-dependence, is it *good* fortune? If truth
makes a man whole even when truth is defeated, *is* it defeated? If
history which seems to be on the "side of the big battalions" suddenly releases a captive Israel and thus gives a turn to events
which neither Israel nor the conqueror could foresee, *does* history
miscarry? Why do we prefer *King Lear* to *The Merry Wives of
Windsor*? "As the heavens are higher than the earth"—How high
is that?—"so are" God's "ways higher than" our "ways."

IV

Now ponder God's ways in redemption. That is the central thrust of this scripture. Israel hardly deserved the sudden deliverance and perhaps was not even ready for it. They, like ourselves, had often lusted after earthy gods. They had forgotten the Mystery without Whom no man can worship. Even in captivity they had not understood or repented, for many of them took their fashion from the conqueror: they had become fat in this world's goods. Nor were they themselves quick to forgive. Are we ever? One of their psalms cries out terribly against the conqueror: "Happy shall he be, that taketh and dasheth thy little ones against the stones!" [10] Yet God delivered them when there was no deliverance in all their sight or circumstance or power. For in redemption God's ways are mercifully not our ways.

Perhaps I should say that though *judgment* may be secretly tragic or dramatic on a vast stage, *redemption* is always quiet and lowly. Redemption comes in "great humility." This same prophet tells in the fifty-third chapter of this same book how the faithful in Israel were led as sheep to the slaughter, but how that very death became catharsis in those who slew them and in the sight of later generations. Not strangely that same chapter has become for us the prototype of Christ. Suppose him to be our redemption. Just suppose it, and then mark the manner of it. God comes to our history in a manger-birth, comes incognito, long ago and far away, in a lowly home and a conquered land. The Babe becomes a Man and speaks words which others had spoken, but with how new an accent, how new an obedience, how new a power! Then a Gallows, but with love's purpose unsullied, and love's yearning unstayed. Then the conviction given to those who loved him that he was not dead, but was with them in death and would be with them beyond death. Then a strange fellowship called a church, as faulty as the first fellowship, but as little able to forget him. Just suppose it. Then what a strange redemption! Who could have guessed that in all the abyss of space and time this would be God's way? But is it not always love's way to be lowly? Can love ever coerce? Must we not always be free to believe or disbelieve, to accept or refuse? Thus God comes, as the "Servant in the House." [11] He uses the back stairs as at Bethehem, not the front stairs of pomp and power, and draws water for us for our cleansing and waits our word.

James Martineau attended the tercentenary of Dublin University as an honored guest [12] but stole away from the pomp to visit the grave of his infant daughter. Mrs. Martineau had died, and Martineau was then eighty-seven years old. For almost his lifetime an ocean had kept him from that grave. But his heart was there, and his hope. Redemption comes in no thunders, though judgment may; for at long last only the secrecies of man's heart are great. Our tears and our hope are also at a grave, an empty grave, across an ocean of years. We would not now forget a lonely cross, even if we could; we could not, even if we would. For he is with us in the secrecy and power of his Spirit. In judgment God may sweep the world, as in our time, and storm the heart for our dismay that we may know that deliverance is not in us; but in redemption there is only an "old, old story" which is never old and never fully told. That story is Presence now—a living spring in all man's history. "Neither are your ways my ways, saith the Lord. As the heavens are higher than the earth . . . ." How high is that?

V

All this has deep meaning for our crisis-time. Is history a sarcasm, and are its ambiguities a fatal flaw? Often we shall wonder and fear. We are on a tiny swinging ball, perchance the only personal ball in the whole cosmos. Why should our hope be hope? We remember a conversation in a Hardy novel:

"Did you say the stars were worlds, Tess?"
"Yes."
"All like ours?"
"I don't know; but I think so. They sometimes seem to be like apples on our stubbard tree. Most of them splendid and sound—a few blighted."
"Which do we live on—a splendid one or a blighted one?"
"A blighted one." [13]

Then we remember Christ. His was no blighted life and no blighted death. If all history be "static," the "old, old story" is clear and lovely music. We could not despair, had we not first hoped. We must choose now to believe either the static or the music. The static *is* static: we know that it is rattle and raucousness. The music *is* music. We could never have imagined such redemption. But then, God's ways are not our ways. "God so loved the world, that he gave his only begotten Son, that whosoever believeth . . . ." [14] We can believe. It is grand and heartbreaking and heart-mending belief. Then we *will* believe and bow before the Mystery, so awe-struck in power, so tumultuous in judgment, so lowly in love.

10

THE AUTHORITY OF JESUS

> "He taught them as one who had authority, and not as the scribes."
>
> *Mark 1:22*

The college woman came with her thoughtful comment: "So many voices! Which shall I follow?" She confronted the babel of our times. Some cynic has said that man gained the power to speak around the world just at the moment when he has nothing important to say. Sound-truck voices, radio voices, platform voices, television voices, pulpit voices, and voices of our endless arguments bedevil our day. Some voices are greedy: the advertising voices sometimes mean "I want your money"; and the political voices, "I want your vote"; and they have scant regard for the persons to whom they speak. Some voices are frantic, especially when discussing Sputnik. Some proclaim too confidently that they know the way. Some touch only the surface of our need. "So many voices! Which shall I follow?" Perhaps a Voice which is never heard, except silently in silence, yet always heard.

I

Some men have proposed that the voice of authority is in the Church. They could be both right and wrong. They are wrong in that the Church manifestly fails and that it is culturally conditioned, but they are right in that the Church has power to stand when governments topple and that people turn to it in crisis, even though with only half a hope. The wrongness is underlined in the story of cardinals who criticized a picture of Peter and Paul as "too ruddy," only to hear Raphael retort, "They blush on seeing the Church governed by such men as you." [1] But the rightness is emphasized even in that incident, for the artist was there using Jesus as criterion by which to judge the Church, the Jesus who would hardly be known among men but for the Church which proclaims him. Someone has said that though the aisles of any church are dirty, only a man on his knees can clean them. The voice of authority speaks *through* the Church, now muted, now clear.

Others have claimed that the Bible is the voice of authority. They also could be both wrong and right. They are wrong in that the Bible cannot be opened at random to provide instanter a drill-sergeant command at every complex juncture of our daily life. If the Bible here counsels the slaughter of all enemies captured in battle and there bids us love our enemies, which voice shall we follow? Furthermore, if life is under printed compulsion, are we not robots rather than men? But the claim of authority in the Bible is right in this: Christ stands there like a mountain peak ruling and judging all the lower terrain, so that the whole country becomes a Holy Land. Beneath the country there are tremors of a holy earthquake, above it an ineffable Sun, and round its shores the thundering tides of an infinite Sea. The voice of authority sounds *through* the Bible.

Others tell us that conscience or "the inner light" is authority. They also may be both wrong and right. They are wrong in that conscience can be perverted and the inner light become an aberration. Crimes have been committed in the name of conscience, and insane people have justified their deeds by "God told me to do it." Because men are finite, conscience is finite: it is more faulty than a ship's compass which is out of true because of a cargo of steel on board. The New Testament is realistic in this matter: it speaks of our need to be cleansed of "an evil conscience." But the claim made for the inner light is right in this: our world has often been guided by prophetic minds who have stood against the world, saying, "Here I stand, I cannot do otherwise." [2] Every reader has known luminous hours when the path of life has stood out sharp and clear like a white road in moon-light. The compass may be faulty, but there is a magnetic north. So authority sounds through a man's conscience, now unmistak-ably, now with much static. Authority sounds *through* a man's conscience but is not locked within it.

The New Testament—prodigious Book!—sums up these issues: "There is no authority except from God, and those that exist have been instituted by God." [3] Man is creature. What other authority but the Creator? With these swift comments on themes that could rightfully ask a lifetime, we turn to our text. "He taught them as one who had authority, and not as the scribes." They quoted authorities, in a bondage of quotation marks to which most writing in our time also is sadly in thrall. They cited the Mosaic law, though they tried hard to adapt it to new times, while he took sharp issue with it and yet fulfilled it at the deep springs of its intention. Was God, the only authority, speak-ing through him? We take certain meanings of the word "au-thority" to see if they are met in him.

II

One meaning is creative freshness. Authority as a word has *author* as its first two syllables, and that word is derived from the Latin *augere*, which means to produce or to create. Thus the word "augury" means a sign of what may next spring from the secret roots of history. Is there this creative freshness in Jesus? His words and deeds are not a dull lesson: they are the sparkling overflow of a fountain. Perhaps we should not speak about the "character of Jesus." Character is a self-righteous word, and we cannot imagine Jesus shaping his character. Perhaps phrases such as the "principles of Jesus" are likewise taboo, for Jesus did not go through our world peddling abstract principles. The Beatitudes are not "principles": they are sparks struck from our earthly road by the racing of his spirit.

Perhaps we have even less right to speak of the "consistency of Jesus." When was he tamely consistent? Always he dared a para-dox: "He who loses his life for my sake will find it";[4] and thus he risked the misunderstanding of "consistent" minds. He was not "puritan," if by that word we mean censo-riously moralistic, for he feasted with the godless and unruly; but he was not impuritan, for his holiness was an unsullied flame. His consistency was always in flashing inconsistencies, like a spring-time. Shall we say that he left us an "example"? That word also can become self-righteous. Translators make him use that word when he took a slave's towel and washed the road dust from his disciples' feet ("I have given you an example" [5]), but the word could as well be translated "symbol." As to example, his word was sharp: "Why do you call me good? No one is good but God alone." [6] That is why we call him good!

Jesus was and is author, fountainhead of ever-creative life. The disclosure of God in him is the flowing spring of new disclosures. Thus music and art and architecture, together with worship and philanthropy, find in him a pristine inspiration. No fret in him, no dull rules, no hankering after titles, no protocol, no water from closed cisterns! As for his being an echo of the leader of the Dead Sea Scrolls community, according to a too-swift and ill-informed guess by Edmund Wilson, [7] a guess adopted by some churches, how could such a theory be true? The Qumram people were legalistic while Jesus was not; and they were militaristic, anchoritic, and apocalyptic while Jesus was not. Furthermore, their leader, the Teacher of Righteousness, wished to be remembered but is known only because of the discovery of the Scrolls, while Jesus deliberately risked oblivion and yet exercises a spell on history though he uses no spell. The spring of origin is in him.

III

Another meaning of the word "authority" is knowledge and insight. We say of a scholar that he is an "authority" on this subject. Our age is rich in such men. We marvel at the astronomers' ability to chart the courses of the stars. The exactness and range of their knowledge humbles us. We trust them and accept their judgments. They know. Can we say of Jesus thus: "He is an authority"? Apparently he had no education beyond that of the synagogue school. His contemporaries asked of him with some amazement, "How is it that this man has learning, when he has never studied?" [8] He had knowledge of a deeper kind without having our modern book learning.

We take one instance, and that not the profoundest: his knowledge of human nature. "He knew all men and needed no one to bear witness of man . . . ." [9] Students of an

English school used to say of their beloved headmaster, "It is no use lying to him, for he always believes you." That is a moving tribute, but it leaves the schoolmaster in naïveté. Jesus knew when people were lying to him, and he definitely did not believe them. He said instead: "Out of the heart of man come . . . murder, adultery . . ." [10] The list given in that verdict comprises thirteen demonisms that writhe in their evil. Yet, though often he did not believe people, he always believed in them. It was a practice in the building of the old sailing vessels to set a golden coin at the seat of the mainmast. Someone, acting on that clue, bought up a number of wrecks and thus gathered a tidy little windfall. So Jesus, knowing us to be wicked, knows also that we know we are wicked: we know it by some eternal thing in us. There is in us always the gold coin of God's image.

So Jesus loved men with a love so pure and uncoercive and undismayed that the New Testament had to find a new word for it: *agape;* a love more binding than that between friend and friend and more passionate than that between man and woman. It was no abstract altruism offered to an abstract mankind. It was lavished on each individual, even while it gathered in our whole human pilgrimage. We cannot read the New Testament in quiet mind without its finding each of us. The census taker asked the woman how many children she had, and when she began to list them—"There's Sally and Jim and Bob"—he impatiently interrupted: "The number, not the names." Then she indignantly: "But they do not have numbers: they have names." Numbers may belong on a military metal disc or in an estimate of "hands" in a factory or in national statistics, but they have no place in the mind of Christ: "He calls his own sheep by name." [11]

Such knowledge is in Jesus: "Come, see a man who told me all that I ever did." [12] This is not the profoundest instance of his knowledge. He knew life in its success and failure, and taught us long before Kipling [13] that both are impostors. He knew a mysterious timing in our human story to which our calendars are blind: "The time is fulfilled, and the kingdom of God is at hand." [14] He knew the deeps of the mystery of God that men cannot fathom. He knew the Mystery can be as intimate and gentle as the touch of a cool hand on a fevered head. He knew which pursuits are central and which move on the far edge. He knew what passes and what abides, what corrodes and what preciously endures. "He taught them as one who had authority."

IV

The other meaning of authority is conferred authority. The student thus says of his college dean: "What can you do? He has the authority." His power and rule are bestowed on him. This is the basic meaning of the word in our text: the authority of Jesus came directly from the seat of all authority. "There is no authority except from God." Jesus' had no title, no miter, no scepter: he was "born of woman, born under the law." [15] But his words struck home. When the crowd would have made him king, he refused them, but he spoke like a king. What *is* authority? Two men drowning and one pushing the other into the arms of a strong rescuer: What gives that act authority? We are now at a mysterious depth.

The word "God" and even the word "Incarnation" have gathered so many connotations that, for our present purpose, the word "Silence" may offer better guidance. Theological words wear smooth and should be withdrawn from circulation until they can be reminted, lest somebody should be shortchanged. There is Silence beyond our noise, beyond our time and space, beyond our life and death. All great speech and all great life come from that Silence. So the Word of Jesus comes from Silence deeper than that of silent prayer. He spoke and lived with the shattering impact of Silence, with the surgical knife of Silence, with the healing balm of Silence. The Nativity stories and the Resurrection stories do not "prove" him: he proves them. In between the Birth and the Resurrection his Cross stands, thrust there out of Silence. There is no "proof" of ultimate Silence except that we know, as we know that light is light.

So we must ask one another: "Do you not know that Silence in him, on a deeper level than that of the busy brain?" Making a final comment on Jesus, H. G. Wells said: "The Galilean has been too great for our small hearts." [16] How are we to prove Jesus? We cannot prove even our human love, though we know when its surge is true. What can we say at last but that he has thrust us into the arms of the Strong Rescuer, that light streams in on our life from his life and death, that Silence grips us through him, and that thereby all our human voices are judged! His authority comes from Authority, nay, is Authority. This he himself said in a lowliness that is itself kingliness: "He who believes in me, believes not in me but in him who sent me." [17]

V

So she came asking, "So many voices! Which shall I follow?" It was the right question, for at last we prove authority only by following, only by our obedience. We profess to seek truth, but would we try to do it if we knew it? If not, what right have we to ask to know? As we listen to Silence in Christ, we know which voices in our time are frantic and which are greedy. We know that our armaments in an atomic age, though they may have had some interim reasons, can now never be any final word. We know that American pride is in the danger that besets any pride, and that the monolithic constraint of Russia is a fetter on a rightful freedom, and that man's dilemma goes far deeper than any economic pattern. We know that if life on our planet is to continue in worthiness, there must be a new spirit. Spell the word with a capital "S": the new Spirit, the Spirit of eternal Silence.

"Which shall I follow?" Again the right question, for what is asked of us is only that we follow. It is not ours to lead, for we are creatures; and we cannot ever be Atlas carrying the world. The world rests on the strong shoulders of a cross, and we are asked to follow as we take up our cross. History is in God's hands, where it has always been; and we can follow, however stumblingly, where His Silence of authority in Jesus may lead us. But can we know the very words of Jesus? No, any honest New Testament scholar is aware of the barriers that beset that task. Yet we can know the *Word* of Jesus within the record of his words, for his silent Spirit is given to those who would follow him. So a German scholar has rightly said of Jesus himself that he is no Stranger: "There is Nobody whom we know half so well." [18] Silence is our true self and the true self of every friend and enemy. As we follow, we stumble; as we stumble, we know his lifting and pardoning grace; as we rise again, his silent Voice takes on a clearer and clearer tone. "Which voice?" A Voice heard in silence, never heard, yet always heard. "For he taught them as one who had authority, and not as the scribes."

FAITH AND LIFE

11

WHO OWNS THE EARTH?

"The earth is the Lord's."   Ps. 24:1

The tense of the verb is a main item: "*is* the Lord's." Not *was* the Lord's at the Creation, not *will be* His at the millennium, not *would be* His if man had not filched it, but *is* His now—land and ocean, by any proper title deed. The idea seems patently absurd. No one would dream of saying, present tense, indicative mood, "The earth is the Lord's," except in the unrealism of a church service. That truck careering down the highway, does God own it? The name of the owner is blazoned there in letters large enough to be seen at the distance of a city block. Try to find a bankbook with God's name as owner! This text is almost comic. But let us look at it: comedy can be entertaining and sometimes hides a truth.

I

Men have said in certain eras, "The earth is the devil's," though perhaps the notion has never been held with complete consistency. The Greeks who devaluated matter nevertheless gave us sculpture which almost breathes. But it was characteristic of Greek thought, especially among the Gnostics, that flesh is prison, matter a misfortune, and the whole cosmos the work of a demiurge. Deliverance comes, they held, by thought. In contemplation a man is less trammeled by the crippling earth, and at death (the real deliverance) he will shuffle "off this mortal coil." [1]

This view persists in many forms. It still cankers the life of the Church, for even preachers insist on regarding a person not as a person but as a vague soul in a fettering body. Do we not tend to think of farming, especially dirt farming, as a lower enterprise than, say, the profession of law? Is not the word "sex" morbid or unclean to some people? They reckon it a pity that children cannot be born in some other way. Things are things to our generation, and we are unaware of the heresy of such a view. Cash is materialism, and bodies are a nuisance: without bodies we could pose as pure mind!

To all this astigmatism the Bible replies quietly, "No, the earth is the Lord's. He made it; and though man may disfigure it and though there are blights on it hard to construe, it is essentially good." Perhaps we ought to add that this typically biblical view validates science and art, for these, without the biblical view, would be but a dabbling in the unclean. Likewise it sets a shining imprimatur on medicine and psychiatry, on marriage and on daily work, which otherwise would only build the walls of the prison.

II

In my time in college thoughtful men were saying, "The earth is the earth's." Just as bright students now read Kafka and Camus, they then read Haeckel's *The Riddle of the Universe* [2]—a book which boldly proclaimed that there is no riddle because there is no essential difference between organic and inorganic life, that man also is derived from matter. There is no riddle, said the book, for naturalism is naturally the only truth. The stream of life is a blind amoral vitalism, and man is pink-colored froth churned up in one of the stream's minor eddies. This view also persists into our time, perhaps because there is a certain poor comfort in it: it relieves us of responsibility.

What to say when thought itself reaches the thought that there is no free thought, thought itself being a remote derivative of ooze? It is amazing froth that can survey its whole river to ponder the river and to debate its own froth-destiny! Amazing froth that can take voice and thought, and say: "I am only froth"! Doubly amazing that science should thus prepare its own suicide, saying, "I am only froth"! The word "only" is the giveaway, for a man could not use it if he were not aware then and there of a higher order of life. Each of us stands astride two orders: the natural order in which our days are inexorably set and a higher order from which we survey both the natural world and our own life in the natural world. Haeckel's book could not have been written on any other terms. Was he not surveying "The Riddle of the Universe"? Meanwhile the Bible says that both orders are God's creation and ownership.

III

Our generation says flatly, "The earth is man's." That truck careering down the highway ("careering" means carving out a career) is man's, and who but a fool could deny it? The language of the truck driver is also man's, though, strangely enough, when he swears, seeking something ultimate by which to seal the oath, he instinctively uses the name of God. All that transpires downtown tomorrow morning is man's. To say "The earth is the Lord's" is religious indoctrination or else pious nonsense. Samuel Adams in a letter addressed to Lord Camden in 1768 was categorical, holding that it is an

essential, unalterable right in nature, engrafted into the British constitution as a fundamental law, and ever held sacred and irrevocable by the subjects within the realm, that what is a man's own is absolutely his own. . . .[3]

There man's ownership is declared "essential," "unalterable," "fundamental," "sacred," "irrevocable," and "absolute." To which the pesky Bible replies that, though man may be a trustee of the earth, he is never its owner, because "the earth is the Lord's."

Now a comment or two, for our digestion or indigestion, on man's alleged ownership in our time. *Comment one:* we seem to have botched the ownership, a likely result when people try to use what does not belong to them. We plough up buffalo grass, and the rich soil runs away down every hillside stream. We cut down forests and thus invite dust storms. On a much larger scale we turn atomic power to what we call "defense," and the whole episode of man's history is under threat. Perhaps the first question should have been: How does the real Owner intend this to be used?

Comment two: If man owns the earth, we must then ask, such is human pride, which man? This man cries "Mine!" (of Middle East oil fields); and his neighbor, who may live there, cries "No, mine!" Does oil belong to those who live on land above the oil field, or to the county, or to the nation—or to God? There is a story somewhere of a cannibal who laid claim to a plot of land on the score of having swallowed the original owner. The story is not too remote from our wars, or even from some of our litigation. A predigested owner can hardly file suit. As for sex, one man cries "Mine!" his neighbor cries, "No, mine!" and Shakespeare makes the comment: "It is a bawdy planet." [4]

There are other comments if our digestion can stand them. *Comment three:* no man can own property without some tincture of guilt. In a Camus novel, *The Fall,*[5] which is a study in guilt, the hero, far from heroic, insists on asking awkward questions of himself and others, such as: Do you have any possessions? Have you shared them with the poor? I ask the question of myself, I who have never lacked a meal, while I remember the millions in the Orient who perchance have never had a full meal. Camus' question does not necessarily argue against private property, if any property is private in a cosmos where "the earth is the Lord's." The Bible hints at times that the real argument for private trusteeship (if we allow, as we must, that there is no private ownership) is its defense against man's incurable rapacities—incurable by any self-doctoring. The point I now make is that we cannot claim ownership without some measure of guilt. The reason for the guilt is our secret awareness that we are not owners but only trustees. *Comment four:* "You Can't Take It With You." [6] We bring nothing into the world; we take nothing out of it. At the nineteenth hole the golf course does not belong to man. It would be more accurate to say that he belongs to it—about seven feet of it, seven feet down. That fact is the sufficient proof that the earth is not man's. So the Bible uses the verb "to be" in its present tense, indicative mood: "The earth is the Lord's."

IV

As for that contention, the evidence is not far to seek. The earth proclaims its Divine Original, at least fitfully, even to our time-bound eyes. Who can escape moments of awe as he contemplates the cosmos? The scientist bridles at the word "revelation," but he could not discover anything if it were not there already waiting to be found, free gift before it could be discovery. The artist sees on earth and sky a light that steals his spirit, beauty that allows him no merely utilitarian aim but rather asks of him an ultimate devotion. Every one of us, with no claim to be scientist or artist, sees in the cosmos—the multiplied lenses in a butterfly's eye, flames leaping half a million miles into space from our poor local sun, our tragedy and joy—both terror and order: justice, if that is the word, that goes clean beyond our justice; and purpose that shames all our tiny purposes. The earth quickens in us a basic fear, "the fear of the Lord," because we are not unaware of Him who owns it. Thus Whitefield, as he preached among the hills and lakes of Cumberland, would sometimes stop, and suddenly point, and cry: "The trumpeters have crossed the hills!" [7]

As further evidence, man has always found in the earth a realm of signs—the signs of Him who made it and owns it. We have a saying that a man should not be treated as a thing, and the saying is truth. But perhaps we should add that a thing should not be treated as a thing, for a thing is a hieroglyphic, a secret code, for those who will ponder it. Water is not mere water, and still less is it mere hydroelectric power, for its very essential nature is cleansing. We do not wash in soil or leaves: water is the type and sign of baptism, the embryo promise that we can be cleansed of our sins. Likewise the hills are not merely hills; they are more even than stone for our building, and wood for our burning: they are a great shoulder against the storm. "Thy righteousness is like the great mountains." [8] "The strength of the hills is his also." [9] The impalpable air is not a mixture of gases merely, which the chemist can analyze, but the symbol of an invisible Presence: "The wind blows where it wills . . . so it is with every one who is born of the Spirit." [10] Jesus said that the sky is God's throne, the earth His footstool, a lost sheep the token of our human lostness, and the springing seed a sign of the miracle of God's new life given to our world. John Hall Wheelock inscribed a poem for me, even me, so that I, poor wretch, may yet reach heaven clinging to his coattails. He tells of the wonder hidden in common earth:

> Deftly does the dust express,
> In mind, her hidden loveliness—
> And, from her cool silence, stream

The cricket's cry and Dante's dream;
For the earth that breeds the trees
Breeds cities too, and symphonies.

Equally her beauty flows
Into a savior, or a rose—
Looks down in dream, and from above
Smiles at herself in Jesus' love.
Christ's love and Homer's art
Are but the workings of her heart;
Through Leonardo's hand she seeks
Herself, and through Beethoven speaks,
In holy thunderings around
The awful message of the ground.[11]

Perhaps we must say in our time that if we persist in treating things as only things and as if we owned them, we ourselves must sink into thinghood.

All of which brings us to the deepest evidence: the earth is fulfilled only in sacrament. A farmer drives a plow through a wilderness, harrows and seeds the land; and soon there is bread for man's hunger. In that way of life one of the purposes of the land becomes clear. Michelangelo takes a hog-bristle brush, greasy pigments, and a stucco wall; and soon men see God or at least glimpse His handiwork. Thus a deep purpose in hog bristles and pigments and plane surfaces is revealed. A man and woman speak words in a marriage vow and then through the sexual act (which is not unclean, but instead sacramental) there are children and a home, and through the heartache and joy of a home a deeper understanding of life. A martyr takes stones flung at him—Shall we say segregation stones flung at Negro riders on a bus in Mississippi?—and soon, through that cruel breach in his mortality, light pierces us, even though we shutter every window against it. Who owns an earth that is fulfilled only in sacrament? Not mortal man! Perhaps all progress is sacrament. Perhaps, despite our modern cult of progress, there is no other progress. Perhaps this is the inescapable proof that the earth is by nature sacred because "the earth is the Lord's."

V

Our journey through a seemingly comic text has brought us a long way—to an Upper Room where Jesus took bread and wine, found on every lowliest table, and there made of them another Table where Hands of Grace give food to still the deeper hunger and thirst of man's lonely and blundering heart. Who could have dreamed that such common things as bread and wine could have that awe-struck use? But that is only a hint of the story: that same Jesus took darkness at noon, the sun's rays striking down like swords, flies buzzing around a helpless head, two pieces of wood, three nails (Rome would not waste an extra nail on him: one nail for the feet), a length of thong, a spear, sounds from raucous throats which mocked his death—and, behold, history's final sacrament. This was done through his body also, his body and these darkest tokens of a most earthy earth. How could it be? Because the earth is the Lord's, and He can use it as He will, Whose will is Love, even through death and desolation.

There is no conclusion to this sermon. Perhaps there never should be any for any sermon, for hearer and preacher alike must write the conclusion, each in his own secret commitment, each in his daily life in the earth which God owns. Suppose Christian Dior and his successors never did own any fashions! Wouldn't that be a revolution? Suppose the money in our pocket was never ours, and suppose the banker never owned the bank! What a change, if we knew it, in our acquisitive society! So each of us writes a conclusion as he may be minded. But perhaps our minds also are not ours. The Bible in its vast ponderings goes far beyond "the earth." It says "The earth is the Lord's and the fulness thereof," meaning everything in the cosmos; "the world and those who dwell therein," [12] meaning you and me, and the whole pilgrimage of man, and all other orders of life. "For he has founded it upon the seas, and established it upon the rivers": [13] it all rests on the Abyss of His eternal nature and is all held in His eternal Grace.

12

THE PROBLEM OF THE RIGHTEOUS MAN

> The word of Jesus: "Unless your righteousness
> exceeds that of the scribes and Pharisees, you will
> never enter the kingdom of heaven." *Matt.* 5:20
> The word of Paul: ". . . not having a righteous-
> ness of my own, based on law, but that which is
> through faith in Christ, the righteousness from
> God that depends on faith." *Phil. 3:9*

Few people think of righteousness as a problem, but it is; and
the righteous man is a trouble both to himself and to his neighbors. The whole issue is implied in the little girl's prayer: "O God,
make all the bad people good, and all the good people nice." She
must have been a precocious child, too precocious for her own
peace; or perhaps an adult prayer was foisted on her. But the prayer
makes sense, for "nice" to a child does not mean sugary: it means
a trustworthy, happy person who gladly and gratefully shares a
child's seriousness and laughter. A "righteous" man by contrast
is often aloof or even capsuled. The "bad" man, Milton's "Satan"
for an instance, is more interesting than a circumspect vestryman.
The bad man is destructive and has little to commend him, but
the righteous man is nevertheless not "nice." Our world is burdened by attractive sinners and stale saints.

I

Jesus said of the scribes and Pharisees that they were righteous. The adjective was in one sense an accolade. They were not the wanton or wicked who muddy life and disfigure it with cruelty. But Jesus as quickly spoke of the need of a better righteousness than they could claim. What could he mean? The *scribes* were jurists, interpreters of the sacred Law, leaders of the synagogue; and it was generally agreed that they were to be held in higher honor by the children of the synagogue school than the honor they gave to their parents. The *Pharisees* were puritans in the best sense of the word, generous to the poor, ardently patriotic, honest to a fault; and they were not narrow-minded, for they tried to moderate the rigors of the Law, not for themselves but for their neighbors, as when they widened the prohibition against traveling on the Sabbath to mean not beyond the bounds of the city. Then why should Jesus warn us against such men when there were plenty worse? Why, why should he say to them: "The tax collectors [collaborators] and the harlots go into the kingdom of God before you"?[1] Thus the problem of the righteous man!

II

Let us look at the case history of a righteous man. His biography begins with: "I will present a good character or reputation before God and men." That resolve seems commendable, but it is a bad beginning, for it begins with "I." The man is looking in a mirror, and a mirror at best has narrow limits. The limits are: "What virtues shall I seek and what sins avoid?" The man's world is now split into "right" and "wrong," a fact which leaves life split. The mirror has become a code. The Talmud had 365 negative commandments, as many as the days of the year, and 248 positive commandments, as many as the bones in the body.[2] Benjamin Franklin kept a ledger of pros and cons in character, and each night added up what virtues he had attained and what vices he had eschewed.[3] A code of conduct never covers life in its newness and surprise. It can give no power for keeping the code, and it has no word to speak when a man breaks it. The man himself, slave now to a code, becomes codified. A codified man is not "nice."

Next step in the case history: the righteous man says, "Not as that bad man." Let us be clear: the bad man *is* bad. What end is there to the entail of his badness? A man defaults in money trusted to him. Then he has to choose between suicide or the district attorney. Then his daughters, now of marriageable age, must decide, when proposals of marriage come, if they shall tell their father's shame. The shadow remains even "to the third and the fourth generation." [4] The Pharisee speaks common sense when he says, "Not as that bad man." Scribes and Pharisees do not default in money trusted to them. The very word "Pharisee" means "separated" in holiness. But that is part of the problem. Should a man be separated from his fellow men? A doctor, however finely trained and skillful, is not much use unless he goes into sickness at risk of contagion.

Next step: the righteous man becomes uncomfortably aware that all goodness is entangled with badness. He must be separated to be a "good" man, but it is wrong to be separated from the world's need. The preacher draws his stipend from the church, but church money is not necessarily clean money. We say, "Money talks." It is a mercy that the collection on Sunday morning cannot talk. That dollar bill might get sassy: "You don't know where I've been!" If we did know, we might be horrified. The great foundations are a blessing; yet we must wonder if such fortunes should have been made, especially in a day when workers were ill-paid. Always there is entanglement of good and bad. Somewhere is the story of the race-horse owner who, having been soundly converted, gave a race horse to the mission in which he had found new birth. The horse began to win, the mission was enriched, its work was thus extended; but—should a mission, of all places, play the ponies? Always the entanglement! The story was called *Faith, Hope and a Horse*.[5] The problem of the righteous man is how to get rid of the horse. If the man goes to jail for a righteous cause, he is still neglecting his family, perhaps to the point of throwing them on public charity. But the righteous man, though he is aware of ambiguity, cannot admit it: it would break his mirror.

Next step in the case history: the righteous man begins to realize that real righteousness goes far beyond his coded mirror. Thus the scientist knows that truth is always beyond his formulas. But the righteous man flogs himself to reach that line where earth and sky meet, for he must be righteous. So day after day he cries, "I'll get there! I'll get there." But he knows he never can. Yet he dare not face the fact that the earth is the earth, and the sky is the sky. Man is man, and God is God; and—how can man be righteous in God's sight? The eternal constraint rests on our human life, but we are mortal; and—how can we ever fulfill the eternal demand? We fail in even the simplest commandment: "You shall not covet." [6] But do we not covet, times in a day? As for heavy commandments, "You shall not kill," [7] do we not daily kill by our indifference? We forget the face of our waiter in the restaurant as though he were robot instead of man, and we do not know the name of our mailman, much less what secret burdens he has to bear. The righteous man begins to understand that he can never be righteous.

Then the denouement: the righteous man may meet Jesus. He will hear Jesus say: "No one is good but God alone." [8] Then the righteous man must confront both the ambiguities of life and the hopelessness of the strictly ethical quest. Then he must either break his mirror or—break Jesus. In many an instance he tries to be rid of the inner conflict by breaking Jesus. Jesus' death was instigated by the religious community, even though it was the Roman Empire which carried out the sentence. After Calvary, we may note, two Pharisees gave him decent burial when his disciples had fled. They, the two, were stricken at the heart, for they were not bad men. Thoreau once remarked that if we see a man approaching with intent to do us good, we should run for our life. [9] He was not speaking about Jesus, for Jesus said in profundity below profundity, "Why do you call me good? No one is good but God alone." [10]

III

Now let us attempt the case history of another kind of man, leaving him nameless except to say that he would never claim to be a good man. He begins by confronting the human dilemma in himself and in his world. It is not a world of black and white: there are innumerable shades of gray. An issue of *The Atlantic Monthly* [11] had a Camus story of a lonely French schoolteacher in Algeria. The French army left an Arab murderer in his charge with orders that he should deliver the culprit to the nearby army headquarters. The teacher was ready to curse both the coercive state and the violent man, but curses solve no problems. He took the murderer to the neighboring hilltop to a fork in the road, saying in effect, "That is the way to freedom; that to prison and death." So he left the choice to the murderer. He returned toward the schoolhouse, looked back at the man against the sky, and then saw him choose prison. Why? For justice' sake? Or to show them that an Arab can die despising French justice? When the teacher reached his classroom, he found an Arab message on the blackboard: he would be killed, as one who had delivered an Arab to death! Thus the crisscross of human motive. Who can unravel it? This other man in our study confronts that snarl.

Then he finds it in his heart to pity man in man's dilemma. Whence that pity? Not from the dilemma, for it is over against the dilemma in pity. Whence? From that Sky which man in his pilgrimage can surely never reach. "If only it were so!" our nameless man exclaims. If we could only believe that all round about the crisscross of our motives and our dilemma there is another Dimension in which all ambiguities are resolved!—just as (there is no "just as," no parable or parallel) a musician takes dissonance and resolves it in great music. Is there any sign? Well, there is that "strange Man upon his Cross." [12] He was baptized though baptism was for remission of sins. The Church has given us an account of that event: "Let it be so now; for thus it is fitting for us to fulfil all righteousness.[13] Is *that* the righteousness that exceeds "the righteousness of the scribes and Pharisees"?—that we make common cause in *love* with all men in the mortal dilemma, because of One who has first loved us? He prayed on the cross for those who slew him: "Father, forgive them; for they know not what they do." [14] Did they not know? Yes, they knew: he meant no sentimental excuse. Yet they did not know either the crisscross of their own motives, or the depth of the human dilemma, or the necessity of God's love in Jesus Christ.

Next step in this strange biography: the nameless man says: "We must live in this faith." Or, rather, he says: "We must try so to live, God helping us." The good man's righteousness does not so believe, for his righteousness ends in self-righteousness. Secularism does not so believe, for it soon breeds its own self-righteousness: it believes nothing that will not give the password to the little logical mind. Perhaps a tortured atheism *does* believe it, for we could hardly deny the light and love of Christ without first believing it: a man cannot say, "All is midnight," unless he has first known the day. In any event, a man must make his choice. Is there not somewhere the story of a husband saying of his wife's infidelity, "Since you and I have done this . . ."? He loved her so deeply that her deed was his deed, and yet not his deed. In Christ we see a Love beyond our human love, stooping to our human dilemma and saying, "Since you and I have done this . . . ." He "who knew no sin" [15] so involved himself with our need that we dimly see God, Who "has laid on him" and therefore on Himself "the iniquity of us all." [16] Thus our nameless man says: "We must believe this." He says it not coercively but as the only sanity.

Then the man gives himself by faith to this same Love. He says again: "I am not righteous and never can be, for righteousness belongs only to God. But perhaps I can keep the channel clear so that God can work through me." He is aware of the crisscross of motives, the strange entanglement of good and evil, but believes that Love is the fulfilling of a deeper Law. Maxwell Anderson's play *Winterset* [17] has the crisscross in very truth. There we see the pitiful man whose views stubborn men condemned as "radical," see him apparently compromised by his nearness to a murder and hung for a crime he did not commit. Then we see his son resolving in fierce sense of justice to clear his father's name. There are others in the cast: the young violinist, knowing that a thug was the real culprit, yet not telling what he knew for fear he would be slain, and for fear his sister and aged father might thus be thrown on the world, yet tortured in conscience by his silence; and there was the sister herself, suspecting what her brother knew and falling in love with the man bent on clearing his father's name. What a crisscross! Should she keep silence to save her brother or speak for justice and the man she loved? She kept silence. Then her lover read the silence and flamed out on her for sharing a brother's guilt. But she, in turn, reminded him of his father's gentleness; and he admitted the pitiful, pitiable thrust: Yes, said he of his father,

> He'd have forgiven—
> Then there's no more to say—I've groped
>   long enough
> through this everglades of old revenges—
>   here
> the road ends. . . .
> the iron I wore so long—it's eaten through
>   and fallen from me. . . .

> They'll say we're children—Well—the world's
> made up
> of children.[18]

That story ended in tragedy, but the tragedy was still apocalypse
—in Love.

The last step in this strange biography? The strange man had
heretofore followed the modern custom of dismissing Paul as an
angular, bigoted dogmatist. He forgot that Paul wrote in tears and
light a poem on Love. Now he read Paul with new eyes. He recalled
that Paul had tried, as few men have tried, to be "righteous." So
he read, and wondered as he read: "For no human being will be
justified in [God's] sight by works of the law . . . . But now the
righteousness of God has been manifested apart from law . . . ,
the righteousness of God through faith in Jesus Christ." [19] He
read again, and wondered still more, knowing now that he had
come upon a revolution in man's thinking: " . . . not having a
righteousness of my own, based on law, but that which is through
faith in Christ, the righteousness from God that depends on faith."
Then the man prayed quietly:

> The best of what we do and are,
> Just God, forgive! [20]

The name of our unknown man? Name unknown, except that
little children called him "the nice man."

IV

Is there a righteous man in the house? No, "not one," as Paul
insisted. We hope there is none who thinks himself righteous, for
righteousness is not the human stance: it belongs to God. The
righteous man easily succumbs to the mirror. Meanwhile the bad
man, realizing that he cannot of himself be good, and stricken at
the heart by the gentleness of Christ, may suddenly turn in a half-
despairing venture of faith—and so enter the Kingdom, while the
righteous man is still capsuled in his righteousness. "The tax collectors and the harlots go into the kingdom of God before you."
But all of us, righteous and unrighteous, are held in another Life,
another Love. Our planet with its endless self-justifyings, which
never justify, is still held in Light. It is what the little girl would
call a "nice" Light.

13

GOD AND OUR MIXED MOTIVES

"For the word of God is living and active, sharper than any two-edged sword, piercing to the division of soul and spirit . . . and discerning the thoughts and intentions of the heart. And before him no creature is hidden, but all are open and laid bare to the eyes of him with whom we have to do. "   *Heb. 4:12-13*

A British psychologist tells of a man who, under hypnosis, was told to take a flowerpot from a window ledge, wrap it in a towel, set it on a sofa, and bow to it three times.[1] This he did, under the hypnotic spell. When he was asked later to explain these strange actions, he said that the plant was cold on the window ledge, and so he had wrapped it in a warm towel and set it on the sheltered sofa; and that then, being pleased with himself for such thoughtfulness, he had whimsically bowed to the plant three times. That account was not the real explanation: he had been hypnotized. Do we always give plausibly false reasons for our conduct? Can our motives ever be unraveled, or even understood? Did Hitler convince himself that he really was the instrument of a "new order"? The crisis of our times has brought a strange doubt: we suspect all human nature, including our own motives.

I

Our motives are always mixed. No man does anything from a single motive, let alone from a completely pure motive. Some people deny that fact, but the very vehemence of the denial betrays them. Other people hardly trouble to examine or question their motives. They are like Ignorance in *The Pilgrim's Progress,* who said chirpingly when Christian warned that a man who trusts his heart is a fool: "Is it not a good heart that has good thoughts?" [2] But most of us are troubled nowadays by this crisscross of motives, perhaps especially students. They say: "Suppose my high-mindedness is really selfish. Suppose my wish to be a doctor or a lawyer is actually a longing for adulation or authority. Suppose my contentment with small-town life is withdrawal or escape." This self-searching has its place. Why do I vote as I vote? Is it because business conditions are reasonably prosperous, or because my upbringing has hypnotized me, or in mere rebellion against my parents? Self-scrutiny is an astringent.

But it can also become chaos and a fatal self-involvement. No man can bathe in strong astringent. Self-scrutiny is an infinite regress. How do I know my motives are pure? All right: I will examine my motives. Then I must ask: How do I know that the examination of my motives is pure? Then I must examine the examination of my motives—in infinite regress. Perhaps Dietrich Bonhoeffer is right in his contention that to be sure of our motives we would have to go clean through "the racial unconscious" to the hidden origin of all things.[3] Soon we are like Milton's fallen angels who in their debate "found no end, in wand'ring mazes lost." [4] They were in hell, and self-scrutiny soon becomes a little hell in which all motives are suspect and all action paralyzed. "Are my motives pure?" may betoken a man feeding on his own fingers: he gains some nourishment, yet he bleeds to death. "But," someone asks, "is not self-scrutiny the realism practiced in modern psychiatry?" No, it is not; for in psychiatric counseling the patient is over against a trained objective mind who governs the scrutiny. Is that our need: to be over against Reality? Our need—and the psychiatrist's need? So to our text. We may find that it is not in a remote "Bible world"; or, rather, that the Bible world is piercingly our world and savingly above our world.

II

For one thing, the Bible knows well that our motives are mixed.

With all honor to Sigmund Freud, who discovered a continent even though his early maps may need revision, the Bible knew about "rationalizing" before the ancestors of Freud were weaned. Many a Bible story, beginning with Adam, shows man making "the worse appear the better reason." [5] Adam said, "The woman gave me fruit of the tree," and she said, "the serpent" was to blame.[6] The Bible says, "The heart"—by which it means central motivation, the energizing will involving thought and feeling—"is deceitful above all things . . . : who can know it?" [7] Our text says: "The word of God is living and active, sharper than any two-edged sword, piercing to the division of soul and spirit." Notice carefully: "soul" there means our checkered humanity, and "spirit" there means that spirit in us by which we try to be sure of our motives. This sword, says our text, is always "discerning the thoughts and intentions of the heart." Thus, our text continues, before God "no creature is hidden, but all are open and laid bare to the eyes of him with whom we have to do." That "laid bare" means like the face of a man thrust back by the two-edged sword at his throat, so that every expression of his face is naked to the light. The Bible knows that our motives are always mixed.

It tells us that God knows why they are mixed and that He has them in control. He knows why a hypnotized man takes a flower-pot from a window ledge, sets it towel-wrapped on a sofa, and bows to it three times. The deeps of the subconscious, still more of the racial "unconscious," always go far beyond our ken, but not beyond His sight. Yet—can we be sure that God knows? Yes, despite the recurrent doubt. When nuclear fission was discovered, we all assumed at the back of our minds that Someone knew. about it all the time and had hidden that prodigious power. Always we make that assumption. We would not try to examine our motives if Truth were not busy in us, "living and active." That very Truth led Freud to his findings. Psychiatry calls it "reality." When Nietzsche insisted cruelly that "one will seldom go wrong if one attributes extreme actions to vanity, average ones to habit, and petty ones to fear," [8] he also was saying, without being aware, that there is in Nietzsche and all men a "spirit" which is above vanity and habit and fear. God, who is Reality, knows our mixed motives and the "why" of them.

We see this Reality coming to the top in history. Life itself soon or late exposes falsity. The stars themselves, together with a "spirit" in man, destroyed the notion that our planet is the geographical center of the universe. To take a tiny instance, fake fireplaces in the lobbies of Park Avenue apartment houses soon betray themselves, because when a man tries to warm his hands at the "coals," he finds that they are artificial coals and that the "flames" are flickering electric lights. Do we not say, "Truth will out"? On a vaster scale, Herbert Butterfield's contention that there is always a history above history [9] validates itself. The British Empire seemed so solid as to be almost impregnable, but erosion set in because empire is not history's central word. The erosion came in part by means of Gandhi's gentle witness. It should appall us and then rejoice us that "nothing is . . . hidden that will not be known." [10] We live in an open universe in which the secrets of the heart are finally proclaimed from the housetops.

In all of this Christ overtakes us, because he has never left us. The "word of God" is in him "living and active," as "the Word" made "flesh." The spirit in him was "sharper than any two-edged sword." Men might escape one edge, only to meet the other. Thus the man who came asking Jesus to divide the inheritance with him, and who thus proposed to flatter Jesus' fairness of judgment, found that Jesus was not fooled. The "word" came like a "sword": "Beware of all covetousness." [11] Perhaps there is no *ultimate* need why we should be concerned to find the very words which Jesus spoke (in Aramaic!), whatever the *proximate* need for rigorous Bible study (yes, by scholars deciphering the early manuscripts), for there is a Spirit at work who fulfills Jesus' promise. "When the Spirit of truth comes, he will guide you into all the truth: . . . for he will take what is mine and declare it to you." [12] A letter has come from a fine girl who is no stranger to the flashing truth in Christ, as is shown by her lowliness: "Since that moment I have tried with varying degrees of success to be worthy of the name Christian, and I find that the human will is a most capricious, lazy, and good-for-nothing instrument." [13] The Spirit with the two-edged sword is become flesh in Jesus Christ.

So back to our question: Can we be sure that God knows and that His light is shed always on our shadowed motives? Sure enough for the venture. Some time ago a congressman confessed that his war record was bogus. We should not quickly condemn him: others had credited him with the heroism, and he let the account pass; and he might, in any event, have found that his denial would not be printed. Besides, he wished to be a hero, and yet he wished to confess the truth. The confession itself may have been in mixed motive. Was it because exposure threatened? Or because he could no longer live in untruth? Or because he coveted inward peace? Perhaps all these motives, and many another unknown motive, were at work in him. The strange, strange heart of man! What we need is the guide who sits on a platform above the famous London maze. People are soon lost there, and some of them become frantic. Then he tells them to "go left" or to "go right," and so guides them to the exit. But our guide must not be dictatorial: we need also to find our own way. We need a Spirit not to coerce but to guide. But can we be sure? We can be sure enough for the brave venture.

III

Now to that venture. It is an act of faith. But so is every experiment in science and every trustfulness in friendship. We cannot see the future, and therefore all life is an act of faith. Faith is not a business of believing what we know isn't true. It is being grasped by the "invincible surmise" that Someone knows and taking our courageous chance on it. The letter just quoted tells how Christian commitment began: "I jumped, and found myself on the other side." Kierkegaard also spoke of "the leap." [14] We cannot disentangle our motives. We lack wisdom to probe the deeps of the subconscious. We cannot go back to the origins of our life. We may from time to time examine ourselves as to why we are acting thus and so, and then unmask any motive that is clearly an impostor. But endless self-scrutiny is endless—an infinite regress. Gordius tied a knot with such tightness and complexity that nobody could untie it. Then Alexander came, too wise to try to unite it, and cut it with his sword. [15] Well, there is a spirit in us and beyond us, "sharper than any two-edged sword." This we know—enough for the venture. We trust God made known in Christ.

The venture is an act of prayer. Silently we pray. We expose ourselves to the Light:

Search me, O God, and know my heart!
Try me and know my thoughts!

> And see if there be any wicked way in me,
> and lead me in the way everlasting.[16]

The implication in that prayer is that we can never know our own hearts or ever successfully test our own thoughts, but that God knows. The passage from which our text is taken reminds us that Jesus came in our very human nature and that he knows therefore the crisscross of our motives. Was he not tempted as we to live in the second best of motives? "If you are the Son of God, command these stones to become loaves of bread":[17] he was tempted to satisfy man's material needs in order to win man's spirit, but knew by Light the dark seduction of such a plan. The New Testament traces the meaning of this sharing of our nature by Christ: God so loves us that He has made common cause with the crisscross of our motives; and Christ, being tempted as we, is able to sustain us in our dilemma, yes, and makes intercession for us, holding our prayers within his prayer. God knows us, our heads thrown back, sword of truth at our throats, but His knowledge is incarnate love. Therefore we pray in the remembrance of Christ, which is more than remembrance:

> Look, Father, look on His anointed face,
> And only look on us as found in Him.[18]

The alternative to endless self-analysis is to locate ourselves in Christ by venture of faith and by the constant act of prayer.

An account has been left to us of a conversation between a theologian and a skeptic. The skeptic asked, "Is it right to pray to God without really believing in Him?" The theologian replied wisely and well: "If you ever have the impulse to pray, that means that you do have some belief in Him." The skeptic then said: "I do have a desire at times to say, 'If Thou existest, O God, hear me. If Thou hast a heart for the desires and cares of a poor mortal, incline Thine ear.' But I do not know if such a prayer would be sinful." Then the theologian bobbled the ball. He said: "It all depends on the motive." He should have seen that the skeptic's motive had some clear measure of honesty. He should have known that all motives are mixed and that no man can read either his own or his neighbor's motives. Charge him with an error!—and with pride of judgment mixed in with his own motives! What do

you think he should have said? This perhaps: "Cast yourself
on God, who is dimly seen in all the mixture of human motives.
You do not know even why you are a skeptic: perhaps pride of
your own mind is involved and perhaps the failure of my church.
You call yourself a 'poor mortal.' My faith holds that God Himself became a poor mortal, so that we may know that He knows.
If that faith seems fine to you, cast yourself on it and keep on
praying!"

IV

Your motives are mixed. So are mine, for I shall not know
this side of death why I became a preacher; and I have no right
to assume that all that moved me in the choice was of angel
brightness. Sometimes we see how incredibly raveled are even our
best desires. I have heard of a priest claiming that, though other
orders might surpass his in learning or prayerfulness or works
of mercy, his was supreme in one regard—in humility! So Tennyson says of the motives of Lancelot in his guilty love for his queen,
King Arthur's wife:

> His honour rooted in dishonour stood,
> And faith unfaithful kept him falsely true.[19]

But two facts hold: Light plays on us, or we would not ever question our motives; and we can cast ourselves on that Light as we see
it in Christ. It will bring us under judgment, but the Judge has
crossed the courtroom floor to stand by us in the dock. The judgment is sharper "than any two-edged sword"; it divides our "human" motives from the Light that ever plays on us, but the very
judgment is love—to bring us to Reality.

So we pray: "Search me, O God, and know my heart!" We
cannot know it. "Try me, and know my thoughts!" We cannot
disentangle them. But faith cuts the Gordian knot, as with a
"two-edged sword." Such prayer is the very purpose of our present
worship. Having prayed, we can then live our life in forthright-
ness, not getting caught in endless self-scrutiny. So let us forget
ourselves and get on with our knitting. The Light shines on us. God
will do His work also, and at long last Christ "shall see the fruit
of the travail of his soul and be satisfied." [20] We shall find our life
in Him.

14

FRUSTRATION AND FAITH

"These all died in faith, not having received what was promised, but having seen it and greeted it from afar . . . . Therefore God is not ashamed to be called their God, for he has prepared for them a city."   *Heb. 11:13, 16*

"These all died . . . not having received what was promised." Thus the stark realism of the Bible. There is no glossing of disappointed hopes, no easy fiction of the happy ending. You and I are not ready to accept tragedy as life's final term, for tragedy, as in the death of Lincoln, is itself apocalypse, the opening of long-closed eyes; but we are obliged by facts to admit, with the honesty of this text, that the promises and hopes of our mortal days are not fulfilled. We die with half our music in us. Thus George Frederick Watts depicts Hope herself as seated atop our planet indeed, but with head forlornly bowed and her fingers plucking one unbroken harp string.[1] We now note that issue: the topic is "Frustration and Faith."

I

Certain words are here pivots. One is "promise." The child reckons the future as always bright. Though a favorite toy may be broken, tears cease with the promise of a new toy. Even the shock of someone's death is assuaged by promise that

> There's a home for little children
> Above the bright blue sky.[2]

This hope does not quickly ebb even with adult years. We say of our political and economic systems what we say about the building of a new house: "I want it to be perfect." Not quickly do we accept the inexorable fact of imperfection. A young economist told me that she almost cried when, early in her economic studies, she found that scarcity is a prime datum. Another friend has recently gone to a remote corner of South America, with his wife and three children, to build there a truly Christian community. Always we try to fashion Utopia. That fact has tremendous meaning. Life holds out promises.

Another word is "faith." We believe the promises. We put our trust in them. Faith has many definitions, even within the span of New Testament writings, and is perhaps never defined. It is not mere intellectual assent to a set of propositions, though the mind is always involved. It is not merely deliberate resolve, the will to believe, even though it is an act. It is far more than emotional surcharge, though it carries with it a certain ecstasy. Our text suggests its own definition: faith is the movement of our finite life toward the beckoning of infinite promise. The Pilgrim Fathers sought on these shores the commonwealth of God. They were not visionaries, or if they were, so are we, for we also seek that selfsame Kingdom. We believe in it, in a far deeper sense than we believe in gravitation or that John Doe is a good teacher. Paracelsus, the German physician,[3] chose that name deliberately: superior to Celsus, who was a cynical atheist; for the physician strove to know all science, all astronomy, all medicine and all theology that he might thus bring perfect healing. Always there is in us some such faith in life's promise.

The other word is "frustration": "These all died . . . not having received what was promised." That word also should be faced. Compare the Pilgrim dream with our modern America: the Santa Fe trail, marked in splotches of hero-blood, now ends in Hollywood. Compare man's long hope for peace with the present Middle Eastern problem and the atomic threat. Does someone say, "The dream will yet be fulfilled"? Perhaps we must say it, for faith is the deepest movement in us, faith in love, the thrust of our finiteness toward its home in the Infinite. But the fact remains that human hopes are not fulfilled. Is the work you have done as great as your early hope? Have your marriage and home fulfilled your dreams? Life has a fatal flaw, and our own culpable failure scores deep the flaw until now it is like a gouge on a polished table. Is anything perfect in this world? *Can* anything ever be perfect in this world? There are fatalities, fate-alities, an irrational and unpredictable streak in history. All historical structures suffer a downward drag, and all discoveries are perverted, as when the submarine, intended for the safe crossing of the ocean, was promptly made a lethal weapon of war. Is finiteness itself a "fall"? Can the finite, in any event, compass the Infinite? There is no Utopia in any America, south or north. Three words preside over our life —promise, faith, and frustration.

II

So what to do? It is a central question. My six-year-old granddaughter, Anne, much wiser than her grandfather, was shown a kodachrome picture on a screen of her small cousin Karen. The picture had been taken as Karen faced a bright sun, so her eyes were almost closed and her face puckered. "Why is she so muddled?" asked Anne. "Muddled"—as are all men's hopes!

> Ah, what a dusty answer gets the soul
> When hot for certainties in this our life! [4]

What to do with man's muddled face? The question is not academic though it involves a theology: it is practical, for we must determine how to live in a world where promised perfection has a fatal flaw.

We can deny the frustration. That is one answer, and many people choose it. We can pretend that there is no imperfection or that it can easily be overcome. This pretense is a false perfectionism, and psychiatrists know its baleful issues. Parents print perfectionisms on their children—"No child of ours must ever fail"— and thus curse them, when failure comes, with a sense of inferiority. University professors are sometimes guilty: one of them in a nationally reported speech hailed "man's invincible mind."

He would have spoken equal sense had he announced that all fences are fenceless. Preachers join the pretense: "What a man dreams of doing he can do." Perhaps he can in some other world, but in this world an infinite hope is laid on finite powers, and therein are the pathos and grandeur of our mortal life. Graduation speakers join the false parade: "Failure is a word found only in the dictionary of fools and cowards." Do they think that graduates will never fail? Do they realize that, in telling graduates to "dream," they invite them to become cleft or remote? Perfectionism finally cripples all action, as in the instance of the would-be writer, one of the characters in Albert Camus' *The Plague*. The writer never got beyond the first sentence because it was never perfect.[5] One answer to life's dilemma is to deny the frustration and escape into perfectionism.

Another answer is to deny the promise—faith. Sometimes this answer comes of cowardice, as when Gérard Roussel believed in the Reformation but was afraid to confess his belief because of marshaled foes: princes, crowds, church, and armies. He asked, "What shall a little man do among so many lions?"[6] More often the answer comes because a man keeps looking at the flaw until he no longer sees the beauty of the world. Defeated perfectionism may thus breed cynics.

> The Worldly Hope men set their Hearts upon
> Turns Ashes—or it prospers; and anon,
>   Like Snow upon the Desert's dusty Face
> Lighting a little Hour or two—is gone.[7]

Then? Then escape into nature worship: "Ah! Moon of my Delight who know'st no wane"[8]—the moon being already a burnt-out coal. Or escape into human culture and human love:

> Here with a Loaf of Bread beneath the bough,
> A Flask of Wine, a Book of Verse—and Thou
>   Beside me singing in the Wilderness—
> And Wilderness is Paradise enow![9]

Imagine such self-crippledness and self-deceit: bread from the supermarket, wine from the ubiquitous liquor store, Miss America, and the latest book of scented verse as the new paradise! The final issue is weariness, "the sere, the yellow leaf," [10] and the cynicism which says that we live in a rotten world.

Then what is the answer? We do not get rid of faith except by getting rid of life. While life lasts, we cannot get rid of the frustration. Then what to do? There is a third answer: to accept the frustration and yet cleave to the faith. "But that," someone says, "spells tension." Yes, the tension of a cello string which sings only when it is taut. This string is stretched between the infinite hope and the finite limitation. Only so can life give forth its best music, which fact shows the shallowness of modern doctrines of "peace of mind." If we deny the promise-faith, we can have peace of a kind, a cynical peace which has surrendered the struggle and the hope and so stands off from life instead of being involved. If we deny the frustration, we can again have peace of a kind, praecox peace living in fantasy-land. But neither of these denials can be sustained by people willing to confront life. The only true peace on earth is in the singing of a taut string stretched between the heaven of hope, which never forsakes us, and the earth limitation, which we can never escape.

III

What happens to the man who makes this hard and worthy choice? Jesus bade us cleave to the promise-faith, even to praying, "Thy kingdom come . . . on earth as it is in heaven." But Jesus never tried to hide from us the sharpness of a flinty earth. He told us that most seed of the Kingdom would fall on inhospitable ground, and prepared his followers for failure, warning them that some doors would not "receive" [11] them; and he himself came at last to a Cross. Then what happens to the man who cleaves to the faith while accepting (with whatever pain of spirit) the inevitable frustration? He is given no tranquilizing drug. Our text gives a better answer, tides of splendor flooding its harbor of words.

The man is found of God: "Therefore God is not ashamed to be called their God." "Not ashamed" is shining understatement for "very proud." Hear a quotation from C. H. Dodd: "As we follow the biblical record, we observe that the encounter with God is apt to take place when a man finds himself involved in a situation of unusual tension in the real world." [12] Notice the language: "involved," no escape; "unusual tension," not "peace of mind"; "the real world," not the world of the perfectionist or the world of the cynic. We think we can find God by argument, and endlessly we ask for "proof." But God is not so found, for He is neither a theorem to be proved nor lackey to our questionings. No, God is found as we face adverse facts and yet keep faith. Electricity glows only against resistance. So faith glows. See an aged pottery maker under royal demand to recant his faith in Christ. Why should faith be so crossed? Why should men be so evil and life so perverse? The pottery maker did not know. He knew only that he must keep faith and meet the contradiction: "I will teach you this royal speech! You can never constrain a potter to bow the knee before images." [13] To such men comes surety of the presence of God. They are born in His image (that is why faith is in them), and now they know it, and they keep the family honor; and God claims them for His own. There, at the point of tension, music breaks.

Such a man knows heaven, a dimension of life beyond this life: "For he has prepared for them a city." The veneer-thinking of our day would persuade us that heaven is "pie in the sky," a mirage offered by rapacious men to the dispossessed. Sometimes preaching takes that poor form—"projection" for the comfort of cowards. But this is not the "heaven" of the Bible, and it is not the heaven deeply hidden in courageous hearts. Perhaps it is inevitable in the finiteness of our minds that new words such as "evolution" or "projection" should, in the flush of new knowledge, be offered as explanation for a range of facts far too vast for them to cover; but sensible people, knowing the deeps of man's spirit and the poignant witness of the generations, need not sell out to clever newness. In the Bible, heaven is for those who keep faith and meet the harsh onset. Because they know God, life's electricity glowing in light and power at the point of resistance, they know also His infinite grace. Is He at His wit's end when He has made this checkered planet? Is He a tinpot-god ruling at last over acres of graveyards? Or is He—God? Men who accept life's thrust and yet keep faith know that God is God and that there is Life beyond life. Thus two monks whom Henry VIII threatened to tie in a sack and cast into the Thames if they did not renounce their faith: "The road to heaven lies as near by water as by land; and therefore it is indifferent to us which way we go thither." [14] Such men, knowing God and known of Him, are sure that God's creative power is not exhausted by this life, and that His love is not cabined by our tiny house of years.

So all roads lead to a Cross. Christ kept the faith, the only Man who ever fully kept it; yet he met the contradiction in bitterer thrust than any other has known or could know. He kept the faith in such surety that he could say, "The kingdom of God has come upon you." [15] He faced the adverse facts and never side-stepped, even though no other ever met such blindness and cruelty. Our failures were all added to his burden, but he asked neither respite nor release: Nevertheless, "thy will be done." [16] How could we ever make him the apostle of a comfortable "peace of mind"? That question answers itself and another question likewise: Where is our world most Godlike, and where do we best glimpse a City? There at Calvary. There light breaks in the deepest darkness where Christ still kept faith: "Father, into thy hands I commit my spirit." [17]

IV

You must judge the truth of what we try to say. What do you really think about people who close their eyes to life's alien facts? Do they really keep the faith? And what do you really think about people who deny the faith to assure us that there is nothing but frustration? You have known some people who have accepted nobly what cannot be changed, not shrinking from disappointment and sorrow, and who all the time have cast themselves on God, not denying the innate faith—Jesus Christ himself being their "pioneer" and the "Captain of their salvation." [18] What do you think about them?

King Arthur's dream was broken, and his Order of the Round Table scattered to the winds. Some of his followers deserted him, some betrayed, and some were lost in battle. But the poet is right: in that shattering, as he still kept faith, he found God and heaven:

> Then from the dawn it seem'd there came,
> but faint
> As from beyond the limit of the world,
> Like the last echo born of a great cry,
> Sounds, as if some fair city were one voice
> Around a king returning from his wars.[19]

"These all died in faith, not having received what was promised . . . . Therefore God is not ashamed to be called their God, for he has prepared for them a city."

15

JUDGE NOT

"Judge not, that you be not judged." *Matt. 7:1*

But can we help it? We judge Khrushchev and Eisenhower, and the rival managers in the World Series, and the worth of this course or that course at college. We gossip, because people, next to God, are the most interesting topic of conversation; and gossip is filled with judgments, mostly adverse, whether at a bridge club or a preachers' conference. Does not the Harvard motto, *Veritas*, involve us in lines of judgment drawn between truth and falsity? How can we help judging?

The trouble is in the meaning of a word. A gangster-politician in a comedy drama said of the newsman who was about to expose him: "I owe him a lot—a lot in a cemetery." There the word "lot" seems to have more than one meaning. So does our word "judge." So does the Greek verb used in our text. It means to distinguish (the real from the spurious), to determine (a course of conduct), and to censure or condemn. That last meaning here prevails. "Judge not": do not act as a censor of men's deeds and motives.

I

Some reasons for the warning are quite clear: we do not know our neighbor's motives. James Smetham, despite his evangelical convictions, refused to join the attack on Harriet Martineau in

117

regard to her Unitarian faith: "I can't unwind her seventy-four years of act and thought." [1] He could not have unwound ten minutes of her life, or even ten seconds. For what we call our "reasons" go down to the depths of dynamic subconsciousness: they do not live on the surface mind. "The man is a liar!" we exclaim indignantly. But a lie may come because the man has been reared in a home careless of truth, or it may be a final defeat after a valiant struggle on the man's part to speak sincerely, or it may be a defense against insecurity. Bobbie Burns pleaded that before we censure, we should know "what's resisted," not only "what's done." [2] The yacht may have a broken mast, but how and why? Has it been content with Back Bay or bravely dared the ocean? Sometimes we completely misconstrue a man's deed. Years ago a captain was rescued from a doomed submarine, and eyebrows were lifted: a captain use the safety hatch and leave the crew to their fate? But he was observer for the construction company on ship's trial voyage and had volunteered to go to the surface fifteen miles from shore, with messages tied to his wrists in the likelihood that he would drown. We do not know enough to act as censors.

Another reason: censure hides our own need and thus delays our own cure, for censorious judgment is always unwitting confession of the censor's own shame. It is always self-judgment. Psychiatry throws light on this issue. Censure is a "transfer." We avoid self-confrontation by blaming our neighbors—for faults that are in us. "He is lazy," we say. But how do we know? Only by experience of being lazy. The story in the Gospel of John about the woman taken in adultery (it is not found in the earliest manuscripts, but is consonant with the word and spirit of Jesus) has him saying of her accusers: "Let him who is without sin . . . be the first to throw a stone.[3] "Sin" there seems to mean the *same kind* of sin, either in the deed or in the lustful longing. Thus condemnation of our fellow men is self-condemnation. Hatred, as in daily vituperation of the "government," stems from self-hatred. Phyllis McGinley describes the "Old Reformer":

> Few friends he kept that pleased his mind
> His marriage failed when it began,
> Who worked unceasing for mankind
> But loathed his fellow man.[4]

—because of the conflict in his own life. We do not like old or young reformers: they are too busy with other people's sins in unwitting confession of their own; but we love the saint, for he is humbly aware of his own sins. Thus condemnation only delays our own redemption.

Further reason: the censure we hurl at the world is hurled back at us, and so strife bedevils all of us. This hurling back is often the human act. Perhaps it should not be so, but human nature is not angelic, and an insult is likely to provoke an insolent retort. The hurling back seems to be also in the nature of things: "Are grapes gathered from thorns, or figs from thistles?" [5] A man sowing skunk cabbage will reap skunk cabbage, not corned beef and cabbage. There is a gruesome story of a murderer who dumped his victim in the lake five miles away from the cottage where he had committed the crime, only to find the corpse washed up against his own doorstep. "Fogarty came back!" said the murderer, and surrendered to the sheriff. [6] It does not quickly follow that if we give good will to men and the world, we shall reap good will. Jesus reaped Calvary. But ultimately? The world now reverences Jesus—and his Calvary. At any rate, we fairly quickly reap censure if we sow it. So much for the plain reasons.

II

I used to think them the whole reason, but there is a much deeper level: man's role is not that of judge. That is to say, the whole business is a perversion and denial of human nature. This we know because censure is instantly a lesion in our life. This separation is total. It is separation from our neighbors. If I say to my friend, "You are always bragging and making a fool of yourself," I may be speaking the truth, and granted I have often proved good will, I may "get away with it"; or if I know that bragging is a symptom as much as a sickness, and if I then address myself in love to the real issue (the insecurity and the lostness), I "may get away with it"; but other factors being equal, the judgment will alienate him because it "rejects" him: it does no proper honor to his status as a center of freedom.

The censure separates the censor also from himself, for he is at least dimly aware that the fault he condemns lurks in him. So my friend brags, and I do not? But why do I refrain? Because I pride myself on poise? Because I wish to be popular and know that the braggart cannot win long-continued plaudits? Because I fear the center of the stage? Because if I bragged, I could no longer censure his bragging? All these reasons point to egocentricity, to hidden forms of bragging. Thus my censoriousness condemns me and makes a split in my own life. This self-estrangement of modern man is evident in any newspaper with its daily record of men and nations in mutual recrimination. In Russia this mutual accusation is a required strategy, sufficient token of a nation self-estranged.

Obviously the censor is separated from God, for he has usurped the role of God Who alone can read men's hearts and alone can judge, and Who, if Christ be in any deep sense God's self-disclosure, holds His judgments always in the depths of sacrificial love. The Pharisees were "good" men, but they were obsessed with the law, with a scrupulous dividing of right from wrong. So life was always cleft into an ethical right and an ethical wrong. They were thus always in conflict, separated from their neighbors, themselves, and God. No man can pose as God without making God a rival. Thus alienated the man becomes a stranger to God's love. The Pharisees were nobler than the godless men whom they condemned, but the condemnation shut them from heaven, so that Jesus was obliged to tell them that collaborators and harlots would enter heaven before them.[7]

III

Censorious judgment, even when the facts seem to justify it, simply is not the human stance. One summer I was overtaken in a lonely round of golf by a student from a Middle Western university. He wished to know all about Harvard—a fact that carries responsibility and "opening" for us who live in Harvard. He drove a ball a country mile straight down the fairway. I asked his help. He did not criticize my game, which is a game even if it is not golf. He said, as if speaking in general, "It's hard to hit a ball from a certain stance." I made the translation: I was standing there like an agonized pretzel. Actually I *had* been hitting the ball, but not a mile due south down the fairway: a hundred yards at best due west across the neighboring fairway. You can understand why he overtook me: my golf is a slow exploration of the surrounding terrain. "Just stand up straight," he said. "Put the club head on the ground, and have fun." You should have seen the next drive! —even if Brother Pretzel did return on the subsequent tee. "It's hard" to live life "from a certain stance." Man is not a judge in the planetary law court, still less the state's attorney.

What is our role? Simply to live as God's finite children. God is our Father. Yes, "Father" is symbol, but we live by symbols, and they foreshadow reality. We are His children, living in the baffling ambiguities of mortal life and always tempted to make ourselves the center of the world. Christ is God's self-disclosure, by whom we may appraise conduct, granted we do not use that living norm to belabor our neighbors. We are God's children, some of us unruly, some cruel; all of us are aspiring and all dependent on the Father's grace; and, therefore, we are members of one family as each strives to honor and keep the family bond in family love. "But we cannot help condemning," someone says: "Are we to condone Russia's brutal subjection of Hungary or 'white councils' in the South?" No, we are not to condone any wrong. But note carefully: these two instanced judgments are first rooted in love—in the one case, for the oppresssed in Hungary and in the other, for Negroes in our own land. Whenever judgment is rooted in love, those condemned cannot bridle, or at least they cannot treat the accusation as if it were simply attack. Lincoln opposed the slave owner, but never merely in accusation: rather, in compassion for the enslaved.

Mark how Jesus refused the role of judge. "Who made me a judge or divider over you?" [8] He was in our human nature, and censure was not the human stance. "You judge according to the flesh" (the phrase means from the order of the natural man, from the fog level of our finitude) "I judge no one." [9] Again he said: "I did not come to judge the world but to save the world." [10] Suppose that he had judged us from the cross. Suppose he had said to the soldiers, "You are violent men, now guilty of murder"; to the traders in the Temple, "You carry your greed to the sin of shed blood"; to the crowd, "You are cowards in your mob sadism"; to the Temple leaders, "Your pride corrupts both you and the house of God." Every charge would have been true, but had the charge been made, Calvary would not have been the focus of our reverence and hope and love. What Christ did say he said to God, for man, in prayer: "Father, forgive them; for they know not what they do." [11]

This earth is not a law court, and we are not God's prosecuting attorneys. We are not good enough by a long shot, and we do not know enough about God's deeper laws, and the man in the dock would in any case be our brother. To judge is not man's role. "But we need law courts!" Yes, as "broken lights" of a Diviner law, as rooted in love, as refuge for the oppressed; but the basic pattern of our world is not a law court: it is a home—"my Father's house." [12] The angle from which to view a law court is that angle from which a man may view the law court in Paris—with the spire of Ste. Chapelle beyond it and above it, pointing to God's mercy. The ethical level of life is important, but not basic; for the man who asks incessantly about an abstract right and an abstract wrong will live as a divided man in a divided world. The basic level is personal, from man to God and from man to man, "right" being His love toward us which fulfills in us His creation-love. If we try to play the role of judge, we lose the chance to be subsaviors within God's saving grace. Psychiatry has helped us to understand, for it says, in so many words: "Love or Perish." [13] Life is not legal, but human; not moralistic, but personal; and at last not merely human, but Divine.

IV

Where shall we find the instance to draw these poor strands of surmise into a knot of truth? In John Masefield's "The Widow in the Bye Street," we see the widow's only son rightfully found guilty of murder. The judge goes to his chambers before pronouncing sentence and there wonders how any man dares to be a judge. He could not unwind even ten minutes of the murderer's act and thought. There was a pretty, wanton woman and her jealous consort, two men's violent anger, a bloody fight—and murder. Why do such volcanic angers brood and flame in human flesh? Why is history so perverse? The judge knew that he did not know. So he prayed, as every judge must or should:

> Show Him Thy grace, O God, before he die;
> Shine in his heart; have mercy upon me
> Who deal the laws men make to travel by
> Under the sun upon the path to Thee;
> O God, Thou knowest I'm as blind as he,
> As blind, as frantic, not so single, worse,
> Only Thy pity spared me from the curse.[14]

The judge thus confessed he had no right to be a judge; he became a brother man. The widow also prayed, in the jail cell, with her condemned son:

> "And God who gave His mercies takes his mercies,
> And God who gives beginning gives the end.
> I dread my death; but it's the end of curses,
> A rest for broken things too broke to mend.
> O Captain Christ, our blessed Lord and Friend,
> We are two wandered sinners in the mire,
> Burn our dead hearts with love out of Thy fire.

> "And when Thy death comes, Master, let us bear it
> As of Thy will, however hard to go;
> Thy Cross is infinite for us to share it,
> Thy help is infinite for us to know.
> And when the long trumpets of the Judgment blow,
> May our poor souls be glad and meet agen,
> And rest in Thee." "Say 'Amen,' Jim." "Amen." [15]

A university is filled with judgments. So is any church or any other community or any lonely life. The judgments are not altogether wrong. Youth is radical, and ought to be: it ought, in the very meaning of the word, to go down to the roots. A young conservative is an affront on nature. Youth is impatient with the old in mind who suck their gums and cling to old ways. They should be impatient, perhaps. But I know a student who left college, never mind which college, saying: "I'm tired of hearing everything taken apart, including me." The word "judge" has many meanings. It means discriminating appraisal. It means a concern for worthy conduct. It means the indignation that springs from love. It means censoriousness, the prosecuting attorney. That last meaning is "out" for human beings. Perhaps each man must decide if this world is a courtroom or a home, if he shall go through life as prosecuting attorney or as a member of the family. And since this sermon, despite its theme or because of it, has dealt in judgment, may God forgive this sermon.

16

HOME TIES AND THE FAITH

> "And he replied, 'Who are my mother and my brothers?' And looking around on those who sat about him, he said, 'Here are my mother and my brothers! Whoever does the will of God is my brother, and sister, and mother.'"
>
> *Mark 3:33-35*

The Bible offers its truth not in cellophane, but in flashes of drama. The family into which Jesus was born did not approve his zeal for the kingdom of God. They reckoned it overwrought, even fanatic. They questioned his sanity and came to take him home: "He is beside himself." [1] Mrs. Poyser in the George Eliot novel said as much about Dinah Morris, the village preacher: ". . . There's a bigger maggot than usual in your head." [2] So Jesus had to choose between the dear familiar music of home and the insistent beat of another drum. He made his choice: "Who are my mother and my brothers? . . . Whoever does the will of God is my brother, and sister, and mother." Thus our topic, which touches every family: Home Ties and the Faith.

I

We speak, therefore, about the renunciation of home. Anyone who counsels college students meets that issue almost daily and

124

yearns for both child and parents. Renan accused Jesus of "trampling under foot everything that is human—love and blood and country." [3] How could Renan be blind to Jesus' love for his home? His parables are again and again drawn from the well-loved incidents of home, and his prayer "Our Father" draws mankind into one family. Yet Jesus had to make his choice, as every man must, between his home town and the mysterious Sea. In that choice Jesus was very lonely: "The Son of man has nowhere to lay his head." [4] Freud confronts our generation to insist that a man is shaped and misshaped by his home environment, and Freud has too much evidence to be disproved. A man must choose between his home —and what? Freud is not so clear about the "what": "the Ego" is a vague term. Years come and go: Jesus falsifies Renan's charge and is "long beforehand" with Freud.

So Jesus, never disparaging home, always grateful for it, always aware of its necessary importance, yet calls for a man to break with home. The breach must come on a human level, that a man may make new earthborn loyalties: A man shall "leave father and mother, and shall cleave to his wife." [5] It must come on a much deeper level, in obedience to a Voice "that never was, on sea or land," [6] but which no man may escape:

> I could not love thee, (Deare) so much,
> Lov'd I not Honour more. [7]

Thus a man is bound, yet never bound, to his home. Psychiatry sometimes seems to propose that parents should not fail their children: only "seems," for psychiatry is not concerned primarily with praise or blame. Parents could in most instances do a much better job, but there are no perfect parents, not even among psychiatrists or preachers; and their children, becoming parents, will in turn fail and bless their children. Sometimes psychiatry proposes that a man break with home in order to be "himself." But what is "himself"? A recent psychiatric conference asked what is a normal man and reached the tentative conclusion that he is not a man without frustrations: there is conflict in him. What conflict? Is it the clash between earthly loyalties and "a distant drum"? Later editions of *The Rubaiyat* read drably:

> Ah, take the Cash and let the Credit go,
> Nor heed the rumble of a distant Drum! [8]

But the first edition has a more haunting sound:

> . . . How sweet is mortal Sovranty!"—think some:
> Others—"How blest the Paradise to come!"
> Ah, take the Cash in hand and waive
>   the Rest;
> Oh the brave Music of a distant Drum! [9]

Perhaps we must say outrightly that human nature is such that no earthly loyalty can long content us. Edith Cavell, executed for what men called treason (history now knows it to have been a wider love), said as she died: "Patriotism is not enough." [10] It is not nearly enough. Home is not enough, nor humanity, nor college, nor science, nor human freedom! Patriotism, if it is unexamined, may say, "Our country, right or wrong," [11] and thus become capsuled. Humanity or humanism as a devotion leaves all unanswered the aching questions of man's hidden origin and hidden destiny, and is confronted with humanity's mixed good and tragic ill, and now must face the chance that the whole human episode may end in atomic death. The "American Way" as a goal, if it is not brought under judgment, becomes a cash register, a comfortable armchair, and a golf course. Every earthly loyalty, if it is made central, becomes idolatry: the worship of the disfigured part for the transcendent whole. All idolatries finally destroy their worshippers. So Jesus said of home, and by implication of all time-bound devotions, "Who are my mother and my brothers? . . . Whoever does the will of God . . . ." Paul spoke the same language: "The Jerusalem above is free, and she is our mother." [12] Thus renunciation.

II

Then the new commitment. When we break with home, shall we ourselves become the new focus? It is plain that if a youth always obeys his parents, he becomes an echo; and it is equally plain that if he always disobeys them, he becomes a converse echo. If a man should go into business because his parents wish it, he would stultify himself; if he should go into business because they do not wish it, he would only add bitterness to the frustration. Then should he follow his own ideas and be himself? He must still ask, "Who am I? What is my true self?" Otherwise he may end by being different for

the sake of being different, in a Bohemian exhibitionism or a grotesque alienation—a momentary meteor burning itself out in an
empty sky. One fact about "himself," any man's self, is that it
is derived, contingent, creaturely; and that, therefore, the focus of
life is beyond the self, even though also within it. "Thou hast made
us for Thyself. . . ." [13]

Then how shall we define the new commitment? And how shall
we justify the break with home? Jesus called it: "The will of God."
"Whoever does the will of God is my brother . . . ." He knew that
sometimes the will of God is hard to construe, and that at other
times it is joyously or painfully clear. He knew that the will of God
cannot be learned except in the long silences of prayer. For our
clarity, conceding to our mortal need for an earthly sign, Christ
offered himself—imperiously, yet in incredible lowliness—as living
banner of the will of God: "'He who loves father or mother more
than me . . . .'" He who loves son or daughter more than me . . . .'" [14]
Thus God made Jesus for us the incarnation of His will, the shrine
of our devotion. Thus Christ, far more than the fabled King
Arthur, "bound" his followers

> . . . by so strait vows to his own self
> That when they rose, knighted from kneeling, some
> Were pale at the passing of a ghost,
> Some flush'd, and others dazed, as one who wakes
> Half-blinded at the coming of a light.[15]

A British theologian put it more modernly: that Christ had a
"numinous magnetism" to draw men into thinking men and wom-
en.[16] They knew then what it is to be a self. They found themselves. They were truly persons.

Yet Jesus bound men to God beyond himself. "The word which
you hear is not mine," he said, "but the Father's who sent me." [17]
He knew our human need for a Sign in history, but carried us beyond history to One whom he called "Eternal Father." Somewhere
is a novel [18] that tells of a lad who haunted an ocean pier, not content with home and city streets. But why the dock when home is
warm and dear, when streets have excitement and cash? One day
the lad, fascinated, watched a ship sailing under sealed orders: it
cleared the harbor not yet knowing whither it was bound. Why
should any lad crave that unknown, the restless lanes of ocean

with their storm and shipwreck, when he could sleep in a safe bed? But we do! Finite streets never content us: we crave the vast and unknown Infinite. The sea for us is Christ in God, the horizon of his words, the stormy venture of his cross; and the journey is under sealed orders, for no man knows the future; and our only sufficient comfort is his presence, which we can neither specify nor lose. His followers in every age have broken with home. They have had "nowhere to lay" their "head." [19]

We shall miss the pathos-grandeur of this text unless we see in it both the homelessness and the new home of the early Church. "They of the Way'" had forsaken both their own kin and their beloved synagogue. But they were not bereft. The Church was the new family. It was held in a love deeper than human love, in a bond stronger than any bond of flesh and time, its new devotion welded in the flame of accepted danger. Thus the words of our text are not alone the words of Christ, but also the direct confession of the Church a full generation after his death. We laugh at the church fashion by which members call one another "Sister Jones" or "Brother Brown." If we remember how the fashion came, we shall not laugh: "Whoever does the will of God is my brother, and sister . . . ." A few years ago we stood, my wife and I, on the steps of a somewhat outmoded plane in the far north of Thailand while a group of Thai Christians bade us good-by, a fine young Thai doctor making the gracious speech of farewell in better than broken English. "You are good to come," he said, we knowing that all the gratitude should be offered by us to them for their brave witness in an alien culture: "You are good to come, for we are orphans." They had broken with home, but were not homeless. They had found brothers and sisters in Christ now all around the world. Thus renunciation, and the new commitment.

III

Then the recovery of our earthly loyalties. In the new commitment they are not lost, or they are lost only to be rediscovered in purer form. Home may once more provide a central instance. Suppose that a mother has been dominant or possessively indulgent and that the father has been aloof or absorbed in business, and that, therefore, the son in his growing years has known no real family love and no honoring of his freedom. Suppose, therefore, that he has renounced home, even though he visits within its walls, and that he has resolved not selfishly to "be himself," but to sail the wide ocean under sealed orders. Does he then curse his home? No, he sees it in a clearer light. He is grateful for its blessings and understands its human failures. He has a gentle norm by which to judge it. He understands still more clearly when he has children of his own. Then he says: "There are no perfect parents. I in my turn shall both bless and harm my children. That is why we must pray: 'Our Father . . . forgive us our debts.' For every home needs the pardoning grace that Jesus came to offer, and every home is held and healed at last in an Eternal Home." Thus the son finds his home again, in a purer bond and with cleansed eyes.

Ask yourselves: Do not all earthly loyalties fester unless held in the astringent light of a Higher Loyalty? A musical comedy song runs, "We belong to a mutual admiration society," sung by a mother and daughter. It has its place perhaps in that setting, but not in real life, for in real life two such people, living such a song, would go soft inside, like overripe fruit. Soon they would begin to sing, "We belong to a mutual *accusation* society." Time-bound love is a stuffy house: not liveable until windows are opened on it from the Time-less. That is the word in the Galsworthy play *Loyalties*,[20] more effectively spoken because the author leaves the word for the audience to speak. An army officer steals money to satisfy a girl whom he has betrayed. He denies the crime, which soon cannot be denied. Then the crisscross of human loyalties. The girl's father is true to her and to their Italian blood. The Jew is loyal to his race, the Gentile to his prejudice, the army officers to their clique, and the lawyer to the law firm's honor. The culprit meanwhile is true to his wife, too late in the day, and she to him. What chance has truth-love? An acid commentator remarks sardonically: "Criss-cross—we all cut each other's throats from the best of motives." [21] She should have said "the second best of motives"! What happens when the crisscross of earthly loyalties has no compass and no North Star? The guilty officer killed himself, leaving a note to say that it was the only decent thing left to do. The note ended: "A pistol keeps faith." [22] But, of course, it was not the only thing to do, and a pistol cannot keep faith or unfaith. Everybody had kept half faith, the time-bound half. Jesus said all this very differently: "Who are my mother and my brothers? . . . Whoever does the will of God is my brother, and sister, and mother."

IV

Well, there it is, as well as I can presently speak it. The word is spoken because in a hundred instances since coming to Harvard I have seen this problem of home. Parents have no right to try to *control* sons and daughters in college, and I have tried to defend them against this undue pressure. But I yearn also for the parents. Have I not failed, I also, along with all parents? The word is spoken also in a much wider context than home. For what son has the right to "be himself," when every self is created and dependent and derived? The universe does not center in our mortal days. No earthly loyalty is vast or deep enough to claim our devotion, because, though we are mortal, we know we are mortal; because we have eternal longings.

> Our little systems have their day;
> They have their day and cease to be;
> They are but broken lights of thee,
> And Thou, O Lord, art more than they.[23]

One Loyalty is of earth, yet of the Sky. It is deep within us, but carries always beyond us. That Loyalty is our true home in an ever-present Galilee, and our only Fealty. But so gracious is Home that, if we are committed to it, all our earthborn affections are welcomed —and redeemed.

17

REALISM AND PRAYER

> Jesus said: "Pray then like this: Our Father who
> art in heaven."   *Matt. 6:9*

On a certain campus two students were discussing religion, unaware that religion is a vague word. One said, in the voice of a
cross-examiner, "You don't pray, do you?" The other confessed, as
though caught in a crime: "Once in a while I say, 'Our Father.' "
The other promptly nailed him: "So you've sold out to a father-
image!" Very little is settled by argument, but the "father-image"
notion of prayer is nowadays so rife and so uncritically accepted
that any would-be honest sermon on prayer must take issue with it.
So let us speak about it, without wasting too much time.

I

It stems from Freud, whom Christian faith should not castigate,
for, by and large, he has left us in debt. His contention
about prayer, which he regarded as "illusion," [1] runs roughly as
follows: When our earthly home disappoints us and our parents
prove to have feet of clay, we shy away from the necessity of confronting an imperfect world and the fulfillment of our own selfhood, and for our cowardly comfort we print on the sky a vast fiction, a Father image; and then we begin to pray, "Our Father."
Let us hint certain answers:

131

This: If Freud says that Christian faith is escape, and Christian faith retorts that Freudian doctrine is escape (a hiding in time from the demand of eternity), by what norm do we determine which charge is true?

And this: The Freudian theory came from a study of neurotic religion; and though such a study has value for any discussion of faith, it does not necessarily follow that what holds of neurotic religion holds also of what William James called "healthy-minded religion." [2]

And this: If an earthly father has failed us by weakness or coercion, and we are thus in business for a fiction-God of our own devising, it would seem that we might fashion the "God" in any guise except that of the father against whom we have rebelled. I know of one boy who refused to pray "Our Father," because his earthly father daily thrashed him.

This, moreover: The Freudian notion about prayer is so hasty and ill-considered that it condemns almost any human endeavor, as, for instance: a university is a place of academic abstractions into which we fly rather than confront our home and the alien world. By that same plea Freudian doctrine itself could be condemned.

This, further: In the raucous planet called Earth, with Buchenwald as an instance, illusions do not long endure, but prayer has a history as long as the history of thinking man. Jesus said that the universe is an open universe: "There is nothing covered" (in the subconscious or in the annals of crime) "that shall not be revealed." [3] Colored water for medicine may "cure" for a time, but not for long. Yet at Buchenwald men of prayer met that terror with better strength than men who had no faith.

And this: Does anyone, deeply pondering life, easily believe that the agelong portent of prayer is explained by a "quickie" such as the word "projection"? Projection on what? Would it ever occur to anyone to project on nothing? To dismiss prayer as "projection" savors of the folly of accounting for a Mississippi flood by proposing that someone must have left the faucet running.

And this again: Is the Lambaréné Forest Hospital of Albert Schweitzer an escape? It came by prayer. Or the music of Bach? That also came by prayer. Or the Cross of Christ? That came from Gethsemane-prayer and the words from the Cross were themselves instinct with prayer.

Argument still proves nothing, but it may serve to show that quick and clever notions need not be accepted out of hand. Close thinking may well hint that the attempt to make Christian faith a childishness is itself doubly childish. But that being said, we should bow in the direction of Sigmund Freud to thank him for reminding us that religion *can become* an escape, as can music or friendship—or psychiatry. Christian faith should never try to evade scrutiny by sociology or psychology or any other of man's tests. Faith needs astringent challenge, and need not fear the onset of Truth. So long as man is in the natural order, he is a proper object of scientific study. But man as subject, man standing above the natural order, still does the studying! Man is subject-object, "and that's the rub"—the Divine rub. Therefore we offer certain avowals for your pondering.

II

Prayer is the instinctive cry of the finite to the Infinite. Fritz Künkel has suggested that a basic pattern of our mortal life is this: the group defends and nourishes the individual, who in his time and turn contributes to the group.[4] The home is the earliest and "classic" instance of this give-and-take. The babe is welcomed and supported by the home, and growing into maturity, helps to sustain the home. But Künkel is honest to admit that every group fails us. This failure, in the home, has rightly been underlined in Freudian thought. The nation fails us: we speak often about the duty of the individual to the state, but what of the duty of the state to the individual? That cities fail the citizen is plain to see in the city's pall of smoke.

This failure on the part of every man is indigenous and constitutional: it is in the grain of our finite nature. So nobody fully understands us, and we do not understand ourselves. Francis Thompson in his poetry retorts to the bride who on the eve of her marriage day promised and pledged her "fondest heart" to the man of her choice:

> Ah, fool! but there is one heart you shall never
> take him to!
>
> .   .   .   .
>
> Its keys are at the cincture hung of God.[5]

So because of finitude, every home fails us. Always there is a cold war in the home, or a hot war, or intermittent misunderstanding amid much love, or dull endurance; and all this because there are no perfect parents, not even among the psychiatrists. To cry out for a Home beyond our homes is not necessarily weakness: it may be wisdom. When the winter's storm strikes, we do not make our bed in the city square. But by what strange light do we know that parents fail us, and that the earth is imperfect? Add this to the "reasons" I proposed contra Freud: we could not arrive at the notion of a perfect heaven by piecing together bits of earthly imperfection, for each piece would still be imperfect. There is already in us the Surmise of Eternity: that is how we know that earth is time-bound and broken.

Thus the immemorial cry of prayer from the finite creature to the Infinite God. William Blake has a picture of a man at the bottom of a ladder which goes dizzily into the sky. The man knows that he cannot climb, for soon he would fall: finite creatures cannot manage the eternal Sky. So the man stands there crying: "I want! I want!" [6] This is elemental prayer. Or should I say that prayer is the Infinite praying in us? Part of the "proof" of Christ is the fact that he so speaks that the Infinite in us answers instantly to his word: "Pray then like this: Our Father who art in heaven . . . ." All the phrases of the Lord's Prayer may be found in duplicate or likeness in earlier Jewish devotion, but the Prayer is new because of Newness in him. The axiom of our nature answers to the Axiom in Christ, which is deeper than logic. We pray, and we are at Home. Our finiteness is not overcome, for we are still men; but it finds its Infinite, and it is girded again for the hazards of this mortal life.

III

Prayer is the cry of our guilt. Human brokenness is not simply constitutional: it is also responsible. Every man lives under conviction that he has abused his freedom. Dr. Johnson's reply when asked how we know that we are sinners is still the existential reply: "Every man knows his own sins." [7] The whole issue is burdened and darkened by the fact that we cannot forgive ourselves or mend the course of history. We cannot forgive ourselves because our sin is not merely against ourselves: it is against our neighbors, and more deeply it is against life and the Source of life: "Against thee, thee only, have I sinned, and done that which is evil in thy sight." [8] We cannot mend history, because we ourselves are shaped by history even as we shape it, and because we cannot reverse history to eradicate the failure at its point of origin, and because if we could go back, we would carry with us a cleft and infirm will. Sin is poison poured into the stream of time. Man's only language in his shame is a cry: "God, be merciful to me a sinner!" [9]

Once again the leading of Jesus "strikes home" to the marrow of our nature: "Pray then like this: Our Father who art in heaven." He is telling us that, despite every shadowed failure, we are still children of God. We know failure for what it is, and so we still have our bond with Eternity. He counsels us to claim the bond and implies that heaven will honor the claim. The only real "proof" is in the venture. Those who have made the venture in the light and leading of Christ testify with tears and joy that there is Love, above history and within it, that gathers in man's culpable folly more profoundly by far than the sky accepts and purifies the smoke of our homes and cities. Masefield read Chaucer, and then said: "I knew then . . . that my law was to follow poetry, even if I died of it." [10] We listen to Jesus as he leads us to the place of prayer, and we say: "I also am a child of God." Thus man raises his Pater Noster from generation to generation.

Our modern psychiatric term "acceptance" may provide the clue. A psychiatrist is slow to take as consultee one of his personal friends, for in that instance acceptance might not easily be demonstrated or accepted. He is slow also to accept for counsel someone for whom he feels some instinctive dislike, and for the same reason. The basis of conversation is this: there is no condemnation of wrong when the patient comes to his office, and no flattery of fancied right. The man is simply accepted under one assumption: he is a candidate for cure. The man is accepted not only for what he is, but for what he may become. Regarding such acceptance the questions throng, and for the most part they are shining questions. Who is to accept the psychiatrist? Since the psychiatrist takes it as his job to bring his patient to face reality and thus help him to make his own praise and blame, shall we say that reality (or Reality?) accepts us? Who shall bridge the estrangement in man between the below-man who sins and the above-man who recognizes the sin for what it is? Whether these questions are answered or unanswered, psychiatric method provides a parable: "Pray then like this: Our Father." We are accepted at our hidden worst and hidden best. We are loved in spite of all and through all; and everything in us, conscious and subconscious, what has been and what is, is understood. A friend of E. Stanley Jones as they watched the day end in India said: "What a wonderful sunset, *especially for such a small place.*" [11]

Not alone our individual lives, but also the structures of corporate life are held in this grace of prayer. Wrongdoing inheres in the group as in the person. The group prays in public worship. Indeed the Lord's Prayer is a group prayer; and when Jesus said, "Pray then like this," he spoke to the group of his disciples. Rollo May describes a mural by Francis Scott Bradford [12] which shows a man chained to a skyscraper, yet peering into the sky and trying to stretch his chains. The title word reads: "Man though chained to earth looks across time and space toward an unknown perfection, which he may never reach but will forever seek." True, man is chained to his skyscrapers, the corporate structures which scarcely yet can scrape the sky, but from them and for himself he peers upward. True, he cannot reach the sky; but the sky can reach him in light and power, centrally in the Man who taught us the Lord's Prayer. So from our lonely guilt and our corporate guilt we pray, and are accepted into the pardoning grace of God.

IV

But prayer remains as realistic demand. Despite Freud, it is not escape. It gives wings, but the wings are weights and require of men new journeyings on new missions. We try to specify some items in prayer's demand. For one thing, it lays on us the burden of the Mystery. The words "Our Father" seem to make God in man's image; but the other words, "Who art in the heavens" (such is the Greek original), imply God's transcendent mystery. God is beyond our little systems of justice and seems at times to belie any justice, as when a fire sweeps through a tenement block. We know far, far less about the immensities and vistas of God's providence, in worlds on worlds, in dimensions beyond dimensions, than a child of a statesman knows about the affairs of the realm. Day after day we must trust where we cannot see. Often we must say of our individual selves: "The universe seems careful of the type and careless of the separate life. But I have been created a person, and God has sought me out in the Person of Christ. Therefore I believe where I cannot see." God is a Mystery profound, and prayer must always carry the burden of the mystery.

Again, prayer must not shrink from the requirements of action nor from times when "our Father" seems almost an absentee stranger. An earthly father sends his growing son into the cruel politics of grade school. There the boy may sometimes say, with Job, of a parent who seems callous: "Oh, that I knew where I might find him!" [13] But the boy continues to grow only by the test of school, and by making his own decisions though these will always involve blundering. Dimly we surmise that, though God is our Father, He is not an indulgent or possessive Father. In my boyhood I wrestled, with minimal success, with problems in arithmetic. If one train started here at 11 A.M., I was asked, and the train traveled at sixty miles an hour; and another train started there at twelve noon and traveled at fifty miles an hour, when and where would they meet? I did not know and could not see that the commonwealth would be enhanced should I ever (by some lucky guess) discover. But my father would not solve the problem for me. "How much do you know?" he would ask. It was not much that I knew. "Could this be true?" he would ask, giving me a hint. Gadzooks, that definitely could be true! So after a while, a long while, the problem was solved. Is that God's way—to seem to desert us in the school of this life, to help us only by hint? Prayer must meet that demand.

There is an even sterner demand: "Our Father" requires that we regard all men as brothers, for the "our" cannot be muted. Beyond race and rank, beyond learning and ignorance (if any man is learned), beyond goodness and badness (if any man is good), we accept our neighbors when we pray, as we ourselves are accepted of God. Perhaps prayer is the only bond of brotherhood. Statesmanship is inevitably compromised as a bond, and windy pleas from public platforms only darken counsel with self-intoxicating words. How can there be brotherhood unless men pray in acknowledgment of one Fatherhood, "Our Father"? Kierkegaard was estranged from his earthly father, not least by the disclosure of his father's shame. But God was not a "father image." When the father confessed the shame and prayed, and the son confessed the alienation and prayed, and they prayed together, "Our Father," father and son were reconciled.[14] As for me, I find it very hard to "love people," as pulpits recommend, until I think on Christ, and how he saw us all from his Cross, and how he bade us pray, "Our Father." Then for his sake I can make some poor beginning at loving my neighbors. The demand is in the word "our":—"*Our* Father," "*our* daily bread," "*our* debts."

V

We know the brokenness of earthly homes because we are already aware of a Home in heaven. "Lord, thou hast been our dwelling place in all generations." [15] Robert Frost has said in an poignant line:

> "Home is the place where, when you have to go there
> They have to take you in." [16]

When a man is sick, or out of work, or when he has shamed his name and every other door is shut against him, home "is the place where," under blood bond, "they have to take you in." Then what of the day when a man seems lost in nothingness, and when he knows he has failed and that his world has failed, and when death comes on with steely tread? Home, a Father's Home, is the place where, when he has to go there, they *wish* to take him in, with that same welcome that men found in Christ in Galilee. Therefore Christ said to us: "Pray then like this: Our Father, who art in heaven."

18

KNOWLEDGE AND LOVE

> "Now we see through a glass, darkly; but then
> face to face: now I know in part; but then shall I
> know even as also I am known. . . . Now abideth
> faith, hope, love, these three; but the greatest of
> these is love."   *I Cor. 13:12-13* (K.J.V.)

The Bible is not a book of dogmatics in any harsh sense of that word. It is often agnostic. Then it matches our modern mood. The Old Testament exclaims, "Oh, that I knew where I might find him." [1] The cry is not a lone instance: it is typical. The New Testament says flatly: "No man hath seen God at any time." [2] In our text the agnosticism is explicit: "Now we see through a glass, darkly"; for "glass" means a bronze mirror which, because of the hammer marks, gave only a broken reflection; and "darkly" is almost our word "riddle": "Now we see the broken reflection of a riddle." We are obliged to say as we go through life, "If only I could see that man's face more clearly!" or "If only I could understand that particular plan of providence!"

I

This agnosticism is true to our knowledge or ignorance of our world. A few years ago such words as "space" or "time" seemed

139

relatively simple, but now we say that space is "curved," and we ask of time if we are in time or if time is in us. Philosophy joins space and time as if they were blood brothers, and speaks of the "space-time continuum." [3] Causality likewise was taken to be a straightforward affair, a chain with alternate links called "cause" and "effect." But now we are told that no new event can be fully explained by its antecedents, not even in nature, let alone in human nature; for in every new event there are items of unpredictable newness. We say of modern knowledge, "That mystery is solved!" and then find that the "solution" has roused six other mysteries from their long sleep. When a librarian at a British university wondered out loud how he could find shelf space for the flood of new books, a scientist advised: "Take any book of science more than ten years old, and put it in the cellar." We launch our sputnik-satellites a tiny distance from our tiny satellite-planet into the tiny space area of our tiny satellite-sun, and even then would have to surround any man in a sputnik with our tiny earth conditions, while we boast about our "conquest of space." In all our science, theoretical or applied, we see an enigma through broken lines.

Agnosticism marks our knowledge of ourselves. Some people try to pooh-pooh the Freudian concept of the subconscious mind, but their very disparagement may show that they are being swayed by the subconscious. Any fracas in any university about the place of "religion" in education or about racial discrimination is never merely a debate of intelligence with reasons offered pro and con: it generates too much heat. We flatter ourselves that we act only from "considerations of rigorous thought," and then find (if we do ever fully find) that we are being governed from "below the threshold." Forgetting an appointment with the dentist is not merely a "slip of memory": subconsciously we do not wish to go. Forgetting a friend's name may come of pride or jealousy. Preaching is a difficult task, never fulfilled, because it must be addressed to the whole man from the whole man: it cannot be an affair only of the "mind." Our doubts, for instance, are not born in the intellect, however we may say, "I do not understand": they are born in the dynamics of depth psychology. The subconscious is only one item in the total mystery of selfhood. How is it that we can talk to ourselves, saying "Why are you cast down, O my soul?" [4] We can and do so speak. Who then is the "soul," and who is doing the speaking? Why did I become a preacher? Why does an empiricist become an empiricist? Or a syncretist become a syncretist? "Broad-mindedness" can become its own dogmatism. These depths in us we cannot sound; or in the language of our text, "We see through a glass, darkly."

It follows that we cannot clearly see our neighbors. Richard le Gallienne tells how he classified his fellow passengers on a London bus.[5] Over there was a man about town, true to type. Near him was a matron, struck off from the matron stencil. There was a businessman, made from the businessman mold. There, a clergyman, stereotyped. Then he said to himself: "But here am I, made from a unique mold, and the mold then broken." Suddenly he realized that every man and woman secretly says what he had said: "I, myself . . . the original one," and knows it to be true. This fact makes every other human being, in part, a stranger and gives some warrant to Sartre's "Hell is—other people." [6] We classify one another, but maybe that very habit is defense against our painful ignorance of other people's secret world. Marriage is or should be the steady fulfillment of a plighted troth, but it reveals to any sensitive husband and wife how little one human being knows about another, even after years of living together in one house and home. There are shrines in every heart which nobody has ever entered or can enter.

Need it be said that agnosticism marks our knowledge of God? There are people who claim to be God's intimates, perhaps even his favorites, but they thus show more of bigotry and pride than of Godliness. Or is their claim a matter of insecurity? We shall keep on saying, "God"; or if not that word, then pale substitute words such as "truth" or "values." But how much do we know about God? Enough perhaps, but not more than enough. The Athenians, in a burst of honesty, built an altar inscribed: "To an unknown god." [7] How and why was the world made, if "made" is the right term? Why is human nature crossed by perversity though it craves love? Why does righteous judgment often miscarry not only when bad men succeed, but also because good men's plans are thwarted, as in Woodrow Wilson's "war to end war"? We say that God's providence is evident in the beauty and order of nature; but when we see a cobra or a tornado, we are no longer sure of providence or order or beauty. How much do we know about God? How much can finite mind hope to know? Carlyle answers in *Sartor Resartus:*

Does the Minnow understand the Ocean Tides . . . ? Such a minnow is Man; his Creek, this Planet Earth; his Ocean, the immeasurable All; his Monsoons and periodic Currents, the mysterious Course of Providence through Aeons of Aeons.[8]

The mystery of God is in the child's question, "Who made God?" It is in the scientist's question, "How can something come from nothing?" Our minds are finite, but their queries run out into infinity. "Now we see through a glass, darkly."

II

But we should notice certain items about our admittedly imperfect knowledge. This: though "we see through a glass, darkly," *we do see.* We assume that the reflection of what appears to be a substantial world does not utterly mislead us. It is faithfully recurrent, socially attested, and does not change by our whim or wish. So to speak is basic speaking and not unrelated to Kant's asking if we ever know "the thing-in-itself." [9] All our knowledge is provisional, but that is a good adjective: it provides provisions for our daily life. The water in the Creek where the human minnow swims is the same water as in the Ocean, and governed by the same Will. The light that strikes into the Creek is the same light as strikes into the Ocean. George Santayana knew the limits of human knowledge:

> Our knowledge is a torch of smoky pine
> That lights the pathway but one step ahead
> Across a void of mystery and dread.[10]

But midnight can be almost redeemed by a "torch of smoky pine," especially on a woodland path. The difference between agnosticism and biblical agnosticism is that the one says, "in a mirror darkly," while the Bible adds, "but we see."

Another item regarding our broken knowledge: we know it is broken. In that item we touch a depth of mystery in our own nature. We know we are ignorant. That is to say, our very ignorance is held in a much deeper knowledge. The minnow in the creek is aware that there is an ocean beyond the river's mouth. To take an instance from the field that I know best, or where my ignorance is not so total: it appears that the Gospels were written in whole or part from one to two generations after Jesus as his followers made their way into the Greco-Roman world, and that therefore the record has been colored by the new setting and the new times, and that the questions which thus arise about the Gospels cannot be fully answered, though archaeology and other studies may enable us to make a clearer and clearer answer. We know that our knowledge about Jesus is partial. But how do we know? Now we can see another difference between agnosticism and biblical agnosticism: the latter is aware that ignorance is always held in a deeper knowledge, and so it says in joy: "but then face to face." The deeper knowledge is prophetic and more than prophetic: "Then shall I know even as also I am known."

Still another item: we must trade bravely on our partial knowledge and on the deeper knowledge of our ignorance, for we must go on living: "The sun also rises." [11] Camus finds life "absurd" in its enigma of pain and its pain of enigma, but when he debates the alternatives of suicide or continued life, suicide seeming to be the better strategy in an "absurd" world, he votes for an agnostic courage and compassion,[12] maybe because life at its depths *has* meaning and is not "absurd." How shall we treat our neighbors: as worthless or worth-ful? We must decide, for day by day we must live with our neighbors. Are they trees which we may use for our selfish shelter when it rains, and which we may "cut down" if that serves our purpose, or are they also centers of freedom? If Jesus says, "Thou shalt love thy neighbour as thyself," [13] and if our denial makes chaos and our obedience makes community, then life itself has spoken. Knowledge is never apart from life, and life slowly or swiftly brings in its verdict on our knowledge. Even a monastery cannot avoid life in the world, if only because it must import ink for its sacred manuscripts, if only because its dinner comes from surrounding fields. Harvard cannot determine truth about Jesus or any other issue by living in a learned stratosphere. The attempt would lead on a straight line from Harvard Square to Mount Auburn Hospital to Mount Auburn Cemetery. The word "know" in our text might better be translated "understand." "Now I understand in part." That partial understanding is always being put to test in the necessary traffic of daily life.

III

So the upshot is *faith*. We must make our venture. The New Testament says: make our venture in response to God's "high calling" [14] in Jesus Christ. Is there any better calling? Faith does not mean faith going counter to knowledge. It means faith in the light of knowledge, and faith as wellspring of new knowledge. The scientist in his limited field finds new facts by drinking of his spring of faith: he "believes" that the universe is trustworthy and that his mind may partly construe the world. Indeed he sometimes believes that his finite mind can fully construe it, and then faith ceases to be faith: it becomes an idolatry of finite mind. Christian faith finds its home always in Jesus. From him and by him it makes its ventures. That faith is not what our modern mind calls "faith in life," for life holds both Rasputin and Camus, pornography and the Sistine Madonna. Likewise Christian faith is not a faith in "all faiths," for "all faiths" harbor contradictions, so that when we ask about the "nature and destiny of man," [15] different faiths give opposite answers. Faith confronts three facts: one, we see in a mirror; two, we do see; and three, we must live and die. Which clue in the mirror shall we follow? It is the crucial question, for the Hitler clue turns the world into desolation and academic freedom into a crime. What of the Christ clue? It shines in a golden light. Life in its deep secrecies does not falsify it. Karl Barth has said that Christian faith means to live as a "man who is faced by Jesus Christ." [16] Our partial knowledge calls for faith.

It calls also for *hope*. The ground of hope is our knowledge of our ignorance, the eternity from which we see the limits of time. We should not bridle if people ask, "Why maintain a university when all knowledge stumbles over the unpredictable and is stopped by walls of mystery?" It is a searching question, even though people who ask it are not always aware of its depths. Basically we go on learning in a finite world because of an infinite hunger: because we must. Meanwhile knowledge is prophetic, even though it is always incomplete. Galileo spoke of the "handles of Saturn" because he saw that circlet of satellites as a man looking at its edge. To him the circlet seemed a straight line or like two "handles" to a globe. But his imperfect guess led on to fuller knowledge not only of Saturn, but of the solar system and the cosmos. Meanwhile the resolve to know reveals us to ourselves, not least when the quest brings us the mountain-land of mystery. The mountains are too high for our attaining, but we are miserable in the valley. Our destiny is of no merely finite kind, and our epitaph must be that of the Alpine guide: "He died climbing." Meanwhile knowledge exposes our life to the Mystery. Einstein once said: "Before God we are equally wise and equally foolish." [17] But the wise know it, while the foolish think they can be as wise as God; and the wise, knowing that our knowledge is as nothing before God, are thus doubly wise; and like Einstein, they keep on learning.

Faith, hope—and *love:* these abide, as the air we breathe in the knowledge-quest and as the only climate for learning; "and the greatest of these is love." Our ignorance in face of Mystery might be an unbearable pain, except that we know we are ignorant. This deeper knowledge (of our ignorance) is thus a saving mercy. It is love. Christian faith and hope find this love validated in Christ: "All the promises of God" in the Bible or the book of our human nature "find their Yes in him." [18] Speaking in practical terms, we cannot endure the life of learning without love. War destroys universities and kills off its best minds. Industrial war may dictate scientific projects, saying, "This we must know to gain advantage of our competitors"; and so it may drive the free mind down paths of coercion. Defect of knowledge spells the need for love. Not our poor human love, which is fragmentary and fractured and marked out for death; not love as an abstract "value," for love by nature can never be abstract; not our love, but the Logos in us and in Christ by which (or whom) we know that all human love is fitful and disfigured. My youngest son was directing a play which had been translated from the French, when he and the cast stopped in rehearsal, wondering of one scene what the playwright intended. A man strode down the aisle, saying with quiet authority: "Look! I know the playwright. This is how he wants it played." Is that the authority of Jesus? Is the Christ-Event how God "wants it played"? In Him we may find the surety of encompassing Love.

V

"Now we see through a glass, darkly." Yes, and we always shall on earth. "But then face to face": we can be sure, as we are sure that our knowledge is partial, and because the ultimate in Christ speaks to the ultimate in us. "Now I know in part." Yes, that fact is beyond cavil. "Then shall I know even as also I am known": we can be sure, as we are sure that "Someone knew" all along about a sea shell of great beauty drawn from a five-mile depth of ocean, or about a child killed in a hurricane; as we are sure that human pity is noble; as we are sure that Christ is true. The old maps had captions over areas not yet explored: "Here be dragons," or "Here be demons," or "Here be sirens." Sir John Franklin wrote instead, "Here is God," [19] and so made his brave ventures. Thus the quest for knowledge, though it can never be fulfilled on earth, rests back on great deeps in us—on faith, hope, and love; and the quest may thus grant something better than knowledge, namely, wisdom; and the wisdom may make us wise to know that "now abideth faith, hope, love, these three; but the greatest of these is love."

19

TWO-WORLD CONVERSATION

"Whosoever therefore shall confess me before men,
him will I confess also before my Father which is
in heaven. But whosoever shall deny me before
men, him will I also deny before my Father which
is in heaven." *Matt. 10:32-33* (K.J.V.)

In a little book entitled *The Screwtape Letters* [1] a devil reports
to headquarters to tell how he diverted a man from God. The
man, deep in thought in a London library, was becoming convinced
that God, the very God, had dealings with him. He kept saying,
"Thou." He knew the mystery of the word: the vast and lonely
cosmos seemed to give very little warrant for it. But he kept saying
it: "Thou." How, then, did the devil divert him? Not by argument: devils wisely know that nothing can be proved or disproved
by argument. No, the devil touched the man on the shoulder of his
thoughts, saying: "Aren't you feeling hungry? It's nearly lunch
time." So he got the man out of doors where he could see the Number 73 bus rumbling on its way and hear the newsboys shouting,
"Extra!" Soon the man was earth-bound once more, wondering
how he could have been such a fool as to be exercised about God.

I

There are two worlds. In that story they are symbolized by the library and the street. Which is the real world? We are sure that the street world is real, even though we cannot understand why its reality (we refer to it as "getting at the facts") should be such boredom. We get out of bed, shave, eat breakfast, read about our real world in the newspapers, and go to work—with a million other men equally commonplace in our commonplace earth. We greet other men: "Hi, Jim." Jim replies: "Hi, Bill." At work a telephone rings, a mailman delivers letters, a stenographer armed with pencil and dictation book opens an office door, and the Number 73 bus rumbles down the street. This is the real world. Why has it become so dull? This swarm of people in street and office will mill around for a while until even smaller microbes get them. We are right: the street world *is* real. Body and cosmos are one term in the paradox of our personhood.

Then is the library world also real? Is the "Thou" a fact or a fiction? Supposing there is a Jacob's ladder set down at every man's door, between heaven and earth, why do we so rarely see it? Is it because we so rarely give ourselves chance for solitude, because we are afraid of silence? If both worlds are real, is there an interworld communication system, prayers ascending, gleams and stirrings descending, in constant traffic more important by far than the one-world traffic of the street? Jesus set his stamp on the two-world doctrine: "Every one who acknowledges me before men" (in the street world), "I also will acknowledge before my Father who is in heaven." [2] That is, when a man walks down the street, saying to himself, "Something in me kindles at the thought of Christ," the shining ones look down, saying, "That man has the secret flame."

II

But that library world, a man saying, "Thou,"—is it really real? Granted that we cannot live immured in the library, granted that we must earn our daily bread, with the help of the Number 73 bus and the newsboy shouting, "Extra!" is it true that we cannot live without the "Thou"-world? "One world at a time," [3] we say, in such a way as to do injustice to the author of the phrase. Thoreau refused to become pious and "spiritual" even in his last sickness. Not even then would he renounce body and "the good earth"; and he was right: "One world at a time." But Thoreau never took his cue from the street or from the crowd. He lived nobly in two worlds at a time. Perhaps we must, despite ourselves, because the two worlds are co-centric in the creative will of God. Then how shall we recover the sense of the reality of the library world? Are there reasons for believing in it? Devils are wise: they don't deal in "reasons." They ask, "Aren't you hungry?" But there may be evidences, better than reasons.

The basic evidence is that the two worlds are in us. The man in *The Screwtape Letters* was not satisfied with street traffic: he *wanted* to think about life from above life; he *wanted* to pray. A man from Eliot House [4] walks through The Yard, saying to himself, "Certainly don't feel like classes today!" whereupon "himself" answers, "I know how you feel, but better not cut classes." There is always that kind of conversation in us, and it is two-world conversation. We live in the street world (and must), but we see ourselves there from a dimension above this time-space destiny. You speak to yourself, perhaps as follows: "Wonderful to have this money to spend on myself"; and yourself replies to you, "Maybe you should not spend it on you." Who could doubt this two-world conversation? It is the moment-by-moment stuff of our life. Sometimes the two worlds themselves seem to take voice. The street says: "You up-there people are a colossal mirage"; and the "Thou"-world replies: "Don't get us wrong or air your self-estrangement: we are not perfectionist up here. This is the place of deepest understanding."

The words of Jesus strike fire because they are so true to this unspoken, unheard, secret conversation. This text is instance. It may well have been colored by the preaching of the early Church, for we now surmise that Matthew's Gospel was not written before the last decade of the first century. The text's metaphor is discredited in our time, with its two-story stage of "heaven" and "earth" which no science could accept, though it must be added, no one has yet shown how people living in space can avoid spatial metaphor. But whatever "may well have" been, the words kindle. We are beings who can judge our own lives—from above our lives. That "above" was called by Jesus "the kingdom of heaven." He said that "heaven" will one day be all in all, and that it is here now, and that it has come upon the world in him, the Christ, and that we should pray for its coming. These avowals cannot be reconciled in logic, but they are clear in life. So the words of Jesus "find" us: "When ye pray, say, Our Father which art in heaven." [5] Despite Sigmund Freud, we do not proceed from our broken homes to devise a vast fiction of a perfect Sky, for we cannot build infinity from broken pieces of finitude. We know our brokenness because we are already aware of heaven. Therefore we cry: "Our Father which art in heaven." The words of Jesus are "right." They give coherence. They are true to our secret dialogue.

Deeper evidence: his words are set in the context of the whole drama of the Christ-Event. He did not despise the Number 73 bus, which in his day may have been a camel train; and he was interested in the newsboy shouting, "Extra!" even though news traveled then largely by word of mouth. His parables are filled with sights and sounds of the "good earth." But his allegiance was given to the mysterious "Thou." Day by day he could say: "I always do what is pleasing to him." [6] In the Garden of Gethsemane the pledge was kept: "Nevertheless, not as I will, but as thou wilt." [7] On the cross he yielded up his whole life, as through the years that led to the Cross he had yielded up life piece by piece, episode by episode, day by day: "It is finished" [8] (the last chord of the music now sounds): "Father, into thy hands I commit my spirit!" [9] The New Testament is awe-struck by the two-world drama in him. It says that at his birth the sky was rifted and angels sang; and that at his death, such was the insensate blindness and cruelty of men, the sky darkened in judgment and grief. He becomes thus the crucial instance: "Whosoever . . . shall confess me before men"—in public on Massachusetts Avenue or at home on Main Street—"him will I confess" in that upper world "before my Father which is in heaven."

So much for evidence. There is much more, but preaching should never overplay it. "Proof" of God would rob a man of the freedom by which alone he can become a man. So Browning wisely tells us:

> White shall not neutralize the black, nor good
> Compensate bad in man, absolve him so:
> Life's business being just the terrible choice.[10]

Terrible if the choice is blackly made, as our present world attests; not terrible, but deep laughter, when the choice is whitely made.

Even then the laughter may not quickly start, for (Browning again) God's books are balanced

> In God's good time,
> Which does not always fall on Saturday
> When the world looks for wages.[11]

So we may choose in free choice, a choice not always quickly ratified and never coerced, to live in this world as if it were the only world, or to live in this world by the light and obedience of the "Thou"-world.

III

"Whosoever . . . shall confess me before men": suppose that were our real business! *Not* making a livelihood, but making a living: the livelihood is the necessary gathering of brushes, paints, and canvas, but the living is—the picture. *Not* making a perfect world, for the very notion that *we* can make a perfect world is an idolatrous denial of our creaturehood; and besides, how can a finite world ever be "perfect"? An issue of *The Globe* [12] had a comic definition of a perfectionist which is too true to be merely comic: "A perfectionist is a person who in his pursuit of the perfect becomes a perfect nuisance." *Not* "expressing ourselves," for we are hardly the center of the universe; and besides, there are so many selves in us that expressing them might easily be bedlam. Suppose our real job is to "confess Christ," to become what the New Testament calls "witnesses of the Resurrection," [13] to testify amid buses and newsboys in this actual world to another World which rules this world in judgment and mercy. Zona Gale has a story about two tadpoles. One stuck his nose above their roadside pool and returning to his friend, said in effect: "There is a wonderful world around our pool, vast, terrible, beautiful; and it undoubtedly controls our little pool." The other said in effect: "You are several kinds of fool. Besides, what you say is otherworldliness." [14]

It is our modern fashion to confess less than we believe. We would rather air our doubts than acknowledge our faith. Perhaps the too-confident faith of sanctimoniousness has made us cautious. We say, "I do not pretend to be a Christian, but . . . ." The sentence trails away. If it were completed, it might run, " . . . but you can bet your buttons, your whole suit in fact, that I would not overcharge my customers as Whoosis does who does claim to be Christian, and I would never be an oily church hypocrite like Bloosis." There we are using the light in Christ to condemn our neighbors. Or we say: "All religions are true in their setting," though it is fairly clear that "setting" is no full criterion of truth, and equally clear that if one religion says that history is illusion or misfortune and another says that history is the vehicle of God's self-disclosure, we are confronted by an existential choice. Or we say, "I do not pretend to be a Christian." A man should not pretend to more than he believes, when mortal life is held in mystery, but he should not pretend to less than he believes; and if he insists on pretending, he might wisely go to church, for there he would be confronted by the realism of Jesus, if only in the reading of Scripture. Atheists among us make their noble witness for academic freedom. Are they then atheists? Truth and freedom are their faith, truth and freedom which exercise a personal claim on their personal selves. Why do we confess less than we believe?

Someone retorts that deeds are better than words. Are they? Or rather, are not words themselves deeds, deeds of the lips? And are not deeds of the hands and deeds of the lips always joined in mutual interpretation? And are not deeds of the lips the most instant, the most frequent, the most flexible, the most freighted with personal witness, of all our deeds? Homer's heroes, it must be granted, move in strong silence while his cowards chatter like blue jays. But the business of "the strong, silent man" can be overdone: a hero need not act like a deaf mute. Sometimes a deed of the hand cannot become current coin without a deed of the lips: if a cure were found for leukemia, it would have to be *told*, or someone would wickedly fail. Sometimes we can do no more than speak, as when Turgenev, wishing to give a coin to a beggar and finding he had no coin, blurted out: "Don't be angry, brother; I have nothing, brother." The man replied, in unwitting testimony to deeds of the lips, "Thanks for this, too. That is a gift too, brother." [15]

To "confess" Christ should enlist all our deeds in such consistency as we can muster. Sometimes words of the lips are almost sure to be misunderstood. Perhaps Western Christianity must be slow to speak in the Orient until other deeds, through hospitals and farms, have shown that Christian faith is not colonialism. Generally, if anything or anybody is generally, the hand-deed is not understood without the lip-deed; and the lip-deed seems empty or even false without the honorable hand. The deed need not be a "great deed." Or rather, deeds are not great according to the size of the stage, but according to the gladness and poignancy of their witness to an unseen world. Deeds on a great stage soon seem histrionic, and history soon deflates them. But a little deed (the very phrase betrays our egocentric itch for "front stage, center, spotlight") is not little. The man who put a hand on Luther's shoulder in the bitterest crux of Luther's battle, bidding him bravely persist,[16] may well have given the battle its turn toward victory. A television dial, moved a fraction of an inch, brings a clear picture. Perhaps we can bring life into focus for one another by tiny deeds, provided they be done in confession of another World.

"Whosoever shall deny me before men"; we shrink from that dark side of the text. But the fact remains that if a man makes himself a stranger to an upper dimension of truth and love, he is a stranger: he is estranged from himself, from his neighbor, and from the God whom he has thus denied. Perhaps we may learn thus why the world of the Number 73 bus and of newsboys shouting, "Extra!" has become dull, so dull that we cannot endure it without a "shot in the arm." The shots are repeated now until we become "addicts" instead of men. An earth without any horizon-mountains and any starry sky is bound to be a prison. It is man's self-appointed hell and leads on to God's self-appointed explation. That is why Christ is crucified in every generation.

IV

"Life's business being just the terrible choice"—whether we shall live only on the street or also in sight of an encompassing Mercy. We *must* live in the street, but that is our chance to confess a Higher Light. The devil in the library, watching a man's lips frame the prayer "Thou," said to a fellow devil: "Before I knew where I was I saw my twenty years' work beginning to totter." [17] We say:

> To-morrow, and to-morrow, and to-morrow,
> Creeps in this petty pace from day to day.[18]

But suppose it is not petty. Suppose every word you speak registers on a seismograph up there. Suppose that wherever you walk, you are watched in holy love. Suppose that when you turn from shabby selfishness, Christ says: "That man is Mine." Life is not petty: it is a two-world conversation and a two-world traffic, an affair between time and eternity, between each of us and the very God.

A story for you rather than any "moral": Abraham Holmes, the Puritan, refused to confess any king but Jesus. He was tried for treachery in London and sentenced to be hung. The horses that took him in a wagon to the gallows became fractious. So Holmes said: "Stop, gentlemen, let me go afoot. Remember how the ass saw God, whom the prophet could not see. There is more in this than you think." [19] There is more in any earthly act than we think. We say, "Hi, Jim"; he answers, "Hi, Bill." We see the Number 73 bus, and sometimes in the library we find ourselves asking about "Thou." There is more in this than we think. A two-world traffic is involved. There are no little deeds, for all deeds are registered in that other World. You pray now in church, even though you can say no more than "Thou," even though the "Thou" seems lost in mystery. There is more in this than you think. For Jesus said: "Whosoever . . . shall confess me before men, him will I confess also before my Father which is in heaven."

THE CHRISTIAN YEAR

20

THE THIRST FOR GOD

(*An Advent Sermon*)

> As a hart longs for flowing streams,
>   so longs my soul for thee, O God.
> My soul thirsts for God, for the living God.
> When shall I come and behold the face of God?
>
> Ps. 42:1, 2

Some years ago a novel named *The Great Desire*,[1] told of a young writer coming from New England to New York City to gather material for a novel by that same title. In his quest he plied people with one question: "What do you want?" He would not let any man take refuge in proximate answers. If the man answered, "I want to be an engineer," he would pursue him with, "But why do you want to be an engineer? What do you really want?" Thus he tracked down the "great desire." Perhaps Rudyard Kipling could have given him the answer, for when he stirred restlessly in a serious sickness and the nurse asked him, "Do you want anything?" he murmured, "I want God." [2] Is that every man's great desire?

I

The thirst for God seems an absurd affair. That a man upon his sick bed, or any other little man in pulpit or pew, his mind dim and his days numbered, should want God is surely absurdity to the

157

pitch of absurdity, presumption built on presumption. The very word "God" is the final mystery, the ultimate reality. A man wanting God? But here is a fact worth noting: our eyes, which soon fade and fail, nevertheless live by the total light of the universe. Is it not strange that all the light of suns and stars travels down the tiny path of the optic nerve? So our bodies feed on the economy of the whole cosmos. As for our minds, the cosmos is not enough, for when we say "the cosmos," we have taken our stance beyond it. From some infinite we view all finite things. Perhaps the great desire *is* the thirst for God—because we have already been found by Him.

This world does not satisfy us, least of all its cash and pleasure. Cash, if we live for it, makes us metallic. Rich men dimly fear that fate: they find a better joy in collecting paintings or in raising money for a hospital. As for pleasure, if we live for it instead of enjoying it when it comes as alternate mercy, it leaves us hopped up—galvanized spasms. Cash and pleasure, when they become the focuses of life's ellipse, cannot hold us. Soon we fly off at a tangent into a dreary void. Life is a circle—with only one Center, which is everywhere, never explored. The scientist pursues a "truth" always beyond him yet within him; the artist lives for "beauty," always fleeting, always found; the saint finds in holy love a passion which is yet his despair; and for these men life does not flag. What do they *really* want? Even human love cannot satisfy us, for it can betray us, and it dies.

Perhaps our modern lostness is the "great desire" in reverse. We could not say, "I am lost," if we had no memory of home. The book title said *The Damned Don't Cry* [3] and might be true of the utterly damned, for they would be beyond any compunction or hope. But modern man cries, if only to tell us that he can find no meaning, that all history is absurd; and, therefore, our modern age is not damned. Perhaps we have been living for cash and pleasure and human love; and perhaps the cash has become bondage, pleasure a fever, and human love a succession of divorces, because these are not life's true center or real desire.

> Where the sun shines in the street
> There are very many feet
> Seeking God, all unaware
> That their hastening is a prayer.

> Perhaps these feet would deem it odd
> (Who think they are on business bent)
> If some one went,
> And told them, "You are seeking God." [4]

Our very frustrations may be but the reverse side of an intense longing: "As a hart longs for flowing streams, so longs my soul for thee, O God."

II

The thirst is for the "living God." Such is the order of the text: "God," then the "living God." "Living" means not as a dead idol. Modern idols are not made of wood and stone: they are made of concepts spelled with a capital letter, such concepts as Values or Progress. But they have as little power as a totem pole at last to answer us. In the crises of life—life itself being always precarious and so always a crisis—these abstractions are almost mockery. When a cottage burns and people within it die, shall we speak to the mourners about Values or Progress? The "hart" comes with distended eye and palpitating flank: his thirst is not quenched by water which is a mere ideal. The man comes pursued by hounds of realized failure or the black rider called death: Shall we talk to him about the Future of the Race? Near our summer home there is a lane with here a horse trough and there a flowing spring. Even horses know that the trough soon is empty and the water in it stale: they pass it for the "flowing spring." Even they want the real thing. This thirst for the "living God" is nowadays dubbed weakness. Perhaps the answer is, "Are we not weak?" We are so weak in body that we must sleep, lapsing into unconsciousness, every few hours; and soon we die. We are so weak in mind that we plot our own atomic death. Our life is obviously contingent and derived: there is no final resource within ourselves. The story of the woman and the psychiatrist has here its sharp point. She complained of an inferiority complex, but he, having examined her, said: "Madam, you are not suffering from an inferiority complex: you just *are* inferior." To deny our constitutional human weakness is not courage, but only blindness. Katherine Mansfield wrote to Dorothy Brett of our human need: "God is now gone for all of us. Yet we must believe, and not only that; we must carry our weakness and our sin and our devilish-ness to somebody." [5] Devilishness: the weakness is both mortal and culpable: we are doubly weak. So our "soul thirsts . . . for the *living* God."

Thus we confront the issue of personality in God. Perhaps we should say "in God" rather than "of God," for we all know that God must not be equated with our finite life. The argument against personality in God is not impressive. Usually it consists of the Greek jest: "If an ox conceived of God, it would conceive Him as a larger Ox." [6] There is a later version, supposed to be clever, "If the triangles made a God, they would give Him three sides." [7] But an ox cannot conceive of God: that is why it is an ox. Still less can a triangle conceive of God. The "if" in both instances is nonsense, so the conclusion is equal nonsense; and there is no good reason to reckon such nonsense as "clever." The argument *for* personality in God is more impressive but not conclusive, for God is never proved or disproved by argument. It could run as follows: the Ultimate, by whatever name, exercises a personal constraint on our personal lives and is to that measure personal. Besides, the creative process has brought forth personality as the highest term we know; and though God is doubtless far greater than the best we know, He cannot be less. The charge of anthropomorphism—that man is making God in man's image—need not trip us: to hold that fear is to be already beyond it. Thus the first phrase of the Lord's Prayer is anthropomorphic and already beyond it: "Our Father who art in heaven." [8]

Man will continue to thirst for the "living God." Could there be thirst without water? Or an eye without light? We do not know, but we guess not. Even Alfred North Whitehead who under student questioning was never quite ready to commit himself to faith in the "living God" used personal language when he wrote, as nobly as Plato, of the ultimate. He calls God the "unity of adventure": [9] adventure is a personal term. He says that that title "includes Eros": again Eros is personal love, though it goes far beyond personal love. He says that this "living urge toward all possibilities" is "claiming goodness as their realization": claim and goodness and realization all beg the question, for they are *our* language. Personality need not be confused with *our* personality: man's prayer is for communion, for the "living God," who nevertheless always goes far, far beyond our mortal ken.

III

Then why should any man carry the prayer to the further stage, asking to "behold the face of God"? That asking seems hardly short of blasphemy. Yet Israel had such awe in the presence of God that they would not write the vowels in the Hebrew of the Divine name. We see that same reverence, with its face covered before the Glory, in the New Testament account of the parables of Jesus: "There is joy in the presence of the angels of God." [10] This means "God is glad," but awe shrinks from that blunt familiarity: therefore the roundabout phrase. Israel knew that "no man shall see 'God' and live." [11] Then why should a man ask: "When shall I come and behold the *face* of God?" Because our longing, which even fear of blasphemy cannot stay, is for God as known Companion of our daily life and as the Redeemer from our sins. When the child asked where is God, and her mother told her that God is everywhere, the child answered: "But I want God to be somewhere." That also is part of the "great desire." When we try to picture God and know we cannot, we still yearn for Him to be somewhere— actual in our actual life.

The psalm gives evidence of this longing in the strange sentence: "Therefore I remember thee from the land of Jordan and of Hermon, from Mount Mizar," [12]—the hill country at the River Jordan's source. Some scholars think the sentence has been interpolated. If the theory is right, an exile, reading the psalm with its longing to "behold the face of God" (to come into the very presence of the King), wrote in: "Here where I am exiled, at the headwaters of the Jordan." Our version would be: "Here on Massachusetts Avenue in Cambridge." Despite the seeming irreverence or overreaching, we long for sign and surety of God in our existential life. Otherwise God must always be—Otherwise. That longing G. K. Chesterton sets on the lips of "The Wild Knight":

> So, with the wan waste grasses on my spear,
> I ride forever, seeking after God.
> My hair grows whiter than my thistle plume,
> And all my limbs are loose; but in my eyes
> The star of an unconquerable praise:
> For in my soul one hope forever sings,
> That at the next white corner of a road
> My eyes may look on Him . . . ." [13]

"The next white corner of the road"—the corner of the cosmos called Earth, the corner of Main Street in the planet Earth where my house is built!

Christian faith holds that in Christ the longing is fulfilled, at Bethlehem, on Christmas Day. No other faith so speaks. Strange fulfillment: Deity once took our constitutional humanity and appeared at the "next white corner of the street," a corner called Nazareth, and there lived out our life! Stranger fulfillment: he bared his life to our sins and died our death—on a gallows! Someone, nay, a multitude of someones, ask for "proof." That word "proof" has become our shibboleth. But it is a slippery word. Even human love, let alone Divine Love, is not proved as a theorem in geometry is proved. What tests shall we set against the Eternal in Jesus Christ? Shall we ask about his power? Gentle power which has yet split time into before and after. Or about his creativity? Music and philanthropy and worship age on age give their glad answer. Or about his gift to gather life into meaning? Suffering is a final enigma, but the Cross has given it a somber glory. Shall we ask empirical "proof"? There are the actualities of the New Testament and the Church: these could hardly have sprung from death and hardly have withstood treachery within and attack without except by very Life. But there is no "proof" as we reckon proof: there is only the onset of God, Who is His own evidence. Do you not know His confrontation in Christ?

People are at home with Jesus: afraid and yet deeply at home. We must never pretend that the heavens were emptied when he came. He does not resolve or dissolve the mystery of God: he reveals God. But could any answer better satisfy our longing to "behold the face of God" than the Event of Christ—at our "corner of the road"? Then have it so, venturing life! Somewhere the story of the daughter of a British Colonial statesman tells how she tired of hearing her father vilified by his political opponents, so that she finally took his photograph to the office of a hostile newspaper, laid it on the editor's desk, and said: "Look, that is what he is really like!" [14] When Russia attacks our version of God as "opium" (not without some tincture of truth), or when some voices in America try to turn God into the chaplain of a cult of "personality" and material success, or when we fear God is a vast Nothing in Nowhere, we turn again to Jesus: "This is what he is really like, though in a mystery which mortal mind cannot fathom!"

Thus Christ is "the Way, the Truth, and the Life." He is Actuality:—the very Road, the very Reality, the Life lived out on the "next white corner of the road." Some may stumble over such particularity, forgetting that life is never abstract. But others, who are baffled by mystery, find in Christ the visitation and the answer. Ericsson, friend of Ole Bull, the violinist, was a skillful craftsman but had no ear for music. He mended the famous violin so that it was almost better than before the mishap, but was still stranger to the song in it—until then and there Ole Bull began to play. Workmen gathered around the shop, ordinary men now spellbound by a thing impalpable, so that even Ericsson cried out at last: "Ole, Ole, I've an ear for music after all!" [15] Faith? It seems a chimera. Faith in God? Nobody has ever seen God, and He may be only a name for an enigma, a maze of riddles in a fog. Then Jesus!—and faith is understood; and if this be God, we believe in God for time and eternity.

IV

So the Church says age on age: "Behold the Man!" The proof is in the stab of spirit, the trouble and the joy. The proof is that we put him to the proof. We try to follow and soon stumble, falling headlong. Then we understand the need for pardon, knowing full well that we cannot pardon ourselves. Then we see his Cross in a new and deeper Light. this is the rent in history through which we see the love of God, incredibly patient, incredibly loving, and not stayed by any death. Then we follow again, not fearing that we may stumble so long as we stumble with our eyes on him. "Look, this is what He is really like!" "God was in Christ reconciling the world to himself." [16] So the longing for God finds answer, and the thirst for God is slaked, and the yearning to see the face of God is satisfied—as much as mortal man may ask, God mercifully veiled in our flesh, until hereafter we see Him face to face.

21

THE NAME OF THE NAMELESS

(A Christmas Sermon)

> "Then Jacob asked . . . , 'Tell me, I pray, your
> name?' "   *Gen. 32:29*
> "And you shall call his name Jesus, for he will
> save his people from their sins."   *Matt. 1:21*

We ask, "What's in a name?" We mean that there is nothing
in it. In truth there is little enough in our names, for they are
hardly more than tags by which the mailman brings Christmas
presents to our house instead of to some alien door. What, for instance, could the name "Buttrick" mean? "George" means a farmer, as in Vergil's *Georgics,* and I scarcely know the right end or
wrong end of a plow. But there was a time when names had meaning, as you would be reminded should you consult that section
of the dictionary titled "A Pronouncing Vocabulary of Common
English Christian Names." The adjective "Christian" there is something of a sunstart. The name "John" once meant "gift of God,"
just as Joshua (Jesus) once meant "savior." In times from which
the book of Genesis is drawn men believed that if they could learn
the name of a god, they would possess the god's very power; for
a name then meant almost a man's or a god's nature.

164

I

All of which brings us to an eerie story in that same book of Genesis. A man tried to cross a river at midnight, and the river-god disputed the passage. This story, you can see, is as old as an early polytheism. The man and the god wrestled, by the river churned white, in the darkness. "What's your name?" asked the ghostly adversary. "Jacob," answered the man. Now it was the man's turn: "Tell me, I pray, your name." Oh, no! Learn the god's secret, steal the god's power? Oh, no: gods are shrewder than men. So the god answered: "Why do you ask after my name?" It was believed in those days that gods feared the light, so the god soon exclaimed: "Let me go, for the day breaks." Now the man had the advantage as they wrestled in the slowly broadening light: "I will not let you go unless you bless me." Thus the man prevailed to win the blessing. A weird story of "calling shapes, and beck'ning shadows dire," [1] and you may well ask, "What has that to do with Christmas?"

It has this to do: God and we hold the same kind of conversation. He asks, "What is your name?" We try to quip our way out of it, saying airily, "What's in a name?" But name means nature, and we begin to ask what our name really is—dust or divinity, perverseness or child of eternity? Then God asks again, "Where do you live?" We are about to answer, "That's a silly question. It doesn't matter, does it? And in any event, You should know." But the answer dies on our lips. Where *do* we live? Not on this little swinging ball called Earth, for we are always strangers in time and space. So we evade the question by turning it back on God: "Tell me, I pray, your name." If only we knew! Is the name "Fear," an invisible shape that seizes us at midnight on the banks of the turbulent river called Time?

> Time, like an ever-rolling stream,
>   Bears all its sons away;
> They fly, forgotten, as a dream
>   Dies at the opening day. [2]

Or is the name "Nothingness"? That would be a worse name than "Fear." Perhaps everything we say and do is an attempt, a groping question, to learn God's name. But since He is God and we are creatures of flesh, how can we ever know unless He tells us?

II

These questions bring us back to the man Jacob. He was afraid that the name of the river-god might be "Judgment." Twenty years earlier he had wronged his blind father and his casual brother to steal his brother's birthright. That is why his name was Jacob: "the supplanter." Meanwhile he had prospered. He was eager now, as he was returning home, that bygones should be bygones; but neither memory nor history was ready to help him. A dirty trick ought not to live any longer than a dog: it should die in twenty years. But in memory and history it refuses to die. Sometimes Jacob had regretted the deception, but usually he had been too busy to think about it. He had lived alternately by his wits and by his heart, like the rest of us; and like the rest of us, he had not been sure which was his name and nature. Now he had to know, for his brother, whom he had not seen for twenty years, was marching toward him with four hundred men. What *was* his own name —"Deception"? What was the god's name—"Nemesis"? This name business became momentous, there at midnight on the bank of an eerie stream.

Conscience is a strange affair. It gives different verdicts in different cultures, but moves through all cultures dividing right from wrong—and with some common judgments as, for instance, about a man's home and the worth of a man's life. It can be in error and needs repeated checking, as a compass needs it, but like a compass, it seems to move in obedience to a mysterious magnetic north. Our shallow modern theory reckons it a hang-over from a childhood fear of our parents, but that makes no sense, for even a child's conscience is sensitive both to his own sins and to parental cruelty. Our shallower theory reckons it a vestigial affair from ancient tribal custom or social convention. But why, then, does prophetic conscience convict both custom and convention, as in the instance of war or the "double standard"? Conscience can become psychotic, but that very fact implies a healthy conscience. "I have abolished sin," said Renan;[3] but he still used the word, and still knew what it meant, and still knew that other men knew. Therefore, we and all men wonder if the name of God is "Judgment"; and as with Jacob, we wonder with sufficient cause.

III

We are back with Jacob and with ourselves, for every man's

name is Jacob. His strategy, after he had crossed his river, resembled the man himself: it was a strange blend of nobility and shabbiness. He divided his company into two groups, keeping closely within his own care Rachel, the wife whom he most loved, and their son Joseph. As for Rachel, "Jacob served seven years for Rachel, and they seemed to him but a few days because of the love he had for her." [4] As for Joseph (his name means "He shall add": to the world's illustrious families), he was the apple of his father's eye. Every Jacob is this strange mixture of shrewdness and love. If God's name is "Judgment" and nothing else, whence comes the love? And deeper question, why does love, as in Jacob's case, try to forestall death? Always we wonder about our own true name. Always we wonder about God's name.

So we press the question: "Tell me, I pray, your name?" If we could learn God's true name, we might thus learn our own. Is His name "Judgment," or "Love," or "Death"? If His name is Love, can it be also final "Judgment" or final "Death"? Sometimes the Christian doctrine of resurrection is condemned as "selfish." That is another modern notion that is as shallow as veneer, for even Jacob in that faraway time cared little what happened to him, provided Rachel and Joseph might be saved. If "social service" cares for men in this life, the Christian doctrine of resurrection cares for men in this life and beyond it. Solon was asked why he wept for his dead son when weeping availed nothing. "That is why I weep," he answered, "because it is of no avail." [5]

> Time, like an ever-rolling stream,
> Bears all its sons away—

where? A professor once said: "He would have been thirty today if he had lived." We asked, "How old was he when . . . ?" letting the question trail off into the unspoken word. "Three months." We know God's name is "Judgment," or we guess it. Then why is such love in us?

Thus Jacob and his god. Thus we and God, God ever asking our name and we ever asking His name. The word "God" comes presumably from the root word for good. But how can that root word be squared with an earthquake or a maniac? Yet the pity in us which asks that question belongs somewhere within the good. Perhaps all the names we surmise about God are partly true. His name

must be for us "Fear," for we think of Him with awe; and "Judgment," for if there were no judgment, man's life might become
trivial; and "Beauty," for black branches against the snow at sunset
almost grip a man's throat in their beauty; and "Truth," for
scientists and witnesses at court must honor truth. The trouble is
that we do not know the central and sovereign name. The trouble
is that no list of abstract nouns can ever fill our longing, for we
yearn to know that God is here where we live. Presumably He has
a supernal name, but that name is beyond our ken; and we dare
not, cannot, take it on our lips. Doesn't God have a human name?

IV

Then Christmas in its gentleness: 'You shall call his name Jesus,
for he will save his people from their sins." The doubts at once
come knocking at our door, but so lovely is the story, we wonder
if we have any right to invite them. God revealed in a Babe in
swaddling clothes—that is, with linen bands around the tiny
shoulders and thighs? God thus made known? God disclosed as a
Babe in a poor and inconspicuous home, a Babe who had a manger
for his first cradle, with all kinds of strange people crowding
in-between the camels and donkeys to look at him? If that be so, the
doubts still thronging and knocking within us, God's name is "Lowliness" and "Emmanuel": "God with us." Perhaps we should doubt
the doubts instead of giving them entrance. For this is true: if
God had kept the whole heaven between us and Him, if always He
had been only ultimate Truth, like snow on some inaccessible mountain, how would we know Him to be "good"? Or if He had come
near as an angel, how could we have worshiped? What do angels
know about human tears and laughter? If the name is "Jesus," we
can account for the love in us, for our love might then be the
broken image of His love. We could account also for the running
fire of glory, beneath the deceit, in any Jacob.

The name "Jesus" is manifestly a human name. "Jesus" or
"Joshua" was as common a name then as "John" or "William" in
our time. There were two or three "Joshuas" then in the wider
family of the High Priest, and manuscript evidence hints that
Barabbas was also Jesus; for Barabbas, as it stands, means only
"son of Abbas." The first name is missing. Did Pilate ask: "Whom
do you want me to release for you: Jesus son of Abbas or Jesus who
is called Christ?" [6] The name is human. Jesus looked out of the win-

dow and said, as we say, "I wonder if it will rain." When his mother cried because in their poverty a coin was lost, he wept with her so poignantly that in man's estate he remembered and turned that desolate moment into a deathless story.[7] When word came that a caravan from Damascus was passing through the valley just over the hill back of Nazareth, he begged to go to see it. He laughed. He prayed. He worked day by day. How else could we know God's real nature toward us? A musician, when he was asked to compose a new national anthem for a European land, is reported to have said: "How can I? I wasn't born there." Jesus was born here. He lived among us. "The Word became flesh and dwelt among us." [8]

But that very phrase shows what most men have believed: the name "Jesus" is more than human. "The Word" is a title with a capital letter: "The Eternal Logos." "Dwelt" means that Jesus was among men as the Ark of the Holy Covenant was set among the huddled tents of pilgrim Israel. In the King James Version of our text the name "Jesus" comes to us in five capital letters, "JESUS: for he shall save people from their sins." Merely human power cannot forgive sins. If you doubt that fact, try it: try going down to the jail and saying: "Thy sins be forgiven thee." [9] You will soon find how blasphemous such words sound on lips like ours. The prisoners who had sensibility and who know their Bible might answer you in the words that one thief (on that second cross) addressed to the other thief (on that third cross): "Thou art in the same condemnation." [10] But the Man on the middle cross, could he not forgive? Who shall go back in history to forgive the deceit of Jacob? Man cannot reverse history's stream or ever rule its strange turns. Man is powerless to mend even the damage done to nature, much less to human nature. Can a man cause a felled tree to blossom, or an amputated limb to grow into a new limb? On the New Jersey flats there is a sign with a certain turn of humor: "Our erasers rub out mistakes in any language." Not in the language of our daily life! *That* language is in only God's power. Yet Jesus forgave sins, and people knew themselves forgiven; and ever since that time people have known, by faith in him.

Thus the miracle of Christmas. Prosy people still ask if the Christmas stories are fact or fiction, and poetic people are foolishly content to count them merely poetry. Stories that tell of events or the Event are always more than stories, and facts that give no meaning to the fact are always less than facts. What we see at

Christmas is Light streaming through an Event. He split history into before and after, so that the atheist dates his letters from the birth of Christ. Anyone here choose to attempt to split history? It is fact also that men have broken into caroling at thought of him, to tell other men that the sky of human hopes was opened when he was born, and that the stars of a comprehended destiny changed their course. A Jewish girl once said to me: "I love the Handel *Messiah*." She might love it even more if Christians by their anti-Semitic prejudice had not often belied their name. In Bangkok we heard Buddhists singing our Christmas carols, or at least the tune. Maybe a physical and ethical regimen is not enough to satisfy man's life. In Hongkong we saw Christmas cards in which the Babe had tiny upraised slits for eyes, for the name of Jesus is understood in every land.

God has many names, for He is the "Nameless of the hundred names." [11] His name is "Mystery," for the heavens were not emptied when Jesus came; and if God were not Mystery, men could never have worshiped. His name is "Power": He lifts the cosmos and will not let the name of Jesus die. His name is "Judgment," for our life is not a jaunty affair in which Jacob-deceit goes unnoticed after twenty years, in which God casually wipes His lips of our wantonness, saying, "Oh, don't mention it"; life is a momentous once-for-all encounter. His name is "Holiness": people who glibly wish they might meet Jesus forget that once his friends cried out in agony: "Depart from me, for I am a sinful man, O Lord." [12] His name is "Enigma": we simply cannot construe the plan which includes earthquakes and maniacs, and should not pretend that we can. But the central name, if only because it starts our tears and joy and deepest resolve, is Jesus: "for he will save his people from their sins."

V

It is not strange that the name has been taken as a talisman. It is a talisman, even though it must never become a magic spell. Bernardino counseled folk in Viterbo to inscribe on their homes the initials "I.H.S.": "Jesus of Men the Savior." [13] Perhaps we shall not become sure of him until that motto *is* inscribed on factory and store and house. It is inscribed in some fashion on our baptisms and funerals and weddings, on the momentous and creative junctures of our life on earth. But perhaps we shall not become sure until it is written also on the ordinary day; for Monday through Saturday, if those days are pagan, may overcome the one worshipful day of Sunday. Or perhaps we should say with better confidence that the Name is now in our history and in our hearts, and that we shall not be able to forget.

A large man on a plane said to me, "The name's Coulter, from Texas. What's your name?" I was mulling over this sermon and almost answered, "Jacob," and might have been right. Jesus meets us. "My name's Jesus. What's yours?" If we are wise, we shall say: "Jesus! Lord, that my sins may be forgiven!" At Christmas time God asks us our name. Then we can tell Him that our name is not now (not at Christmas time) "dust" or "pride"; for our name is now lost in the name of Jesus, and thus forever found. God asks us then: "Where do you live?" We can tell Him since it is Christmas, "I live at Harvard, in Cambridge, on the tiny ball called Earth, in a universe that goes clean beyond my mind. But not beyond Yours: I live in the Father's house because an Elder Brother has led me home." Everything good and joyous is in one name—the name of Jesus.

22

PENITENCE AND PARDON
(*A Lenten Sermon*)

> "Seek ye the Lord while he may be found, call ye
> upon him while he is near: Let the wicked forsake
> his way, and the unrighteous man his thoughts:
> and let him return unto the Lord, and he will have
> mercy upon him; and to our God, for he will
> abundantly pardon."   *Isa. 55:6-7* (K.J.V.)

Must God be "found"? Is He not always near? Must we "seek" Him in San Francisco, only to hear that He has gone to the Gobi Desert; or in one decade in history, only to learn that such an era is not His visiting hours? A strange notion about God! Strange God, if the notion be true—God playing a nasty game of hide-and-seek in which man is always outwitted. But that is not Isaiah's notion. He is telling us, rather, that though we are self-enthralled or busy with our transient world, there are times when we realize our helplessness and God breaks through our distraction. Then we know God's nearness. Then we should "seize the day."

I

History reveals God. Isaiah was pointing to a juncture in history of which people were obliged to say: "This is not man's doing." Cyrus the Persian, having conquered Babylon, had released captive Israel from the long Babylonian exile. Who knows why? Cyrus certainly had no love for, perhaps even no knowledge of, Israel's covenant faith. He was not concerned about the "one true God." Who in Israel could have guessed such a turn of events? Israel, returning to Zion, could now re-establish the covenant community. Is history merely a game of political chess? Is it merely the play of economic and sociological forces? Or is there also a deeper meaning? Isaiah said, "There is a deeper meaning. God keeps His covenant. Seek Him now while He may be found." So after the battle of Waterloo, Victor Hugo said of Napoleon, "God was bored by him." [1] Isaiah said likewise to his people, "God has now shown His long-hidden hand and has made an unwitting Cyrus His own messenger. We must return to God, as we return to Zion."

Truth is always in some sense through history; and history always has its deeper meaning, even though we cannot always decipher it. Truth is never abstract: it cannot be abstracted from the human situation. We can shape history, but only as we are shaped by it. We think we think and that then by our thinking we re-mold the world. But that is not the order of events. On the contrary, things happen to bring gifts (such as release to captive Israel) or to cuff us over the ears (as in the atomic threat), and then we begin to think. History and the world are slightly beforehand with our clever little minds! A boy not yet adolescent was asked about the movie he had seen, and he answered: "Oh, it was about some sloppy dame." Some months later he was in a canoe with a girl, in the track of the moonlight; and she was not "sloppy," but decidedly attractive. Why had the lad changed his mind? He hadn't: history, the course of events, the coming of adolescence, had changed it for him. History will always have ultimate meanings, if only because men are more than political and economic, if only because every man confronts life. Our history has cuffed us on the ears, and we begin to think. It would seem that we must rethink our whole way of living, our total civilization.

This rethinking is painful business. Our scientific wisdom has misfired—or backfired. Our calculated risks have been badly miscalculated. Our cult of "self-expression," after we had dismissed Christian faith as "repression," has not made a pretty world. Hans Schemm's Nazi proposal that we come to God only "through our *Volk*" has given no supernal light! [2] All this we now dimly know. Two world wars sandwiching an acute depression, so acute that in the world's richest nation people went hungry, are evidence of a virus in the blood of mankind. They have led, for further evidence, to widespread delinquency and international snarling, with a bomb now suspended over us that may terminate the whole episode of man's life on this planet. Some interpreters may dismiss this vast portent as a passing cloud, but they hardly convince us. Such optimism is a small boy whistling past a graveyard—with how many million graves! We intended a brave new world—and were sure that our own brilliance could conjure it, a secular world contrived by secular brilliance. We never intended our kind of world. Then who did intend it? For Israel history broke in deliverance; for us it breaks in wrath. That being so, the word of Isaiah may have sharper pertinence: "Seek ye the Lord while he may be found." History reveals God.

II

Then man acts, or surely ought to act. His act, our act, is always response; the initiatives are in God's hand. But we can view our world and our path in the world (*that* is our human distinctiveness), and we can measurably redirect our lives as history brings us joy or warning. In this sense we can seek the Lord. Who is this Power? Often His ways are hidden; sometimes they are terrible in righteousness, sometimes gentle in deliverance. In time of crisis, "crisis" being a Greek word which means judgment more than it means cruciality, we suddenly know that we are like a man lost at sundown in deep woods.

> Alone, alone, about a dreadful wood
> Of conscious evil runs a lost mankind. [3]

Who among us has more than tentative wisdom for a tentative next step in our present crisis? We look ahead and see only deeper darkness. We cannot go back: the road has been too "dreadful." Then we see, or think we see, a clearing: there is a Will, not our will, behind present events. Can we learn that Will? We must "seek" Him, for already He has found us. We must follow down that clearing. What else can we do? The present darkness is not easily endured. So we may "seek."

Then we may "call": "Call ye upon him while he is near"
We thus cry aloud in the clearing, hoping that Someone may
hear us who knows our name. Men have always prayed, especially
in crisis; or perhaps I should say, especially when they have understood that life by nature is crisis. There is no proof of prayer apart
from praying. Meanwhile if we do not pray, no works of ours can
solve our dilemma, for the man who does the works is himself the
problem. Basil fled the city for the desert, as we flee to a ranch
house in the country, though our motive is earthier than his; but he
was obliged then to confess, "I have not yet been able to leave myself behind." [4] If we ourselves are the sickness, the cure must come
from beyond ourselves. Therefore we "call" on God. If someone
should ask, "How can a man pray when he does not believe in God?"
the answer is perhaps this: every man believes in God, if only
fitfully, if only in the doubt which itself testifies to a prior faith.
No man doubts a nothing: he doubts only what he first believes.
In crisis we "call," the word "God" coming instinctively to our
lips, though we do not yet know if there is Anyone hidden for
deliverance in our "dreadful wood." So we "seek" and "call."

Then we may repent: "Let the wicked forsake his way, and the
unrighteous man his thoughts." Repentance is not a "pious" word,
at least not in our usual meaning of the word "pious." It is not
mere fear in crisis. It is not centrally remorse, even though it involves sorrow for our failures. It is never a morbid self-flogging.
True repentance is an act of will, a "change of mind," as we re-
view our whole life, in faith that our will is then held in a Higher
Will. It is a turning and returning: "Let him return unto the Lord."
We turn our backs on the way of life that has brought our wars
and delinquencies. We may not know where we are going, but at
least we know then where we are not going: we are not going to
selfish chaos and obscene death. We now renounce the lackluster
way which has brought only fear and frustration—the taken-for-
granted egocentricity with no flags flying, no trumpets sounding,
and no impassioned aim. Sir Edward Grey, British Foreign Secretary, who said at the outbreak of the First World War that lamps
were going out all over Europe, spoke a sharper word when uneasy peace was declared—that penitence best becomes us.[5] If only
men had listened and heeded! Repentance, by the very meaning of
the word, is a rightabout-face—a turning away from a world in
which thinghood is reckoned success and nobility of spirit is ac-

counted folly. There is as yet no "religious revival" in America because as yet there is no deep penitence.

III

History speaks, man turns; and then God responds. Why not earlier? Because every man is a center of freedom. He is free even to make his blunders, while God waits and with an unseen hand makes a hedge beyond which man cannot go. We have latterly used the word "secular" as if it were sainted. We plead for a "secular university." The word itself means "of the age," and thus carries its own despair: man is of the age, dust and to dust returning. But we could not use the word "secular" if we were not already aware of an ageless life. Even H. G. Wells, not a prejudiced witness in favor of biblical faith, said that "the religion of the atheist has a God-shaped blank at its heart." If so, only God can fill it. Thus Helen Keller, when communication had been made by touch of hand through long and patient love and when she could learn about God in Christ, replied in her new and strangely indirect language that she knew all this before, but did not know His name.[7] Sometimes we call God by the name of "truth," which even for the scientist is not a formula on a page, but rather a constraint of rigorous honesty. New Testament faith calls God by the name "the Word . . . made flesh,"[8] for the light in Jesus judges all prior light; and it is seminal, always breaking in new light. We dimly believe in God. Meanwhile He waits and works behind history, until we turn. His initial response is an honoring of our freedom.

Then "he will have mercy upon him." "Mercy" is more than a Red Cross word though often it is mediated through Red Cross deeds. The wounds of man struggling in a "dreadful wood" are dressed and healed, but with a deeper mercy: he now knows that he and his folly and the wood itself are held in mercy. The Bible is not "sermonizing": it is a transcript of experience. That Book never evades "the tragic sense of life,"[9] and therefore never sentimentalizes or makes false promises. Our age, knowing it must "turn" if it would live, proposes that since there is no deliverance, there is at least some respite in human love. Thus Matthew Arnold, seeing no hope in man's dilemma but only a "darkling plain . . . where ignorant armies clash by night,"[10] turns for respite to human love:

> Ah, love, let us be true
> To one another! for the world . . .

Hath really neither joy, nor love, nor light,
Nor certitude, nor peace, nor help for pain . . . .[11]

He is right. But human love also fails, if only because in this
world it is marked out for death. The Bible points us to a Love by
which we know that human love is but a broken light; to the
Christ who, being dead at the hands of man's self-hate, yet constrained his own from beyond death and who thus made us sure that
his life and love are stronger than hate and death.

God makes further response: "He will abundantly pardon." The
Hebrew reads: "He will be great in pardon." Pardon does not mean
only that He tears up an I O U. He does that, as a New Testament insight tells us in actual I O U language: "Having canceled
the bond"—the I O U—"which stood against us with its legal
demands; this he set aside, nailing it to the cross." [12] But more:
"He is great in pardon," as great as in His power of creation: He
delivers Israel from bondage in ways no man could have dreamed.
He grants a new spirit, in which we no longer desire an old life. He
turns the very memory of our sins into the memory of His mercy,
so that the legacy of sin becomes a precious discipline. There is no
suspicion of us for our unruly failure, no probation, no fumiga-
tion, no quarantine. "Bring quickly the best robe"—the robe kept
for a visit from a prince—"and put it on him." [13] Here words
fail: "Nor tongue nor pen can show." [14] When a wayward son
finally came home and sat shamefaced near the door, his father
said gently, "Nay, lad, come up to the fire." Calvary-fire, where
Jesus breathes God's pardon on all mankind: "Father, forgive
them." [15] The forgiveness is no mere laying aside claim for re-
quital. It is outrightly the gift of a new spirit unto eternal life—
"All This, and Heaven Too"! [16]

IV

We are in history, in our history. Has history nothing to say to
us? Does it commend a secular world? Each man must answer, and
each must honor his neighbor's answer under the claims of truth.
We did not intend this present world. Why have our intentions so
miscarried? Hitler said conscience is a Jewish invention.[17] Russia
has said, "God is opium." [18] We can lay no flattering unction to our
souls, for we said: "We'll pay Him lip service and keep the cash."
In point of fact, we have been our own God:

> Glory to Man in the highest! for Man is
> the master of things.[19]

Our present world is the legacy which mortal pride, now mortally stricken, has left us.

Has the time not come for us to "seek" and "call" and "turn"? To make the issue specific: competitive arms, whether in sputniks or death rays, is now seen to be a hopeless road. If we were to win atomic war, we would hate ourselves for vast incineration; if we were to lose, our culture, for good or ill, would vanish or sink into a new dark age; and if all men were to lose, we would affront the God of history by bringing history to such an end. To build bridges instead of "defenses" would admittedly be risky. But would it be more risky than being trigger happy with an atomic gun? Or more risky than playing Russian (and American?) roulette with inter-continental missiles? To take our chance and die might be better than the blasphemy of a world-wide Hiroshima. In any case individual decisions must be made—as to how and for what a man may rightly live. In all there is an act of faith—that God pardons those who turn to Him, in such abundant pardon that He can make new history in our world and a new world beyond this world. Perhaps we live at a time when men will soon see God in fires of judgment or in the gentleness of a new obedience, and perhaps all that matters is—that we see God.

23

EXPIATION

(A Holy Week sermon written after reading Albert Camus' novel The Fall)

"In this is love, not that we loved God but that he
loved us and sent his Son to be the expiation for
our sins."   *I John 4:10*
". . . we have an advocate with the Father, Jesus
Christ the righteous; and he is the expiation for
our sins, and not for ours only but also for the sins
of the whole world."   *I John 2:1-2*

I have been reading the Camus novel *The Fall.*[1] That title is
the name of a traditional Christian doctrine, the fall of man, which
many people both inside and outside the Church have rejected as
being either obsolete or an affront to human dignity. The hero-
scoundrel of this novel is Jean-Baptiste Clamence, and his name
also is biblical: John the Baptist, the forerunner of Christ. The
novel itself (it is monologue rather than novel, the various characters being seen only by reflection in the monologue) is a study of
sin. Why should that word come back? It was but recently thrown
on the village dump as a vestige of coercive custom or as a useless
remnant of our childhood fears. Why should it come back through
a French existentialist? The novel keeps talking about God, though

the author might call himself an atheist. It keeps returning to the figure of Christ, not in any devotion, but at least to ask questions. History has strange turns.

I

What was the sin of Jean-Baptiste? He is prototype, and therefore we are really asking what is sin. It is a relief to find that he does not charge it to his parents. Neither does a competent psychiatry. Our home does both bless and disfigure us. Sometimes it so disfigures us as to bring dissociation of mind, and then psychiatric healing is needed. In most cases the home, though it may condition our conduct, does not determine it, or we would have a Calvinism far worse than the doctrine (as usually misunderstood and misconstrued) of Calvin himself. Understanding of the way in which home influences have shaped us has as a main purpose a clearer knowledge of the self-material with which we work. Competent psychiatry moves toward that purpose. Responsibility remains for those who are not insane. It is grace in Jean-Baptiste that he did not deny responsibility.

At first he would not have called himself a sinner. As an eminent lawyer he was ready to give his services to the poor. He was quick to represent in court the unfortunate and the oppressed. He spoke eloquently and not insincerely about freedom and justice. He helped blind men across the street, though not less willingly if there were spectators. He would at once give his seat in a crowded train to an old lady. It could even be said of him that he was not ambitious except in these generosities. Certainly he had no consuming itch for cash or a cheap fame. Our psychology and some of our preachers would have called him a "well-adjusted man."

Then what was his sin? He himself might not have known except for a sequence of events which broke the urbane façade. He was caught in a quarrel in a traffic jam, and the guilty driver struck him while a spectator yelled at him and called him a dope; and Jean-Baptiste brooded for days over the double insult, rehearsing again and again the bludgeoning which he would visit on the culprits if he had the chance. Thus he discovered in himself a *violence of self*. Next, one of his love affairs soured. He was a sophisticate in love: the word for him meant sex adventure in a cultured guise, and he dimly realized that he might be incapable of real love. But when this woman turned from him, he could not bear the rejection but laid renewed siege to her heart, in an affair that had no heart. Thus he discovered in himself a shallow *vanity of self*. Next, as cruelest blow to his self-satisfaction, he noticed a woman standing on a bridge of the river late at night and then heard a thud on the river. If he had jumped at once, he might have rescued her. But he delayed for a fraction of time and stood there telling himself that it was too late now, while her drowning cries came from downstream. Thus he became aware of the *cowardice of self*. The violence, the vanity, and the cowardice of self. What was his sin? Self-centeredness, the pride of the creature, the little sun lamp posing as the sun. That, not some breach of some code, is always the essence of sin.

II

The novel thus confronts us with another question: How to get rid of the self of sin? The novel says in effect that there is no deliverance. With that verdict we may not agree, but its realism has value for both the conventional churchgoer who trusts some little salvation-formula without ever understanding the depth of the human dilemma, and the modern man who trusts his own mind or some unexamined doctrine of "progress." The novel at least shows us how we *cannot* get rid of sin. For instance, it reminds us that we cannot just forget. Jean-Baptiste tried that expedient only to hear mocking laughter (not now a drowning cry) as he crossed a bridge at midnight. Once, from an ocean liner he saw a dark bobbing object far ahead. Surely it could not be . . . ? When the ship overtook it, it was seen to be debris. How foolish of him to imagine it could have been . . . ! Yet he had treated another human being as debris. Memory is a strange affair. How deep is it? As deep as all men's memories, as deep as eternity?

Jean-Baptiste found that he could not will himself into deliverance any more than he could forget his sin. His trouble was "The Fall"—the fall, not from some animal ancestry, for animals are neither cruel nor humane, but the fall into the will itself, the human will that can assert itself against both man and God. The trouble was precisely that he had willed his own self-esteem, to find that thus he could only despise himself. Do we not all say, "Nevertheless not *Thy* will, but mine, be done"? [2] Is not the will crippled by many a failure? Emmanuel Kant rightly held that the only good thing is a good will.[3] But who among us has a good will? There is no refuge in aesthetics, for beauty demands our willed action or it festers. There is no refuge in ethic, for the infirm will (or even the good will) cannot meet the ethical demand, the fulfillment of "all righteousness." We cannot will ourselves into goodness, for the will itself is cleft or vulnerable, and it is marked by failure. We *will* to do evil, as Jean-Baptiste had found.

There is no hint in the novel that the course of history brings deliverance by some vague "progress." The book is too honest to sell out to that nonsense. Once at a lecture at the Grand Canyon, in which the lecturer pointed to the marks of agelong erosion plainly to be seen on the canyon wall, a man sitting behind us exclaimed after the fashion of our time, "Give the race another million years!" He meant presumably that thus and then there would be heaven on earth. Such exclamations are almost sheer euphoria. Leaving aside the ominous possibility that by our misuse of atomic power the race may not have another million hours, what evidence is there that mere flow of time brings deliverance? Time and history bring legacies of bad as well as good, as witness the fact that history is now darkened by the entail of two world wars. If man is free (he will always take some measure of freedom for granted), he can wreck "evolution," and does! Meanwhile what is any Jean-Baptiste to do about "The Fall"? Topsy in *Uncle Tom's Cabin* said: "I never seed dat ar" (ribbon),—"it must 'a got in my sleeve." [4] But she did see it! Don't we all—all the way down history and all the way across it? Total depravity does not mean that anyone is totally depraved, for if anyone were, he would not know himself depraved. It means that history is cankered in every culture and every person, as Jean-Baptiste found life to be cankered.

The novel honestly confronts the predicament of mankind. That is why existentialism may mean more to the Church when the books are balanced than what Baron von Hugel called "little churchinesses." [5] A modern poet has said starkly what Camus is saying:

> I have long since come to the firm and considered conclusion
> That love, all love, all kinds, descriptions, and shapes,
> Is but a mask to hide the brute face of fact,
> And that fact is the immitigable ferocity of self.
>
> .   .   .   .
>
> There's no forgiveness for our being human.

> It is the inexpugnable error. It is
> . . . the one thing we have overlooked
> In our outrageous dreams and cunningest contrivances.[6]

Jean-Baptiste would have agreed with that dread verdict. In his monologue of confession he keeps asking his hearer if there are not disconcerting episodes in *his* life, and knows there are—in every life. Jean-Baptiste is judge-penitent: he is penitent, but in a "ferocity of self" which still took perverted joy in being first even in confession, yet he is judge in that he must always torture himself and other men in condemnation.

III

Then is there "no forgiveness for our being human"? The novel cannot escape the name of God. If "the fall," even if it be no more than a fall into finitude and therefore into inevitable ignorance and anxiety (with accompanying guilt?), is as long as history and as wide as the earth, what other name offers hope? Camus has elsewhere proposed that suicide is a main issue.[7] So it is: suicide— or God—or a stoicism that waits tidings of God. One fact Camus has not grappled. This: Jean-Baptiste had in him a terrifying honesty by which he knew his own mortal sickness. He had some root of purity by which he recognized his stain. Whence that honesty? Whence that purity? When we consider this dual fact in human nature, that a man can be both judge and penitent, we can understand why some ages stress the dignity of man and other ages his "immitigable ferocity of self." Both stresses are valid, for man's life is both misery and grandeur. He walks a narrow line, with one leg in time and its failures and the other leg in eternity and its judgments. The honesty in Jean-Baptiste was the divine "image" in him. That is why any novel must ultimately speak about God. Only God, in history yet above it, can cure history.

We must add, in whatever dimness of mortal sight, that not even God can use a casual cure, nay, God least of all. The violence, vanity, and cowardice of self are not easily healed. They are no trivial hurt, especially the cowardice that betrays a fellow creature because the river is cold at night; and so there can be no trivial deliverance. Camus was a member of the French underground during the German occupation. Through the lips of Jean-Baptiste he tells the horror of that time. Men were held in a strait jacket but with head exposed, so that members of the "new order" could spit on the helpless face; and a German officer would ask a French mother which of her two sons he should shoot because he was about to shoot one of them. This appalling "fall" can know no casual lifting. One theory of atonement pictures Christ on the cross as ransom paid to the devil. We cannot accept the doctrine because Christ fought evil with whatever gentleness of weapons: he did not parley with the foe. Another theory proposes that Christ bought off the wrath of God. That also we cannot accept, for if God is not "in Christ reconciling the world to himself," [8] we would be at a loss to know where to look for God. But these theories at least know that there must be some abysmal sorrow and travail in God before sin can be atoned. Such theologies are far more profound than theories that trust to science or humanitarianism or intelligence or progress. There is no easy forgiveness.

There can be, so we surmise, no distant pardon. The "laws of nature" cannot save us. They condemn as well as save. The drunkard dies of cirrhosis of the liver under the laws of nature. Is salvation of any kind ever "in general"? Is it not always an event? Supposing God is ready and able to save us, could we consent to His salvation, as free beings, unless we see Him busy in our world at the work of deliverance? How else could we be stricken at the heart and cleansed? How else could we say "yes" to His mercy? The only language we know is human language, even though that always carries accents of the beyond-human. If these questions have their pith and point, we are in sight of both Bethlehem and Calvary. Does Bethlehem mean that inasmuch as there can be no distant cure, God has revealed Himself in "the Word . . . made flesh"? Does Calvary mean that here we see, thrust into the forefront of history, the eternal travail of God for our salvation? Such is Christian faith: "God of God, Light of Light . . . who for us men and for our salvation came down from heaven . . . and was made man." [9] Jean-Baptiste says bitterly that Christ must have died in agony to know that at his birth the child-innocents were slaughtered. That comment obviously oversimplifies the issue and raises other questions, more than it answers—if it is an answer. But taking our cue from the comment, should we not say that Christ in agony voluntarily took the burden of every crime and sin: "Father, forgive them; for they know not what they do." [10]

Always the Church must ask: Does Christ have this saving meaning? Always the Church must admit the doubt and always cleave to the faith. It is a faith. But so is the assumption that Christ has no meaning or that he is only one more man making one more guess. Faith in Christ has bred life in the secrecies of the heart as well as in painting and music; the other faith breeds chaos or nothingness. That Russia should trust in what our poet has called "outrageous dreams," and America in "cunningest contrivances" is still a faith, for we cannot escape some faith, since we cannot live by supernal sight. This is Christian faith: "Not that we loved God" (we have loved ourselves) "but that he loved us and sent his Son to be the expiation" (the covering and overwhelming forever) "for our sins; . . . and not for ours only but also for the sins of the whole world," because sin is as long as history and as wide as the planet. A certain picture shows a gap in the sky and in the gap a cross tilted so that the Man on it can look down on all our life on earth.[11] The wood of the cross is still there, and the nails; but the wood now is merged into infinity and the nails have gone clean through the wood into . . . ? Into the Eternal Ground and Heart of Life. That picture is Christian faith; God has thrust Christ against the sharp horizon of history that we may know God's nature and trust His grace.

IV

This expiation gives the one, new, and only motive for our daily life. Jean-Baptiste speaks scornfully of people who liquidate their sins at Calvary. But man is the sickness: he cannot liquidate his sins. Yet if God, through the Calvary-rent in history, has shown us His Love by which our sins are liquidated, that liquidation cannot leave us unchanged. By faith His love must find a channel through us. What strange motives rule us! We must defend our culture, we say; but how can any culture become an ultimate? Or we must establish a "new order." But every order decays. Or we must prove our intelligence. But intelligence is encompassed by mystery, which always thwarts intelligence. Or we must preserve freedom. But the freedom which knows not its own ground is a burden too heavy to be borne. The only motive is to accept ourselves as God has accepted us in Christ and so to accept our neighbors—to return to God the love by which He has loved us, directly in prayer and worship and indirectly by loving His other creatures. We ask, "What's the use of religion?" God does not "use" us, and we may not "use" Him. The "use" is to save us from the utilitarian blasphemy of asking, "What's the use of religion?"

This novel moves around the edges of a doctrine of redemption. The four Camus novels when read in their sequence seem to show an author in pilgrimage. This novel is certainly "not far from the kingdom." [12] There is the title: *The Fall*. There is the name of the hero: Jean-Baptiste. There is the picture, a stolen picture once on a time, *The Adoration of the Lamb*, depicting the judges of the earth riding, riding to that adoration, since judgment ceases even to be judgment unless it is held in love. There is repeated reference to the " circle of hell," manifestly a Dante term for that region from which the pilgrim found his way to the "circle of heaven." There is, besides, a symbolism that is the very pain of beauty and truth. Jean-Baptiste went to live near Amsterdam. Was it to suit his despair—a flat land, a flat ocean, a flat sky, a shrouding mist rolling in, so a man could not know which was land or ocean or sky because for judge-penitents all landmarks disappear? But Jean-Baptiste tells us that he sometimes imagines that far up in the sky there are millions of white doves. Why that imagining? Is it that one day they may cover our bloodstained earth with white and gentle wings? "The Adoration of the Lamb," and now, "The Descent of the Dove"! Does Camus dimly see that there is Grace encompassing our disfigured history? By his stark honesty he has helped us to see it as we make the "leap of faith": "In this is love, not that we loved God but that he loved us and sent his Son to be the expiation for our sins" —"and not for ours only but also for the sins of the whole world."

24

OUR TIMES AND THE RESURRECTION

(An Easter Sermon)

> "But in fact Christ has been raised from the dead,
> the first fruits of those who have fallen asleep."
>
> *I Cor. 15:20*

There is gain of realism in our present crisis, for now not even we who live in America can evade the fact of death. Death obtrudes, in war's grim harvest, in highway traffic that becomes a shambles, and ominously in our monkeying with atomic holocaust. A magazine article suggests that we are unmoved. Unmoved? Morals are in the discard, nervous ills multiply, and the rush to gather the flowers of life before they die has become a stampede in which both men and flowers are crushed. All this because we are "living beyond our means" in much more than money. Oscar Wilde once said pathetically that he was "dying . . . beyond my means," [1] and that may be the deeper reason for our frenzy. We cannot now evade death, and we have no faith in which to face it.

I

There is a further gain in realism: we know in our apocalyptic time the hollowness of proposed substitutes for Christian faith.

We have been advised to live for the "progress of the race." The phrase never carried conviction. Can there be infinite progress in a finite world? Or any guarantee of progress if men are free? Is not the phrase callous in any event: a proposal that each vital person shall be manure to fertilize the planet for an abstraction called the "race" which never arrives? But now the counsel becomes non-sensical as well as dubious and callous, for if a bomb falls, the "race" may end. To use race-track parlance, it may end because all the human horses have been scratched. What then becomes of our pretty phrase about the "immortality of the race" or its companion phrase about the "immortality of influence"? The Bible does not evade the word "death." The Bible knows that finite history can have no permanence.

Other goals such as the "ongoing of the truth" are now adrift on the same sea of atomic threat and man's perversity. What truth? Not our dull factualisms, the new scientific discoveries which all live by eating their parents. Not practical truth in science, which now threatens us with the last curtain. How do you suppose the ongoing of truth would fare in the air mass from a cobalt bomb? If someone says that it might fare well in a world beyond this world, the retort is: "Of course: that is now a crucial issue." Is personality precious? We become aware of the "race" and the "truth" and "values" only in and through the vitalities of personal life. Is the person worth-ful? Not if at death he is snuffed out like a cheap candle. That is the issue. An honest agnosticism or even a stoic hopelessness is better than hopes which, despite their pretentious phrases, are anchored to a doomed planet.

II

Let us specify Christian faith in resurrection. It is not mere continuance of this present life. Of that continuance we grow weary even in this world. Hopes always partly mocked, spurts of true fire always doused by evil habit, the day of peace always eclipsed by some new war? Men might soon welcome death in such a world:

> For men must work, and women must weep,
> And the sooner it's over the sooner to sleep,
> And good-bye to the bar and its moaning.[2]

The findings of the Society for Psychical Research bring double dismay: that loved ones should visit us through mediums previously unknown to them and us seems an outrage on love's intimacies; and furthermore, the heaven described is not heaven, but only a drearier extension of this earth with a drearier chitchat and even less consequential doings. Resurrection is precisely *not* the "wages of going on," [3] but the lifting of personal life into a new dimension of light and power. It is resurrection. It is the harvest field, not the continuance of seed in the bin.

By the same token resurrection is not the "immortality of the soul." A man is not a "soul." He is, in our jargon, a psychosomatic unity—psyche-soma, self-body in indivisible paradox. The body is not a prison from which the "soul" escapes at death: it is an essential term in psyche-body selfhood. That is why the creeds speak about the "resurrection of the body," [4] which means, not the revival of bones and muscles or the resuscitation of the flesh, but just what it says—the raising of personhood, in both terms of the paradox, into a new dimension of life, better than our present life as our present life is better than its prenatal prelude. So a gulf is set between Christian faith on the one hand, and on the other, those faiths which, like the Gnosticism against which the New Testament always does battle, promise "absorption into the universal Soul." Absorption is not life: it is retrogression from the vivid personal into the vague and abstract impersonal.

III

Then how and why may we honorably hope in resurrection? The inner evidence is in the structure of our personal life; the outer evidence, meeting the inner evidence as light meets the eye, is in Jesus Christ. As for the inner evidence, we are even now in an eternal order from which we view our mortal life with "compassion and new eyes." [5] The scientist bridles at the word "supernatural," and such are the arbitrary meanings which the religious man sometimes pins on the word, as if "supernatural" meant an alien meteor falling on green fields, that the scientist cannot always be blamed. But whenever the scientist says the "order of nature," he has taken his stance beyond that order and thus is himself "supernatural," above nature. Already we know the disfigurements of our mortal life. Already we sense that it *is* mortal. Already we are in a shining land. Already we are aware that here we have no abiding country, and that our citizenship is in heaven.[6] This prime fact is the beachhead in us by which God in Christ makes His gracious invasion.

As for the outer evidence, the resurrection of Christ, the gospel record is not a scientific manual in rigid "consistencies": it is a rapture, from this man and this man, which exclaims: "Our sun is risen in the west!"[7] It is not a law-court transcript with exact items of time and place: time and place are "lost in wonder, love, and praise."[8] The accounts agree in essentials. For one thing, they agree that this was an act of God: "Now has Christ *been raised* from the dead" . . . "whom God hath raised."[9] Man of himself could never have wrought this deliverance. Thus the presence of angels in the resurrection stories, as in the William Blake picture which shows their wings meeting over the broken body of Jesus,[10] not only to shield him but to point upward to heaven's imminent mighty act. For another thing, the accounts agree that Christ confronted his disciples: they did not conjure up a fiction of a happy ending. If they previously believed in resurrection, we do not know. If a crucified man, crucifixion being a curse, could by their faith bless anyone by his "return," we cannot tell. All the stories show them taken unawares by One who arrested them in their sadness. For another thing, the accounts agree that the event, whatever its objective form and subjective daybreak, changed the lives of Christ's friends from cowardice to valor, from self-seeking to life in his love, from small views to the mighty vistas of resurrection. This redemption was *done* in them—by the *deed* of God in triumph over death in Christ.

Today we have the testimony of both the New Testament and the Church. As for the Book, it was not written by men who took refuge in illusions. To such an interpretation, popular in our time, they would say again: "Why stand we in jeopardy every hour"[11] of our lives? They were not such fools as to face hunger and crucifixion for an imagining or an idle tale. Moreover, they were not liars: they called Christ "the Truth," and made resolve to "speak the truth in love,"[12] so that they became a bastion of truth in an evil-speaking time. They wrote the New Testament without any "in memoriam" line. Men quote it now, even men without faith, as a fount of wisdom, and newspapers print from it the "text for the day." But the wisdom is rooted in the surety that Christ had been raised from the dead. Maybe the wisdom will vanish unless we cleave to that faith. *As for the Church,* it is not a funeral-benefit society, and its hymns are not dirges round a grave. How has it endured? In cannibal islands it should have been swallowed. Its secret is not in numbers, for often it has been the persecuted minority; nor in power, for its foes have had the swords and the thrones; nor in the righteousness of its members, for they have again and again led their Lord to some new Calvary. Then? It began and has continued as the Body of Christ, indwelt by his regnant and present Spirit.

IV

But we should be quick to admit that faith in resurrection, Christ's and ours, is still a faith. Why should we shrink from that admission? The New Testament does not shrink. The beckonings of God are just that—beckonings, not bludgeonings, not batteries of irrefutable "evidence," not the tyranny of unanswerable logic. Always there is freedom for our choosing and response. One item about the resurrection of Jesus has sometimes been overlooked: he showed himself after death only to those who loved him. He did not "appear" in Pilate's palace, for empire politics give him no welcome; nor in the High Priest's court, for churchly pride leaves him no room; nor in the market place, for money-itch is not reverence. Easter sermons must not be overpreached, and their "proofs" should never overprove, for God's beckonings are always by hint and gleam, lest we be coerced. Do we love Him? Are we ready to follow at some risk? Then we shall know some quickening of His Spirit. He will "find" us from beyond death. On the Western Front the fighting stopped on Easter Day, and Easter greetings, amplified across no man's land, replaced the noise of bombs. Then men knew the Easter truth. But the next day bombs fell again, and the Easter truth again grew dim. So we look now at the response. It is just below the surface of the phrase "the first fruits of those who have fallen asleep." [13]

"The first fruits": Christ himself has made response in his obedience. By ancient Israelitish law a farmer brought to the Temple the first sheaf of harvest, and the priest there "waved it before the Lord" as token that the whole field and the farmer himself were now dedicate to God. Christ is the first sheaf of our humanity in the new age. Through him we are now all of us dedicate. We are not our own, though in stubborn will we may still try to act as if we were, for Christ has offered himself as "first fruits" of the whole harvest field of history and of every man at work in the field. The sheaf itself is promise of new seed for a new harvest. "God gives it a body as he has chosen, and to each kind of seed its own body." [14] Here is no vague "immortality of the soul," as if each human life were like each other, as if persons were indistinguishable drops of water sinking at last into some abstract and impersonal ocean. No, each seed is different, and each is precious; and though each must die, each is "not quickened, except it die," [15] and each is changed into the new dimension of harvest "from glory to glory." [16] Thus the whole of our life has already been offered to God in dedication.

The "first fruits": we may dedicate our life within the dedication which Christ has already made. Not our "soul" only, for we are not soul: we are body-psyche, and the body is as holy a term in the paradox of person as is the psyche. Our lathes and our notebooks are to be dedicate, our laboratories and our stores, our food and our homes, our weddings and our funerals. The clothes we wear are now not our own: they also are "first fruits." Thus the custom of new clothes at Easter time. You find it in *Romeo and Juliet*: "Didst thou not fall out with a tailor for wearing his new doublet before Easter?" [17] The festival has too profound a meaning to excuse any casual mind, even in regard to clothes—or to anything else that is part of a worthy life on earth:

> At Easter let your clothes be new
> Or else be sure you will it rue.[18]

Let everything else be new, because God has raised Christ from the dead, as first fruits of all who live and die on earth.

Even if we fail to choose God's Easter beckoning in glad response to His grace, we cannot get rid of Easter. Soon or late we must come to terms with the Resurrection. The Mosque of St. Sophia in Istanbul was originally a Christian church, though the Christian symbols and inscriptions have been overlaid. A visitor noticed, as he stood under the great dome, that a picture of the ascendant Christ, his arms outstretched in blessing, was showing through the covering paint; and the visitor exclaimed, almost despite himself, "He is coming back. You cannot blot him out"! [19] If you wish to prophesy, with some chance of success, in a world which seems to falsify all man's guesses, prophesy that Christ will come back when the cruel simplification of Communism, the greedy self-entanglements of capitalism, and the dull average of socialism have all been forgotten. Even if men fail the Easter beckoning, God in the present Spirit of Jesus will not fail us.

V

Our Times and the Resurrection! We have placed our faith in human leadership. So Hitler's "new order" has ended in Buchenwald. We have trusted in science to make a "brave new world," so it now poses an atomic threat. Now we know that the "progress of the race" may prove to be a vast incineration. The second law of thermodynamics, if man's calculations are correct (we do not know), may bring a day when this planet, by discharge of heat energy, may be too cold to sustain life. Our poor humanisms falter on the edge of an icy wilderness. The "immortality of influence" in such a world is a mockery and a mirage.

Now our jibes about Christian faith die on our lips. "One world at a time" [20] no longer makes sense, for we dimly realize that the two worlds are not in chronological sequence: the one world lives within the Other, and this world becomes a prison unless held within eternal sanctions. "Pie in the sky by and by" is an even cheaper jibe in a generation that has seen millions of men killed in war. Besides, the Sky is already in us: we know space and time for what they are only by means of a dimension of life beyond space and time.

The central issue is—God and the worth of personality. If all men die, and that is the end of them, there can be no "progress of the race." Personality then is not precious: it is a dreary path to final death. The honor of God is also at stake, for He is not God if His Kingdom on earth is an endless cemetery. There remains for our choice and loyalty *either* a stoic agnosticism which lives in some blind trust in decency, *or* faith in the resurrection. The woman who broke her crucifix exclaimed pathetically: "Now I shall have to trust in God alone!" But He has always been man's only trust; and "this shall be a sign":[21] the life, death, and resurrection of Jesus Christ.

VI

Our world is dark and frantic; and it would appear that if history continues, it will be in spite of human leaders, not because of them. There are few gleams of political hope. But then, hope never was political. Its only ground is God, who raised Christ from the dead, "the first fruits of those who have fallen asleep." We would never have learned the vastness of the universe if night had not come. Perhaps our present darkness will reveal providences and powers in God which otherwise we could not have known. Bombs may fall, but God does not fall. History may end, but God never ends. So we choose now a faith for our times. We choose Jesus and the resurrection, and thus we shall know that "everything matters, nothing matters." "Everything matters," in glad obedience; "nothing matters," because nothing can thwart the love and power of God.

25

BABEL AND PENTECOST

(*A Whitsuntide Sermon*)

> God said: "Come, let us go down, and there con-
> fuse their language, that they may not understand
> one another's speech."   *Gen. 11:7*
> The men of Pentecost said: "And how is it that we
> hear, each of us in his own native language?"
>   *Acts 2:8*

The world traveler marvels at the babel of tongues. How could hundreds of languages ever have come from what must have been at the beginning a few instinctive sounds and gestures? He realizes, perhaps for the first time, that international relationships are crossed and cut by Chinese walls of speech. How are these walls to be leveled or set with gates? Is Esperanto the answer? Or will one language, let us say English or French, finally prevail? Or will Babel continue to the end of history? World friendship must climb many barriers. Not the least is this "confusion of tongues."

The book of Genesis has an etiological story (nice fat word for a myth which explains the cause or origin of something) which purports to tell how and why our babel of modern languages began.[1] This Hebrew myth has apparently been conflated with a Babylonian myth, for the word "Babel" is a shortened form of

Babylon, which here represents man's pride in his own exploits. Thus pride is proposed as the direct cause of man's confusion of tongues. "That is not the cause," says some student of linguistics. Perhaps not. But pride causes a worse babel. So we look at the fascinating story.

I

A word is in order about story and myth as the vehicle of truth. Our scientific age takes for granted that truth is best found and shared by argument and proposition, but we could be wrong. Such a method cannot bridge the generations, Abraham's generation and ours, because science and its formulas are in continuous change. It cannot bridge different temperaments in any given generation, an artist's temperament and that of a chemical engineer, for it leaves the artist cold. It cannot stir in us the awareness of God, for God is not a theorem to be proved or an object to be analyzed. But story is a universal language. It conveys truth where a syllogism or an equation must fall. What we call "modern knowledge" is always truncated. Jesus spoke in parables, and "indeed he said nothing to them without a parable." [2] We should not dismiss myths (of Asgard or Olympus or the book of Genesis) as "primitive," for they may be both universal and profound. So to this dramatic myth of the Tower of Babel.

II

Men knew that God was "up there" above "that inverted Bowl they call the Sky," [3] and that we humans are "down here" in a very finite earth. But men were not content with their low estate. They wished to be gods. Don't we—always? So they said: "Come, let us build ourselves a city, and a tower with its top in the heavens, and let us make a name for ourselves . . . ." [4] This virus of pride (man's resolve to build his own paradise) was aided and abetted by another virus—or are the two only different types of one bug?— anxiety-fear. They instinctively feared the hazards of their earth-born lot: ". . . lest we be scattered abroad upon the face of the whole earth." [5] They meant lest they should be defenseless against ravening beasts and the lonely dark, against storm and death. Thus they sought both security and fame. They trusted their own god-like ambition and self-confident skill. They began to build a tower that would reach to the plaque of sky, so that they could clamber over the edge of heaven and seize God's throne. God knew their thoughts and let them build for a while. Then He looked down over the rim of the sky and pushed aside their tower with scarcely a move of His hand. He demolished their city, and for punishment He laid on them the confusion of many languages.

What happens to us when we read the story, which may well have been both history and myth? We pooh-pooh this "outmoded three-story world of the Bible." We laugh at these "childish, prescientific pictures which Christians accept." Then we sell out to the really ridiculous myth of "inevitable progress" and "man's invincible mind." Then we may or may not realize that *our* myths are written in Babel-pride. Then we may suddenly say to ourselves that *our* towers *have* fallen, by bombs in Berlin and London and Hiroshima; and that confusion *has* come upon *us*, worse than any confusion of languages, so much worse that we cannot understand one another—democracy meaning one thing in Russia and almost the opposite thing in the United States. Then not knowing what to do with an atomic threat which we ourselves have fashioned, we wonder and wonder at God's word in an old story: "Nothing that they propose to do will now be impossible for them." [6] Then we decorate our cities with the ominous word "Shelter," even while we know that there is no hiding place. "These childish, prescientific pictures!"

No need to point the moral of the history-myth of the Tower of Babel. It points itself at sword point. But we should confront elemental facts about human nature. Man is a creature. His life is contingent, derived, dependent, and even though he is a center of freedom, the freedom is always within an ordained destiny. His intelligence trips over the unpredictable and bumps into walls of mystery. His passing days are under the sovereignty of a seeming impassive sky, and he cannot climb the sky. Yet he is never content to sink into the earth. If he tries to be an animal, he is worse than an animal; if he tries to be an angel, he is a grotesque and arrant fake. So his little planet is littered with ruined towers, pyramids made pathos by time's erosion, obelisks crumbling in desert sand, empires that now are but the rumor of a name.

> Imperious Caesar, dead and turn'd to clay,
> Might stop a hole to keep the wind away.[7]

There is a modern version:

> The great God Ra whose shrine once covered acres
> Is filler now for cross-word puzzle makers.[8]

Meanwhile in our confusion India does not understand America, and London does not understand the Middle East. Have we yet learned what chaos comes of human pride?

III

So let us look at another history-story, this one at the New Testament end of the Bible. It may save us from the folly of saying, "The Third *Reich* will last a thousand years," or "There will always be an England," or, "America, God's country." Yes, Pentecost is myth in certain elements, as well as history; and without much doubt, it was written with the Genesis myth in mind. But that fact heightens rather than lowers its value as a vehicle of truth. It is better than a syllogism or a formula and far more true than *our* myth of the purity-impartiality of man's mind. Most of us know something about Pentecost. The followers of Jesus were huddled in an upper room after tragic Calvary. They were there to await his word, the story tells us, they being now strangely persuaded that he was not dead but alive beyond death. They prayed to the Abyss of Mystery, as all men must pray, yet to the Abyss now made luminous and intent in Jesus Christ. Suddenly a terror and a rapture! There swept down on them "as it were" (notice the language of symbol) a tempest! "Tempest" is a favorite Bible metaphor for the inrush of God's Spirit: it winnowed the grain of reality from their well-loved chaff. There fell on them "as it were" ("like" or "as of" in acknowledged symbolism) a wave of fire! "Fire" is a favorite Bible metaphor for God's judgment-purity which rids us of our dross. The wave of fire divided so that a tongue of flame rested on each praying head. Babel was canceled! For each man, a Scythian let us say, heard every other man speaking in the Scythian tongue!

We cannot honestly deny either the mythological factors in the history-story or the stanch historical event. We should not blink that repeated "as it were." Moreover "speaking in tongues" [9] was a portent in the early Church. "Glossolalia" is the Greek word, the sound of which is index to the meaning: frenzied, ecstatic mumblings and exclamations of supercharged emotionalism in the religious field. One of the thousand unsolved problems of Bible study is the apparently naïve way in which the Pentecost story deals with glossolalia. As to the ability of a Persian or an Egyptian to speak instantly in the Scythian language, which language until that moment he had not understood and could not speak, the New Testament nowhere suggests that such a power was afterward employed. In fact there was no need for it, for *koine* Greek was already spoken as a common language across the New Testament Middle East. The Pentecost event is given to us partly in story form: the list of countries is taken in proper order as the writer checked a map of the Mediterranean. Why should we shy away from the symbolic elements in the Pentecost account? Symbolism can build a bridge between the generations, between man and man in differences of temperament, and between man and God. History-myth is still the best language vehicle of truth.

What truth? The truth regarding the gift which cancels the confusions of Babel. Man's self-centeredness, which builds a tower of pride and thus invites division and destruction, is melted as by fire in the gift of the Spirit of Christ. The Cross had shown the Pentecost men, as it shows us, the end result of the perfidy of man's ambition: pride so darkens judgment that the holy community in Jerusalem betrayed Christ and reckoned it as the service of God. What, then, were Pentecost men to do? God had apprehended them to make them sure that Christ had triumphed over death. That event was not illusionary comfort: it was both cauterizing judgment and arresting love. What were they to do? Nothing now to do but to give themselves to the Spirit of Christ, who by death had revealed their own ignorance and shame, who by resurrection had triumphed over the utmost conspiracy of man's wickedness. Thus they prayed at Pentecost. Then the tempest and the fire. Within the elements of myth there is history so stanch that Pentecost, originally a harvest festival in temple faith, centuries old, now became by revolutionary change the birthday of the Church. A lovely old story [10] tells of a city that was to be built by music. One man tried to build it by his harp, another by his trumpet; and all of them failed until all played in symphony. But with all honor to a lovely tale, it moves only on the surface. Togetherness is not enough: the crowding of our brokennesses cannot save us. We need the gift of Music, and the Leader, and the Tempest, and the Fire.

IV

Our present world stands irresolute between Babel and Pentecost. It knows dimly that man's pride and skill have somehow miscarried, but has not yet turned in the surrender of prayer to God in Christ. We confront the ruined confusion of our world. The Crystal Palace,[11] we recall, was built as a monument to enduring peace because, so men then imagined, man by the wisdom of his mind had come to know that war is folly and by the strength of his will had turned from war; but, we recall again, the Crystal Palace burned, though made of glass and steel; and under Hitler's bombers in a later time half of London burned. We realize that our tower has fallen. Vaguely we know that worship of our own work is first idolatry and then demonism. But we have not yet come to a new Pentecost. In this tardiness of indecision the Church is not without blame, for the Church also has trusted in its own mind and its own systems. The gospel has been offered, here and there and in many places, in coercive creed and a worse moralism. Thus a college man described the God he had met in church: "A little railroad station, Victorian and moldering, at the end of a branch line." Beneath our lip service to that poor kind of faith Buchenwald lurked. So our world stands irresolute between Babel and Pentecost. Babel we begin to disown; Pentecost we do not yet understand.

There is need of a new Pentecost. Our phrase is, "We need a new spirit," as if there were a choice and assortment of spirits, whereas for man's solace and strength there is only God's Spirit. Perhaps the new art, despite its sour sharpness, has turned unwittingly toward God. It knows that our formalized art is too tepid for an apocalyptic time and too blind to the demonic-tragic in man's life; and it sees that symbolism, not photograph, is the universal language. The new music also, offending our urbane ears, has honest dissonances and percussions, though its discords are not yet resolved. The New Pentecost cannot ever set *Jesus* anywhere but at the center of devotion. Bethlehem is the answer to our longing to see the Face of God. Calvary is both the interpretation of our sufferings and the apocalypse of God's grace redeeming our sins. Easter is our hope in death's blank misgiving. He abides as history's fount of inspiration, the wellspring of life in each succeeding generation. "The night has a thousand eyes," *His*

200

"day but one." [12] The New Pentecost will not eschew *prayer*: it could not, even if it would. A man must confess his blundering pride, if he would live, as an abscess must be lanced. A man cannot reach God by any tower he can build and cannot ever devise his own heaven, but he is not content with earth and so must live by heaven's light and power, else he will make the realm of nature an unnatural hell. Thus the New Pentecost can come only on those who pray, for both themselves and their world, that God's Spirit may be given. The New Pentecost cannot come without the *Church*, a new Church in every age, yet always springing from the old Church, as the old Church sprang from the Christ-Event, whose Spirit is ever new because Eternal; the Church always blundering in human pride and always redeemed as being the Body of Christ. No man can live an atomized life: he lives by community. But every community fails unless—unless it is indwelt of God:

> There is no life that is not in community,
> And no community not lived in praise of GOD.[13]

Yet the New Pentecost cannot sell out either to obscurantism, such as the doctrine of a literally infallible Bible that would make the "word of God of none effect";[14] or to scientism, which would make even God a theorem to be argued or an object to be studied; or to moralism, which would imprison life in a censorious "thou shalt not." It will honor honest atheism, the kind which is sad because it is atheism, as itself a form of faith; yet it will call men to the venture in Christ "in scorn of consequence." And always its life will be grounded in prayer and love.

V

So two stories, compounded of history and symbol, and our world halting between them. We are horrified by Babel, for we see what desolations human pride has made in the earth, but we still half believe that we can build our tower to heaven; yet we long for Pentecost, for the winnowing of the Tempest and the cleansing of the Fire, and sometimes we are almost ready to pay the price. Almost we ask directions to the Upper Room, where once men prayed and then knew the Storm that drove away the chaff of life and the Fire which purged them of their dross. Where is our Upper Room? Years spent in university study can be the Upper

Room: there are walls round Harvard Yard. The silence in which a man hears a sermon or reads a book may be the Upper Room; the church service—this church service—may be the Upper Room, for both the group and the individual, for once the corporate fire became a flame resting on each head. So we wait for the promise: ". . . before many days you shall be baptized with the Holy Spirit." [15]

26

DIMENSION OF DEPTH

> "Deep calls to deep at the thunder of thy cataracts."
> Ps. 42:7

Imagine a man who has never left his village. Once I actually met him—in England. Far from feeling impoverished, he derided people who scurry over the face of the earth. There was not much to see, he hinted, and almost nothing to learn. Here is another man, the man of this psalm. We know about him, though not his name. He was in exile "because of the oppression of the enemy." [1] He yearned for the still and surging heart of public worship in the homeland: "I went with them to the house of God, with the voice of joy and praise." [2] He had suffered for his faith: "All thy waves and thy billows have gone over me." [3] The place of exile was near the twin peaks of Hermon, a wild mountain country where the River Jordan takes its rise. He would wake at night to hear cataracts sounding in tremendous antiphon from their fastnesses of rock. Sense of the terror and mystery of life overwhelmed him: "Deep calls to deep at the thunder of thy cataracts." This is not the parochial life. This is a wider horizon than the village pump.

I

Now: I propose to you that our civilization has become our village, and that we are afraid to leave it. Civilization is electrically lighted (we forget that our nearby light comes from a cosmic furnace called the sun); it is hygienic and policed. It is graphed, charted, and understood—with cultivated fields crossed by paved roads. At one end of the village street is the hospital in which we are born; at the other end, the hospital in which we die. Not only do we brag about never having left the village, but we insist that there isn't anything else: there is no truth beyond our slide-rule tests.

Auguste Comte, who is still quoted in our humanisms, argued that we have progressed from religious mythology (he used the word with a lift of the eyebrows), through the abstractions of philosophy, to the certainties of logic and science.[4] The fallacy in the description is the word "progressed." Progressive shallowing is not progress; and we have no right to assume, under euphoric words such as "evolution," that flow of time necessarily means enrichment of mind. For myself, I do not find in Buchenwald, or in the inanities of our advertising, Exhibit A of an evolving nobility. In any event the cataracts of God thunder round our village. Our patterned days are encompassed in mystery. "Deep calls to deep," and brave men do not shrink from exile beneath the twin peaks of Hermon.

II

Instance? The deeps before birth call to the deeps beyond death. We pretend that birth and death are only natural process. We dare not go beyond this hospital and that hospital at either end of the village street. We foresee a day when biochemistry may be able to create human life. If we so succeed, and the human life we create has no power to view itself, if it has no dimension above life, the hordes of merely naturalistic men may destroy us; and if, on the other hand, the life we create is genuine life, we have but done after painful centuries what the mystery of life has already done in us. Besides, and this is the thunder of the cataracts, we know that space and time are limits. Why were we born? For what purpose are we in life? What is beyond the limits of birth? Biochemistry cannot tell us, though its gifts may ameliorate our village life. For that we are grateful. To Whom? To Life—and isn't that a strange friendship? Why do *we* purpose things? We do, and cannot help it. What purpose has flowed into us from the Before-birth?

As for death, it is not a natural event. Cows die, but men "have to die," [5] and that is just the difference. Cows do not weep when cows die, but men weep when men die. Jung said that he found that faith in an afterlife brought healing to his patients.[6] Well might he say it! If frustration thwarts personality, as all psychiatrists would agree, death is the final and invincible frustration, unless . . . . Unless! What *is* beyond that mystery of death? We decry faith, but perhaps faith is the only language by which we can converse with encompassing Mystery, since every country has its own language. As we crossed beyond the Rockies a few weeks ago, the train stopped near a tiny desert town, and almost the only green spot in the neighborhood was—a cemetery. Why do we keep *that* green? You would wish it kept green if someone you deeply loved was buried there.

So we salute the deeps that call from beyond birth and beyond death. We surround birth and death with what we call "religious ceremonies." Dimly we realize that our village called "Civilization" is still fed from hidden mountains and the vast sky. Always we shall ask about the two beyonds. If we do not ask, we shall soon begin to fear, and then we shall fall on one another in insensate strife. What does the Mystery require of us, in any war for an instance? The Bible is a great Book, all other books but little adjectives to its vast noun, because it says: "From everlasting to everlasting thou art God." [7] The words mean "from hidden time to hidden time," namely, the beyond-history. Jesus acted as slave to his followers, washing the road dust from their feet, and John's Gospel gives the reason: "Jesus, knowing . . . that he had come from God and was going to God, . . . girded himself with a towel . . . ." [8] "Deep calls to deep at the thunder of thy cataracts." *Thy* cataracts!

III

Can you stand more of the thunder? Then the deep beyond the stars calls to the deep below the mind. What is beyond the range of our telescopes? What is beyond the limit of space? We do not always ask: often we prefer to live in the neat measurements or neater logic of the village. We try so to live, but we cannot. That is why we have telescopes; that, not because we hope ultimately to subdivide the stars. We try to live an earth-bound life, and because we have come to no terms with that Beyond, our space-man-fiction is often in terms of terror, and an Orson Welles broadcast sends multitudes into the streets frantic for fear of the arrival of men from Mars.[9] We try to live the village life, so astrology flourishes: we surrender freedom to the supposed governance of some planet under which we are born. It would seem fairly clear that we are born under all of them, and under the Beyond-space. Christian faith says: "Nor height, nor depth, . . . shall be able to separate us from the love of God, which is in Christ Jesus our Lord" [10]—"height" there meaning the highest point reached by any star, and "depth" there meaning the abyss from which stars take their rise.

As for the deeps below the mind, Freud, whose benefactions go far beyond his theories, perhaps to point us at last to the faith which he reckoned "illusion," [11] has taught us that below the conscious mind with its neat criteria there is a vast subconscious. He seems to describe it as a dubious realm: fears and repressions and early coercions sway us from below that threshold.[12] Whence then the good in life, the Freudian honesty? That also rests on the hidden realm, on the racial unconscious as well as on the individual subconscious. So we begin to explore that depth. Perhaps that quest is a next great departure in psychology. Jung has made a beginning: the mythologies which Comte tried to laugh out of court are, he suggests, the archetypes of the subconscious.[13] The myth of Pandora's box, or the Genesis story of the Garden of Eden with its tree of knowledge and the snake and man's impious desire to be as God, adumbrate the hidden structures of man's deepest mind.

So we salute these two mysteries, the mystery beyond the stars and the mystery below the mind. Once more the Bible offers language which the village cannot speak: "He healeth the broken in heart. . . . He telleth the number of the stars." [14] Or again: "Search me, O God, and know . . . my thoughts," [15] since we cannot know them. We can speak to the planet by slide rule: we speak to the mysteries by faith. So Jesus said: "Swear not . . . by the earth; for it is his footstool." [16] From beyond space God rests His feet on the cosmos! What then of His mind? As for the deeps of *our* mind, Jesus said: "Ye know not what manner of spirit ye are of." [17] That abyss of good and evil cannot be sounded by us, except . . . . Except what? Not by any village strategy! Our electrically lighted civilization still draws its power from a vast hinterland. Our batteries are still charged by the sun, and the sun is in the thunders of the cosmos, and the cosmos . . . ? "Deep calls to deep"!

IV

We have not yet spoken of the deepest deeps: The deeps of God's judgments call to the deeps of man's agony and joy. "Thy judgments are like the great deep." [18] There the word "judgments" does not mean punishments: it means all God's acts whether of brightness or darkness. Who can understand them? Nobody, if by "understand" we mean logically construe. The proper language now is not village arithmetic but the mighty language of faith or, if you will, the venture and pain of man's deepest spirit. We were told as we crossed the Atlantic: this is where the "Titantic" sank. Why should the "Titanic" sink, majestic liner on its maiden voyage? It is easy to curse God. But that tragedy had its glory. The ship's band played hymns as the waters gathered! In the novel *Of Human Bondage* the lad argues from his clubfoot to a demonism in the universe [19]—a demonism or a nothingness; but Helen Keller does not so argue from her blindness, deafness, and dumbness; and if she had, Harvard would not have given her a degree, and fourteen thousand people would not have leapt to their feet as one man to greet her. [20] There is no neat explanation of God's judgments. Somewhere is the story of a man asking the Russian novelist Tolstoy how God can be good when there are cholera germs, and of Tolstoy looking at him aghast and saying, "Don't be flippant!" [21] Dimly below the mystery of God's judgments we see a dimension of life and an ultimate justice—or glory—which shames our petty schemes.

Meanwhile there are deeps of joy and agony in our life. Sex? Students come for counsel in that regard and really need none, for they say two things in one breath: first, sex is only natural, and when you're hungry you eat; and second, it doesn't seem right to tinker and tamper with the specifics of the origins of the mysteries of life. Then I say, "So?" I am tempted to say: "So you must judge this from the village street or from the encompassing mystery." But that would be to rob a fellow human of freedom of decision. Therefore I say "So?" But what agony! Agony of decision in an ambiguous world, agony of sorrow when a friend dies, agony of guilt when we do tamper with primal mysteries, agony and glory of trying to live in a time-bound earth beneath an eternal constraint. So the deep in us calls to the deep of His unsearchable judgments.

That is why we worship and look for signs of what that Deep is saying to our deep. We worship because there is a great gulf between our space and time and His Beyond space and time. How can space methods ever hope to get beyond space? By the step after step of human learning? You do not go step by step across an ocean or even across a gulf, much less up the steeps of the Sky. Adding together fragments of time will never sum up eternity. But perhaps His Deep wills to stoop to our deep, "in great humility." Eternity can reach time when time cannot reach eternity. Has He stooped in a man who was the "Servant in the House," [22] who came down the backstairs at Bethlehem, lest he blind us by excess of light; who answered our agony of guilt by bearing it; whose resurrection is no neat little comfort but the pain of a new dimension of life, a bringing us to the end of our mortal village street to see a strange, unknown land, so that his first followers at the resurrection were "afraid"? The proof of Jesus is that great deeps sound in him. There is no explanation of pain and sin and death: there is simply Calvary. "Deep calls to deep": the judgments of God, the thunder of His cataracts, call across the void to the deeps in us; and we call back to Him—in a da Vinci canvas, in a Bach *B Minor Mass,* in this morning's worship.

V

The Bible therefore in echoing thunder: "Can you find out the deep things of God? Can you find out the limit of the Almighty? The heights of heaven—what can you do? Deeper than Sheol— what can you know?" [23] Or again: "O the depth of the riches and wisdom and knowledge of God! How unsearchable are his judgments and how inscrutable his ways! . . . For from him and through him and to him are all things. To him be glory forever." [24] Or again: "For I am persuaded, that neither death, nor life, . . . nor things present, nor things to come, nor height, nor depth, nor any other creature, shall be able to separate us from the love of

God, which is in Christ Jesus our Lord." [25] That Love is a fierce, deep, and awful Abyss.

The university needs the Church to keep the dimension of depth. Beyond our careful sciences and clever "ologies"—Mystery. Beyond our patterned days and the blank misgiving of death—Mystery. Beyond our neon-lighted civilization and our biochemical explanations—Mystery. Beyond the height of the sky and the depth of the mind—Mystery. Our real life is there, not here: the Mystery governs us as sky and earth govern a village street. "Knowing that . . . he had come from God and was going to God," [26] "from everlasting to everlasting," [27] He lived—how? In such encompassing mystery "it is not in man . . . to direct his steps." [28] Therefore we pray.

VI

So either we choose to live in our hygienically conditioned village called Civilization, or we risk exile under the twin peaks of Hermon where at night we wake in fear and wonder and prayer, while "deep calls to deep." There are atheists in church: they think the creeds are village formulations, and that in them men can be safe and content. There are profoundly religious men beyond the church who cannot accept what they think are village creeds: they have not yet learned that creeds are a vast and necessary symbolism, a calling of the deeps in man to the deeps in God, in thunderous antiphon: "God of God, Light of Light, Very God of very God; . . . Who for us men and for our salvation came down from heaven, . . . and was made man." [29] What do you want—the neat answer, nothing that cannot be reduced to village slide rules, a poor sophistication and a tiny street bounded by two hospitals? No, you cannot forget the Mystery. It is better to live in the dimension of depth.

NOTES

Chapter 1 LONELY VOYAGE

1. Edward Marsh, *Rupert Brooke: A Memoir* (New York: John Lane Co., 1918), p. 95.
2. Title of a book by Soren Kierkegaard, tr. Walter Lowrie (Princeton, N. J.: Princeton University Press, 1952).
3. See David E. Roberts, *Existentialism and Religious Belief* (New York: Oxford University Press, 1957), pp. 149-91, especially p. 154. Also Martin Heidegger, *Existence and Being* (Chicago: Henry Regnery Co., 1949), especially pp. 62 ff. and 90 ff.
4. For example, Albert Camus in *The Myth of Sisyphus, and Other Essays*, tr. J. O'Brien (New York: Alfred A. Knopf, Inc., 1955).
5. Charles Kingsley, "The Three Fishers," st. III.
6. Deut. 33:27.
7. (New York: John Lane Co., 1909), pp. 43-44.
8. *Poems* (New York: The Macmillan Co., 1953), p. 211.
9. Luke 23:46.
10. Bishop Thomas Ken, "All praise to thee, my God, this night" (1709), st. 3.

Chapter 2 FAITH AND DOUBT

1. Refers to a fictional account of a meeting between Hume and La Roche, published in the *Mirror*, 1779, by Hume's friend Henry Mackenzie to prove the real nature of the man. See John Hill Burton, *Life and Correspondence of David Hume* (Edinburgh: William Tait, 1846), I, 58-61.
2. *The Letters of Katherine Mansfield*, ed. J. Middleton Murry (New York: Alfred A. Knopf, Inc., 1929), II, 389 (a letter written in 1921).
3. Henrik Ibsen, tr. R. Farquharson Sharp (New York: E. P. Dutton & Co., 1922), Act III, scene 1, and Act V, scene 3.
4. New York: Charles Scribner's Sons, 1936.
5. "O World, Thou Choosest Not the Better Part," *Poems* (New York: Charles Scribner's Sons, 1923), Sonnet iii.
6. *Pensées*, sec. 4, Fragment 277. The actual quotation reads: "The heart has its reasons, which reason does not know."
7. *The Quest of the Historical Jesus* (New York: The Macmillan Co., 1957), p. 403.
8. Gracie Hegger Lewis, *With Love from Gracie. Sinclair Lewis: 1912-1925.* (New York: Harcourt, Brace & Co., 1955), pp. 301-2, criticizes the Associated Press interpretation of Sinclair Lewis' dramatic action answering a letter signed "A Believer in Hell." She says that Lewis was intent to show that "God is not the avenging god of this man's imagination."
9. "Bishop Blougram's Apology."
10. *Ibid.*
11. Mary B. Cheney, *Life and Letters of Horace Bushnell* (New York: Harper & Bros., 1880), especially pp. 57-59, which report a sermon preached at Yale University describing Bushnell's battle with his skepticism.

12. I have not rediscovered this as a quotation, but it fully accords with Augustine's argument in *De Trinitate*, Bk. X, sec. 14.

Chapter 3 IT SHALL COME BACK

1. The Madison Avenue Presbyterian Church, New York City, supported for many years the mission station at Nansuchow, Anhwei Province, China.
2. See Jer. 32.
3. Edward Gibbon, *Decline and Fall of the Roman Empire*, ch. xxxi. The edition edited by the Rev. H. H. Milman refers in a note to the Jeremiah story.
4. Title of a book by Dale Carnegie (New York: Pocket Books, Inc.).
5. This sentence consists actually of two quotes: Lam. 3:41 and Rev. 19:6.
6. Frederick William Faber, "The Right Must Win," from "On the Field."
7. Feb. 27, 1933; and see Heywood Broun, *It Seems to Me, 1925-1935*, (New York: Harcourt, Brace and Co., 1935), p. 191.
8. I Cor. 11:25.
9. "Abt Vogler," st. 7.
10. *Ibid.*, st. 9.
11. I Cor. 13:8.

Chapter 4 ANXIETY AND FAITH

1. An interesting discussion of this broadcast is found in Halford E. Luccock, *In The Minister's Workshop* (Nashville: Abingdon-Cokesbury Press, 1944), p. 156; and see Cantril Hadley, *The Invasion from Mars* (Princeton: Princeton University Press, 1952).
2. Matt. 12:1-8; Mark 2:23-28; 3:1-6; Luke 6:1-11.
3. Title of a play by Eugene O'Neill (New Haven, Conn.: Yale University Press, 1956).
4. Quoted in *The Great Texts of the Bible*, ed. James Hastings (New York: Charles Scribner's Sons, 1912), XIX, 351.
5. Title of a book by Paul Tillich (New Haven, Conn.: Yale University Press, 1952).
6. John 3:16 (K.J.V.).
7. Phil. 2:7.
8. Rowland Taylor, Vicar of Hadleigh. See John Richard Green, *History of the English People* (London: Macmillan & Co., 1890), II, 258.
9. Plotinus, Ennead, VI, 9. *The Essence of Plotinus*, comp. Grace H. Turnbull (New York: Oxford University Press, 1934), p. 222; and Evelyn Underhill, *Mysticism* (4th ed.; London: Methuen & Co., Ltd., 1912), p. 281.

Chapter 5 PERSONAL WORTH

1. Matt. 10:29.
2. In *Scenes of Clerical Life*, ch. v.
3. Clement Wood, *The Glory Road*; and, *The eagle sonnets* (New York: Greenberg, 1950), Eagle Sonnet vii, p. 65. Used by permission of Chilton Company—Book Division.
4. See Emil Ludwig, *Lincoln*, tr. Eden and Cedar Paul (Boston: Little, Brown & Co., 1930), Bk. V, ch. v, p. 409.
5. Sir Joseph Norman Lockyer (1836-1920), an English astronomer who in 1868 identified helium. Sir William Ramsey (1852-1916), a British chemist who in search for the gas argon obtained helium.
6. See *Diogenes Laertius*, tr. R. D. Hicks (New York: G. P. Putnam's Sons, 1925), Vol. II, p. 43 (Bk. VI, sec. 40).
7. Title of a book by William H. Whyte, Jr. (New York: Simon and Schuster, Inc., 1956).
8. Luke 19:5.
9. John 8:11.
10. Luke 12:32.
11. Originally painted for altar piece of Paradise Chapel of Podesta Palace. The palace burned in 1332. This picture is therefore probably a copy; see *Masters in Art* (Boston: Bates & Guild Co., 1900-1909), Vol. III, Part 32.

12. In a speech delivered during the Bicentennial of Columbia University, 1954, and published (Columbia University Press) in *Man's Right to Knowledge*, 2nd. ser., "Present Knowledge and Prospects in the Arts and Sciences."
13. *The Journal of John Woolman* (Boston: Houghton Mifflin Co., 1871), pp. 238-41.

Chapter 6 GOD AND LAUGHTER

1. *The Boston Daily Globe*, November 6, 1957.
2. See Green, *op. cit.*, IV, 6.
3. Job 38:7.
4. Isa. 55:12.
5. See Ps. 114:4, 6.
6. *The Complete Works of Friedrich Nietzsche*, ed. Oscar Levy, tr. Anthony M. Ludovici (Edinburgh: T. N. Foulis, 1909), *The Will to Power*, Vol. I, Bk. I, p. 74.
7. The undergraduate daily newspaper in Harvard University.
8. Hymn by Lizette Woodworth Reese from *Songs of Praise* (London: Oxford University Press).
9. Ecc. 3:1, 4.
10. "Saul," st. 9.
11. "Christ in the Universe," *The Poems of Alice Meynell* (London: Hollis & Carter, 1947), st. 1.
12. *Laughter* (New York: The Macmillan Co., 1911), chs. 1 and 2, particularly pp. 57-58, 87.
13. *The Emotions and the Will* (3rd ed.; New York: D. Appleton & Co., 1886), pp. 256-63. Also quoted in *ibid.*, p. 124.
14. Bergson, *op. cit.*, ch. 1, especially p. 3; pp. 119-20 describe an incident in a comedy by Labiche. The wording of the quotation has been slightly changed, but not its meaning.
15. *Ibid.*, pp. 40-41.
16. Homer, Bk. I, l. 599.
17. Quoted in *A Treasury of Sermon Illustrations*, ed. Charles L. Wallis (Nashville: Abingdon Press, 1950), ¶ 186.
18. John Bunyan (New York: Fleming H. Revell Co., 1903), The Puritan Ed., Part II, pp. 230-31.
19. Luke 23:40 (K.J.V.).
20. Matt. 18:3 (K.J.V.).
21. Tennyson, *In Memoriam*, sec. cxxvi, st. 1.
22. John 16:33.

Chapter 7 FOOTNOTE ON FREEDOM

1. *No Exit and Three Other Plays* (New York: Vintage Books, 1955), p. 47.
2. (London: William Heinemann, Ltd., 1895), Act IV.
3. *Confessions*, Bk. I, sec. 1.
4. John Milton, *Paradise Lost*, Bk. II, l. 561.
5. *Human Being* (New York: Doubleday, Doran & Co., 1934), p. 77.
6. Ps. 42:5 (K.J.V.).
7. See Roberts, *op. cit.*, especially pp. 155-57, and Heidegger, *op. cit.*, especially pp. 79 ff.
8. Ps. 121:1-2 (K.J.V.).
9. Victor Hugo, *Les Miserables*, "Fantine," Bk. II, ch. xii.
10. "On Growing Old," *op. cit.*, p. 166, st. 2, from John Masefield, *Poems*. Copyright, 1953, by The Macmillan Co. and used with their permission.
11. "Collect for Peace," *The Book of Common Prayer*.

Chapter 8 HAS CHRIST LEFT US?

1. John 1:46 (K.J.V.).
2. *Treasury of the Christian World*, comp. and ed. A. Gordon Nasby (New York: Harper & Bros., 1953), p. 40.
3. William E. Barton, *President Lincoln* (Indianapolis: Bobbs-Merrill Co., 1933), II,

602. Also William E. Barton, *Lincoln at Gettysburg* (Indianapolis: Bobbs-Merrilll Co., 1930), pp. 114-15.

4. John 13:7.

5. Walt Whitman, "Darest Thou Now, O Soul?" from *Whispers of Heavenly Death, Leaves of Grass* (Boston: Small, Maynard & Co., 1899), p. 338, st. 1.

6. *Ibid*, st. 4.

7. *Journal of the Rev. John Wesley*, entry of June, 1739. These words were also used on the tablet in his memory in Westminster Abbey.

8. John 1:14 (K.J.V.).

9. Reference is to the grave of Father Powers in the Holy Cross Cemetery, Malden, Mass., in the fall of 1929.

10. Quoted by Viola Meynell, *Alice Meynell: A Memoir* (London: Jonathan Cape, 1929), p. 284. Used by permission of Burns, Oates & Washbourne Ltd.

11. John 3:16.

12. Luke 12:57.

13. See Rom. 13:1.

14. From a hymn by Adelaide Anne Procter, "My God, I thank thee, who hast made," st. 3.

15. Ps. 119:105.

16. In a letter to Melanchthon, August 1, 1521, M. Luther's *Werke*, Briefwechsel 11 (Weimar, 1931), p. 372; and in *Luther's Correspondence and Other Contemporary Letters*, ed. and tr. Preserved Smith and Charles M. Jacobs (Philadelphia: Lutheran Publication Society, 1918), II, 50.

17. John 16:8 (K.J.V.).

18. Quoted by James S. Stewart, *The Strong Name* (New York: Charles Scribner's Sons, 1941), p. 259, in a chapter entitled "The Strong Name of the Trinity."

19. Hymn, "Eternal Light! Eternal Light! How pure the soul must be," by Thomas Binney, st. 3.

20. I John 2:1.

21. Binney, *op. cit.*, st. 4.

22. Hymn by Mrs. Jemina T. Luke.

23. Matt. 18:3 (K.J.V.).

24. I Cor. 13:11 (K.J.V.).

25. Hymn by Sabine Baring-Gould.

Chapter 9 GOD'S WAYS AND MAN'S WAYS

1. "Heaven," *The Collected Poems of Rupert Brooke*, copyright, 1915, by Dodd, Mead & Co., Inc. Used by permission of Dodd, Mead & Co., and McClelland & Stewart, Ltd.

2. Subtitle of lecture "The Gods."

3. Alfred Tennyson, "The Higher Pantheism," st. 6.

4. A well-known saying of the astronomer Johann Kepler. See Alfred Noyes, *Watchers of the Sky*. (New York: Frederick A. Stokes, 1922), pp. 102-30, especially p. 115.

5. Quoted by Thomas S. Kepler, *A Journey into Faith* (Nashville: Abingdon Press, 1954), p. 35.

6. Ps. 111:10.

7. *De Profundis* (New York: G. P. Putnam's Sons, 1905), p. 41. His exact words: "There is enough suffering in any one narrow London Lane to show that God did not love man."

8. *The Rubáiyát of Omar Khayyám*, tr. Edward Fitzgerald (New York: George H. Doran Co.), First Translation, st. 73.

9. Tr. H. L. Mencken (New York: Alfred A. Knopf, Inc., 1931), sec. 52, p. 140.

10. Ps. 137:9 (K.J.V.).

11. Title of a play by Charles Rann Kennedy (New York: Harper & Bros., 1908).

12. James Drummond, *Life and Letters of James Martineau* (New York: Dodd, Mead & Co., 1902), I, 60-62; II, 176-77.

13. *Tess of the D'Urbervilles* (London: Macmillan & Co., 1927), Phase the First, ch. iv.

14. John 3:16 (K.J.V.).

Chapter 10 THE AUTHORITY OF JESUS

1. J. D. Passavant, *Raphael of Urbino and his Father Giovanni Santi* (New York: The Macmillan Co., 1872), p. 133.
2. Heb. 10:22.
3. See Roland H. Bainton, *Here I Stand: A Life of Martin Luther* (Nashville: Abingdon Press, 1950), pp. 185, 386.
4. Rom. 13:1.
5. Matt. 10:39. See also Matt. 16:25; Mark 8:35; Luke 9:24.
6. John 13:15.
7. Mark 10:18; Luke 18:19.
8. *The Scrolls from the Dead Sea* (New York: Oxford University Press, 1955), also in the *New Yorker Magazine*, May 14, 1955.
9. John 7:15.
10. John 2:25.
11. Mark 7:21; see also Matt. 15:19.
12. John 10:3.
13. John 4:29.
14. See his poem "If," *Rudyard Kipling's Verse, 1885-1932* (London: Hodder & Stoughton, 1933), p. 560.
15. Mark 1:15.
16. Gal. 4:4.
17. *The Outline of History* (New York: The Macmillan Co., 1926), I, 327.
18. John 12:44.
19. Quoted by Paul Tillich, *Systematic Theology* (Chicago: University of Chicago Press, 1957), II, 116, a sentence of Adolph Schlatter.

Chapter 11 WHO OWNS THE EARTH?

1. William Shakespeare, *Hamlet*, Act III, scene 1.
2. Ernst Haeckel, tr. Joseph McCabe (New York: Harper & Bros., 1900).
3. *The Life and Public Services of Samuel Adams* (Boston: Little, Brown & Co., 1888), I, 160, also in Governor Bradford's State Papers, January, 1768.
4. *The Winter's Tale*, Act I, scene 2.
5. Tr. Justin O'Brien (New York: Alfred A. Knopf, Inc., 1957), p. 9.
6. Title of a play by George S. Kaufman and Moss Hart (New York: Farrar & Rinehart, Inc., 1937).
7. See Hugh Walpole, *Rogue Herries* (Garden City, N. Y.: Doubleday, Doran & Co., 1930), p. 337. Also quoted in *The Interpreter's Bible*, IV, 131b-f.
8. Ps. 36:6 (K.J.V.).
9. Ps. 95:4 (K.J.V.).
10. John 3:8.
11. "Earth" in "Dust and Light," *Poems, 1911-1936* (New York: Charles Scribner's Sons, 1936), p. 117. Used by permission of Charles Scribner's Sons.
12. Ps. 24:1.
13. Ps. 24:2.

Chapter 12 THE PROBLEM OF THE RIGHTEOUS MAN

1. Matt. 21:31.
2. Rabbi Simlai, *The Babylonian Talmud*, Makkoth 236.
3. *The Works of Benjamin Franklin*, comp. and ed. John Bigelow (New York: G. P. Putnam's Sons, 1904), I, 188 ff., especially pp. 192-93.
4. Exod. 20:5.
5. Title of a book by John Benton (New York: D. Appleton-Century Co., 1940).
6. Exod. 20:17.
7. Exod. 20:13.
8. Luke 18:19.
9. *Walden, or Life in the Woods*, ch. 1, "Economy," a few paragraphs from its close. The exact quotation reads: "If I knew for a certainty that a man was coming to my house with the conscious design of doing me good, I should run for my life."

10. Luke 18:19.
11. "The Guest," issue of December, 1957, p. 51.
12. George Tyrrell in a letter to Baron Friedrich von Hügel, February 11, 1900, quoted by von Hügel in "Father Tyrrell: memorials of the last twelve years of his life," *The Hibbert Journal*, VIII (1909-10), 238.
13. Matt. 3:15.
14. Luke 23:34.
15. II Cor. 5:21.
16. Isa. 53:6.
17. Washington: Anderson House, 1935. Copyright, 1935, by Maxwell Anderson and Anderson House.
18. *Ibid*, Act III.
19. Rom. 3:20-22.
20. William Wordsworth, "Thoughts suggested the day following, on the Banks of the Nith," near the Poet's Residence, last st.

Chapter 13 GOD AND OUR MIXED MOTIVES

1. W. Fearon Halliday, *Psychology and Religious Experience* (New York: Richard R. Smith, 1930), p. 75.
2. Part I, pp. 152-56.
3. *Ethics*, ed. Eberhard Bethge (New York: The Macmillan Co., 1955), pp. 58-59.
4. *Paradise Lost*, Bk. II, l. 561.
5. Aristotle, *Rhetorica*, Bk. II, ch. 24, sec. 11.
6. Gen. 3:12-13.
7. Jer. 17:9 (K.J.V.).
8. *Complete Works*, ed. Oscar Levy, tr. Helen Zimmern (New York: The Macmillan Co., 1925), VI, *Human, All Too Human*, 83
9 An idea central in *Christianity and History* (London: G. Bell & Sons, 1949), and particularly in ch. 5.
10. Matt. 10:26.
11. Luke 12:15.
12. John 16:13, 14.
13. Quoted with permission.
14. See discussion of this phrase in Walter Lowrie, *A Short Life of Kierkegaard* (Princeton, N. J.: Princeton University Press, 1942), pp. 88-89, 174.
15. Thomas Bulfinch, *The Age of Fable* (New York: The Hermitage Press, 1942), p. 50.
16. Ps. 139:23-24.
17. Matt. 4:3.
18. Hymn by William Bright, "And now, O Father, mindful of the love," st. 2.
19. *Idylls of the King*, "Lancelot and Elaine," l. 871.
20. Isa. 53:11.

Chapter 14 FRUSTRATION AND FAITH

1. In his picture entitled "Hope."
2. Hymn by Albert Midlane, "There's a Friend for Little Children," st. 2.
3. Refers to Philippus Aureolus Theophrastus Bombastus ab Hohenheim, c. 1490-1541. See Robert Browning's poem "Paracelsus" with its biographical note (Riverside Ed., I, 123) and the *Encyclopaedia Britannica*, ed. 1956, Vol. XVII.
4. George Meredith, "Modern Love," *Poems* (London: A. Constable & Co., 1898), Vol. I, Sonnet 50. Used by permission of Constable & Co., Ltd.
5. Tr. Stuart Gilbert (New York: Alfred A. Knopf, Inc., 1948), referring to Rambert, especially pp. 147-48.
6. Canon of Meaux in a letter to OEcolampadius, quoted by Henry M. Baird, History of the Rise of the Huguenots in France (New York: Scharles Scribner's Sons, 1879), I, 86 n.
7. *The Rubáiyát of Omar Khayyám*, st. 14.
8. *Ibid.*, st. 74.
9. *Ibid.*, st. 11.
10. William Shakespeare, *Macbeth*, Act V, scene 3.

11. Matt. 10:14.
12. *The Bible Today* (New York: The Macmillan Co., 1947), p. 100.
13. The French potter Bernard Palissy, 1510-89. See Henry M. Baird, *The Huguenots and Henry of Navarre* (New York: Charles Scribner's Sons, 1886), II, pp. 8-9; and C. L. Brightwell, *Palissy the Potter* (New York: Carlton & Porter, 1858), p. 234.
14. Words spoken by Friar Elston. See Jeremy Collier, *An Ecclesiastical History of Great Britain* (London: William Straker, 1840), IV, 244.
15. Matt. 12:28.
16. Matt. 26:42.
17. Luke 23:46.
18. Heb. 2:10 (K.J.V.). The word "pioneer" is in the R.S.V.
19. Alfred Tennyson, *Idylls of the King*, "The Passing of Arthur," l. 457.

Chapter 15 JUDGE NOT

1. *Letters of James Smetham* (New York: The Macmillan Co., 1891), p. 367, in a letter to J. E. V., July 1, 1876.
2. "Address to the Unco Guid."
3. John 8:1-11.
4. *The Love Letters of Phyllis McGinley* (New York: The Viking Press, 1954), p. 42. Used by permission of The Viking Press, Inc.
5. Matt. 7:16; see also Luke 6:44.
6. Refers to a certain Alvin Lindequist in 1911. Told by Gordon Hurlbutt, *Windows and Wings* (Louisville: The Standard Press, 1928), p. 27.
7. Matt. 21:31.
8. Luke 12:14.
9. John 8:15.
10. John 12:47.
11. Luke 23:34.
12. John 14:2.
13. Title of a book by Smiley Blanton, (New York: Simon and Schuster, Inc., 1956.)
14. Part VI, st. 7.
15. Part VI, st. 29, 30.

Chapter 16 HOME TIES AND THE FAITH

1. Mark 3:21.
2. *Adam Bede*, ch. vi.
3. *Life of Jesus* (Boston: Little, Brown & Co., 1910), ch. 19, especially p. 313.
4. Matt. 8:20; Luke 9:58.
5. Matt. 19:5; see also Mark 10:7.
6. Wordsworth, Elegiac Stanzas, "Suggested by a picture of Peele Castle," st. 4.
7. *The Poems of Richard Lovelace*, ed. C. H. Wilkinson (Oxford: Clarendon Press, 1925), "To Lucasta, Going to the Warres," st. 3.
8. Fifth Translation, st. 13.
9. *Ibid*, First Translation, st. 12.
10. In a conversation with the Rev. Mr. Gahan on the night before her execution, October 11, 1915.
11. Alexander S. Mackenzie, *Life of Stephen Decatur*, Library of American Biography, XI (Boston: Charles C. Little & J. Brown, 1846), 295; and see Burton Stevenson, *The Home Book of Quotations*, p. 63, for other instances.
12. Gal. 4:26.
13. Augustine, *Confessions*.
14. Matt. 10:37.
15. Alfred Tennyson, *Idylls of the King*, "The Coming of Arthur," l. 261.
16. Cecil John Cadoux, *The Historic Mission of Jesus* (New York: Harper & Bros., n.d.), p. 69.
17. John 14:24.
18. William McFee, *Casuals of the Sea* (The Modern Library, 1st. ed., 1931), pp. 505, 512.

19. Matt. 8:20; Luke 9:58.
20. (New York: Charles Scribner's Sons, 1922).
21. *Ibid*, Act II, scene 2.
22. *Ibid*, Act III, scene 3.
23. Alfred Tennyson, *In Memoriam*, Prologue, st. v.

Chapter 17 REALISM AND PRAYER

1. See *The Future of an Illusion*, tr. W. D. Robson-Scott (New York: Liveright Publishing Corp., 1953), for his discussion of religion as illusion.
2. *The Varieties of Religious Experience* (New York: Longmans, Green & Co., 1902), Lectures IV and V, entitled "The Religion of Healthy-Mindedness."
3. Matt. 10:26; see also Mark 4:22 and Luke 8:17.
4. See *In Search of Maturity* (New York: Charles Scribner's Sons, 1947), particularly Part II, ch. vii.
5. *The Poems of Francis Thompson*, "A Fallen Yew" (London: Oxford University Press, 1937), sts. 18 and 23.
6. See Richard Garnett, *William Blake, Painter and Poet* (London: Seeley & Co., 1895), p. 28.
7. Sir John Hawkins, *Life of Samuel Johnson* (2nd. ed.; London, 1787), p. 563.
8. Ps. 51:4.
9. Luke 18:13.
10. Described in *In the Mill* (New York: The Macmillan Co., 1941), pp. 94-97.
11. Quoted in *A Treasury of Sermon Illustrations*, ed. Charles Wallis (Nashville: Abingdon Press, 1950), p. 17.
12. *The Springs of Creative Living* (Nashville: Abingdon-Cokesbury Press, 1940), p. 124.
13. Job 23:13.
14. Lowrie, *op. cit.*, particularly the chapter "Father and Son United," pp. 118 ff.; in greater detail in Lowrie, *Kierkegaard* (New York: Oxford University Press, 1938).
15. Ps. 90:1.
16. "The Death of the Hired Man," *Complete Poems of Robert Frost* (New York: Henry Holt & Co., 1949). Used by permission of Henry Holt & Co.

Chapter 18 KNOWLEDGE AND LOVE

1. Job 23:3.
2. John 1:18 (K.J.V.).
3. As in the philosophy of Samuel Alexander.
4. Ps. 42:11.
5. In an essay, "Life in Inverted Commas," *Prose Fancies* (New York: G. P. Putnam's Sons, 1899), pp. 18 ff.
6. *Op. cit.*
7. Acts 17:23.
8. Bk. III, ch. viii.
9. See John Watson, *The Philosophy of Kant* (Glasgow: Jackson, Wylie & Co., 1934), pp. 27, 31, 129-33.
10. "O World, Thou Choosest Not the Better Part."
11. Title of a book by Ernest Hemingway (New York: Charles Scribner's Sons, 1928).
12. In *Camus, op. cit.*
13. Rom. 13:9 (K.J.V.); see also Matt. 19:19; 22:39; Mark 12:31; Luke 10:27.
14. Phil. 3:14 (K.J.V.).
15. Title of a book by Reinhold Niebuhr (New York: Charles Scribner's Sons, 1943).
16. *The Knowledge of God and the Service of God*, tr. J. L. M. Haire and Ian Henderson (London: Hodder & Stoughton, 1955), p. 104.
17. Albert Einstein, *Cosmic Religion, with other Opinions and Aphorisms* (New York: Covici-Friede, 1931), p. 105.
18. II Cor. 1:20.
19. Quoted by Edward Beal in *Treasury of the Christian World*, comp. and ed. A. Gordon Nasby (New York: Harper & Bros., 1953), p. 109.

Chapter 19 TWO-WORLD CONVERSATION

1. C. S. Lewis (New York: The Macmillan Co., 1947), Letter One.
2. Matt. 10:32 (R.S.V.).
3. *Familiar Letters of Henry David Thoreau* (Boston: Houghton Mifflin Co., 1895), reporting a conversation with Parker Pillsbury during Thoreau's last illness, p. 439.
4. One of the resident houses in Harvard College.
5. Luke 11:2 (K.J.V.); see also Matt. 6:9.
6. John 8:29.
7. Matt. 26:39.
8. John 19:30.
9. Luke 23:46.
10. *The Ring and the Book*, sec. 10, "The Pope," l. 1231.
11. "Prince Hohenstiel-Schwangau, Saviour of Society."
12. *The Boston Daily Globe*, one of the city's regular newspapers.
13. See Acts 1:22; 4:33.
14. Quoted by Sidney Dix Strong, ed., *We Believe in Prayer* (New York: The Press of the Pioneers, 1935), p. 68. The text is a paraphrase of the Zona Gale story.
15. Ivan Turgenev, *Dream Tales and Prose Poems*, tr. Constance Garnett (New York: The Macmillan Co., 1920), p. 250.
16. Refers to Georg von Freunsberg, who said: "My dear monk . . . if you have right on your side . . . then proceed in God's name, and be of good courage, God will not forsake you." Moritz Meurer, *The Life of Martin Luther* (New York: Ludwig & Co., 1848), p. 195; and E. G. Schwiebert, *Luther and His Times* (St. Louis: Concordia Publishing House, 1950), p. 502.
17. Lewis, *op. cit.*
18. William Shakespeare, *Macbeth*, Act V, scene 5.
19. *The Bloody Assizes*, ed. J. G. Muddiman (Edinburgh and London: William Hodge & Co., 1929), pp. 84-87.

Chapter 20 THE THIRST FOR GOD

(An Advent Sermon)

1. Alexander Black (New York: Harper & Bros., 1919).
2. Told by Strother A. Campbell, *Grit to Grapple with Life* (Nashville: The Broadman Press, 1942), p. 35.
3. Title of a book by Harry Clay Hervey (New York: Greystone Press, 1939).
4. Mary Carolyn Davies, "Feet," *The World's Great Religious Poetry*, ed. Caroline Miles Hill (New York: The Macmillan Co., 1923), p. 34.
5. *The Letters of Katherine Mansfield*, ed. J. Middleton Murry (London: Constable & Co., 1928), II, 131-32, a letter written August 29, 1921.
6. A saying of Xenophanus and quoted by Herbert G. Farmer, *Toward Belief in God* (New York: The Macmillan Co., 1943), p. 43; and Albert C. Knudson, *The Doctrine of God* (Nashville: Abingdon Press, 1930), pp. 213-14.
7. C. L. De Montesquieu, *Persian Letters*, tr. John Davidson (London: privately published, 1892), I, 134, in Letter LIX (1714).
8. Matt. 6:9.
9. *Adventure of Ideas* (New York: The Macmillan Co., 1933), p. 281, and a discussion thereof in David Elton Trueblood, *Philosophy of Religion* (New York: Harper & Bros., 1957), pp. 263-65.
10. Luke 15:10.
11. See also Exod. 33:20.
12. Ps. 42:6.
13. *The Wild Knight and Other Poems* (5th ed.; London: J. M. Dent & Sons, Ltd., 1945), Used by permission of E. P. Dutton & Co. and J. M. Dent & Sons, Ltd.
14. Quoted by Norman N. G. Cope in Nasby, *op. cit.*, p. 133.
15. Quoted by Joseph T. Kelly, *ibid*, p. 141. This story does not, however, appear in Mortimer Smith, *The Life of Ole Bull* (Princeton, N.J.: Princeton University Press, 1943), or William Conant Church, *The Life of John Ericsson* (New York: Charles Scribner's Sons, 1890). It must come from some friend known to each of them.

Both lives report a piano which Ericsson made for Ole Bull.
16. II Cor. 5:19.

Chapter 21 THE NAME OF THE NAMELESS

(A Christmas Sermon)

1. John Milton, "Comus," l. 205.
2. Hymn by Isaac Watts, "O God, our help in ages past," st. 5.
3. Madame James Darmesteter, *The Life of Ernest Renan* (Boston: Houghton Mifflin Co., 1897), p. 268.
4. Gen. 29:20.
5. Laertius, *op. cit.*, I, 65; Bk. I, sec. lviii; also quoted in Miguel de Unamuno, *The Tragic Sense of Life in Men and Peoples*, tr. J. E. Crawford Flitch (London: Macmillan & Co., 1931), p. 17.
6. See Matt. 27:17.
7. Luke 15:8-10.
8. John 1:14.
9. Matt. 9:2; Mark 2:5; see also Luke 5:20; 7:48 (K.J.V.).
10. Luke 23:40 (K.J.V.).
11. Alfred Tennyson, "The Ancient Sage," l. 49.
12. Luke 5:8.
13. Alan George Ferrers Howell, S. *Bernardino of Siena* (London: Methuen & Co., 1913), pp. 157-58; see also F. R. Webber, *Church Symbolism* (Cleveland: J. H. Jansen, 1938), ch. vii.

Chapter 22 PENITENCE AND PARDON

(A Lenten Sermon)

1. *Les Châtiments*, 1853, cited in H. L. Mencken, ed., *A New Dictionary of Quotations* (New York: Alfred A. Knopf, Inc., 1942), p. 833; and more fully, *Les Miserables*, Cosette, Bk. 1, end of ch. 9.
2. John Pitts, *Religion and the New Paganism* (London: Independent Press, 1950), p. 212
3. W. H. Auden, "For the Time Being," Advent iii, Chorus, st. 1, *The Collected Poetry of W. H. Auden* (New York: Random House, 1945), p. 411. Copyright, 1945, by W. H. Auden and used by permission of Random House, Inc.
4. Basil, *The Letters*, tr. Roy J. Deferrari (New York: G. P. Putnam's Sons, 1926), I, 9, Letter ii, to Gregory.
5. Edward, Viscount Grey of Fallodin, *Twenty-five Years, 1892-1916* (New York: Frederick A. Stokes Co., 1925), II, 20.
6. *God the Invisible King* (New York: The Macmillan Co., 1917), p. 84 in a chapter entitled "The Religion of Atheists."
7. Alexander V. G. Allen, *Life and Letters of Phillips Brooks* (New York: E. P. Dutton & Co., 1920), II, 806.
8. John 1:14 (K.J.V.).
9. Title of a book by Miguel de Unamuno, *op. cit.*
10. "Dover Beach," st. 5.
11. *Ibid.*
12. Col. 2:14.
13. Luke 15:22.
14. Latin hymn of eleventh century, tr. the Rev. Edward Caswall, 1849, "Jesus, the Very Thought of Thee," st. 4.
15. Luke 23:34.
16. Title of a book by Rachel Field (New York: The Macmillan Co., 1938).
17. See *My New Order*, ed. Raoul de Roussy de Sales (New York: Reynal & Hitchcock, 1941), p. 45.
18. *A Christian's Handbook on Communism* (National Council of the Churches of Christ in the U.S.A., 1952), p. 44 quoting Lenin.

19. *Swinburne's Collected Political Works* (London: William Heinemann, Ltd.). "The Hymn of Man," last l. Used by permission of William Heinemann, Ltd.

Chapter 23 EXPIATION
(A Holy Week Sermon)

1. *Op. cit.*
2. See Luke 22:42.
3. Watson, *op. cit.*, p. 225 (from *The Metaphysic of Morality*).
4. Harriet Beecher Stowe (Boston: Houghton Mifflin Co., 1896), Vol. I, ch. **xx**, "Topsy."
5. *Letters from Baron Friedrich von Hugel to a Niece*, ed. Gwendolen Greene (Chicago: Henry Regnery Co., 1955), p. 122, in a letter written September 17, 1919.
6. Robert Penn Warren, *Brother to Dragons, a Tale in Verse and Voices* (New York: Random House, 1953), pp. 47, 24, words given to Thomas Jefferson. Copyright, 1953, by Random House, Inc., and used by their permission.
7. *Op. cit.*
8. II Cor. 5:19.
9. The Nicene Creed.
10. Luke 23:34.
11. "The Christ of St. John of the Cross," originally sketched by a medieval monk, St. John of the Cross. This picture was reproduced by the contemporary artist Salvador Dali. I saw it in the study of the Rev. Daniel G. Axt, East Jordan, Mich., to whom I am indebted for the information in this note.

Chapter 24 OUR TIMES AND THE RESURRECTION
(An Easter Sermon)

1. Hesketh Pearson, *Oscar Wilde, His Life and Wit* (New York: Harper & Bros. 1946), p. 331.
2. Charles Kingsley, "The Three Fishers," st. 3.
3. Alfred Tennyson, "Wages."
4. The Apostles' Creed.
5. Masefield, "Biography," *op. cit.* p. 200.
6. See Heb. 11:13-16.
7. The quotation from which these words are drawn reads: "Glory to the Almighty, the sun has risen in the west!" It is attributed to an Oriental poet by Joseph Fort Newton in a sermon included in *If I Had Only One Sermon to Preach on Immortality*, ed. William L. Stidger (New York: Harper & Bros., 1929), p. 191.
8. Hymn by Charles Wesley, "Love Divine, All Loves Excelling," st. 4.
9. Acts 3:15 (K.J.V.).
10. Picture titled "Angels hovering over the body of Jesus," 1808; see Laurence Binyon, *The Drawings and Engravings of William Blake* (London: The Studio, Ltd., 1922), Plate 77.
11. I Cor. 15:30 (K.J.V.).
12. Eph. 4:15.
13. I Cor. 15:20.
14. I Cor. 15:38.
15. I Cor. 15:36 (K.J.V.).
16. II Cor. 3:18 (K.J.V.).
17. William Shakespeare, Act III, scene 1.
18. An Old English rhyme, quoted by Mencken, *op. cit.*, p. 328.
19. E. Stanley Jones, *Christ at the Round Table* (New York: The Abingdon Press, 1929), p. 325.
20. Thoreau, *op. cit.*
21. Luke 2:12 (K.J.V.).

Chapter 25 BABEL AND PENTECOST
(A Whitsuntide Sermon)

1. See *Interpreter's Bible*, I, 565.
2. Matt. 13:34.

3. *The Rubáiyát of Omar Khayyám*, Fifth Translation, st. 72.
4. Gen. 11:4.
5. *Ibid.*
6. Gen. 11:6.
7. William Shakespeare, *Hamlet*, Act V, scene 1, l. 236.
8. Keith Preston, "The Destiny That Shapes Our Ends," *The Top o' the Column*, (Chicago, Pascal Corvici, 1925), p. 36.
9. Cf. I Cor. 14.
10. Raymond MacDonald Alden, "The Palace Made by Music," in *Why the Chimes Rang* (Indianapolis: The Bobbs-Merrill Co., 1924).
11. Designed by Sir Joseph Paxton, first erected in Hyde Park, London, 1851; removed to Sydenham, 1854, as a museum. Burned in 1936.
12. Francis William Bourdillon, "Light."
13. T. S. Eliot, "Choruses from 'The Rock,'" *Collected Poems*, 1909-1935 (New York: Harcourt, Brace & Co. 1936), p. 188. Used by permission of Harcourt, Brace & Co. and Faber and Faber, Ltd.
14. Mark 7:13 (K.J.V.).
15. Acts 1:5.

Chapter 26 DIMENSION OF DEPTH

1. Ps. 42:9.
2. Ps. 42:4 (K.J.V.).
3. Ps. 42:7.
4. *The Positive Philosophy*, tr. Harriet Martineau (2nd ed.; New York: Calvin Blanchard, 1856), ch. 1.
5. John S. Whale, *Christian Doctrine* (New York: The Macmillan Co., 1941.), pp. 171-74.
6. *Modern Man in Search of a Soul* (New York: Harcourt, Brace & Co., 1933), pp. 124-31.
7. Ps. 90:2.
8. John 13:3-4.
9. See Chap. 4, n. 1.
10. Rom. 8:38, (K.J.V.).
11. See Chap. 17, n. 1.
12. *The Basic Writings of Sigmund Freud*, ed. and tr. A. A. Brill (New York: Modern Library, Inc., 1938), especially pp. 528-29, 540-49.
13. *The Integration of the Personality*, tr. Stanley M. Dell (New York: Farrar & Rinehart, Inc., 1939), pp. 52 ff., chapter on "Archetypes of the Collective Unconscious;" also *Psychology and Alchemy*, tr. R.F.C. Hall (New York: Pantheon Books, 1953), pp. 17-18.
14. Ps. 147:3-4 (K.J.V.).
15. Ps. 139:23.
16. Matt. 5:34-35 (K.J.V.).
17. Luke 9:55 (K.J.V.)
18. Ps. 36:6.
19. W. Somerset Maugham (Garden City, New York: Doubleday, Doran & Co., 1936), story of Philip Carey.
20. At the commencement, June, 1957.
21. Herbert H. Farmer, *The World and God* (New York: Harper & Bros., 1936), p. 283 n.
22. See Chap. 9, n. 11.
23. Job. 11:7-8.
24. Rom. 11:33, 36.
25. Rom. 8:38-39 (K.J.V.).
26. John 13:3.
27. Ps. 90:2.
28. Jer. 10:23.
29. The Nicene Creed.

The Library of Congress has
cataloged this book as follows:

Buttrick, George Arthur. Sermons preached in a university church. New York, Abingdon
Press [1959] 222 p. 22 cm. Includes bibliography. 1. Universities and colleges
Sermons. 2. Sermons, American. I. Title. BV4310.B85 252.55 59—8194 ‡